AGON Institute of Sports Ministry Series, vol. 8

The Life of the Shoe:
Sports Outreach for the World

P. F. Myers

Overwhelming Victory Press
Canton, Ohio

Copyright © 2021, Overwhelming Victory Press

ISBN: 978-1-952222-01-6

All Rights Reserved. No part of this book may be reproduced or transmitted in any form or by any means, electronic or mechanical, including photocopying, recording, or by any information storage and retrieval system without written permission from the author, except for the inclusion of brief quotations in a review.

For any reproduction rights, including federal copying, computer reproduction, etc., contact:

Dr. Greg Linville, CSRM International
P. O. Box 9110
Canton, OH 44711

Email: sportsminresources@gmail.com

To my beautiful daughters
who have had to share their father with the world.
When I am with you, just seeing your smiles lights up my day.
When I am away from you, just a single text brings joy to my heart.
My greatest joy is to see you following Jesus!

Other books in the Institute of Sports Outreach Series:

- Christmanship: A Theology of Competition and Sport

- Sports Outreach Fundamentals

- Putting the Church Back in the Game: The Ecclesiology of Sports Outreach

- The Saving of Sports Ministry: The Soteriology of Sports Outreach

TABLE OF CONTENTS

III	Dedication Page
VII	Foreword
IX	Endorsements
XIII	Acknowledgements
XV	Preface
1	Chapter 1: The Life of the Shoe
9	Chapter 2: The Impact of Godly Vision
21	Chapter 3: One of The Greatest Strategies to Reach This Generation: Sports Ministry
41	Chapter 4: The Church and Sports Ministry
61	Chapter 5: Evangelistic Disciplemaking, The True Measure of Our Success
67	Chapter 6: Evangelism Through Sports Ministry
81	Chapter 7: Discipleship Through Sports Ministry
93	Chapter 8: Persons of Peace: A Long-Forgotten Strategy
101	Chapter 9: "Tell Me A Story:" The Modern-Day Tool of Sports Parables
111	Chapter 10: Sports Ministry, the Unreached and Persecution – This Present Reality
125	Chapter 11: Missional Sports Communities And A Response To The Present Reality
135	Chapter 12: Building Sports Ministry
143	Postscript

Table of Contents

ADDENDA

145	Appendix #1: Explanatory Notes for the *Institutes of Sports Outreach Community* Book Series
153	Appendix #2: Sports Ministry and the Mission of the Church
155	Appendix #3: Sports, Recreation, and Fitness Ministry (SR&F) Activity List
157	Appendix #4: The Mansfield Graph of Evangelism
159	Appendix #5: Evangelistic Event Planning & Programming
161	Appendix #6: Sports Parable Worksheet
163	Appendix #7: Sample Sports Parables
169	Appendix #8: Personal Testimony Example from Paul and Worksheet
171	Appendix #9: Let's STRIVE together in Evangelistic-Discipleship
173	Appendix #10: Practical Steps to Build Sports Ministry
177	Appendix #11: Building Sports Ministry Worksheet
179	Appendix #12: Sports Ministry Pyramid
181	Appendix #13: Recommended International Ministry List
183	Appendix #14: Glossary
203	Appendix #15: Works Cited

FOREWORD

Sport and faith has played a very significant role in my life. That is why I am so excited to endorse this book that brings together these two elements in such a practical and relevant way and will make a world-wide impact on both.

My first love was baseball. I received a scholarship to play at Wake Forest University where I graduated in 1962 with a degree in physical education. In 1968 I got into basketball for the first time, and from there God blessed me with much success, including... co-founding the NBA's Orlando Magic and serving as general manager of the Philadelphia 76ers, Chicago Bulls and Atlanta Hawks. Winning the 1983 World Championship with the 76ers was certainly a career highlight; only to be eclipsed by being named as one of the 50 most influential people in NBA history and being inducted into the basketball Hall of Fame! Speaking of the Hall of Fame…

In 2012, I received the John W. Bunn Lifetime Achievement Award from the Naismith Memorial Basketball Hall of Fame; an honor that surpassed all my dreams. Now, as I reflect on the dream of the man who the Hall of Fame was named for, I believe this book fulfills the dream James Naismith had for basketball. When he invented basketball during the winter of 1891-92 as a physical education instructor for the YMCA, his original intention was to create a game that would naturally communicate the Gospel of Jesus Christ and promote both physical-fitness and character-fitness. In fact, Naismith's game did indeed become the catalyst for what became known as Muscular Christianity that enabled millions around the world to be both spiritually and physically fit. I believe this is exactly the kind of book that James Naismith would have endorsed.

As a sports professional, I have seen how sport provides some of the greatest opportunities to engage and impact our communities on many levels. The exhilaration of being a part of championship teams is great but nothing compares the victory and joy that I have found in Jesus. Through the ups and downs of professional sports and life, my anchor in Christ empowers me to rise above circumstances and in the midst of the routine demands of life it remains my highest priority to get the Word out to those who need to accept Christ and invite Him into their lives. I believe no one is an accident and that God really knows, loves, and cares for each one of us. That's why Jesus came into the world; to take care of the problem we call sin. We all know that we sin, but Jesus came to clean it up so that we can have a fresh start. It makes sense that sport should be used to reach this generation with this message, the Great News and to that end, The Life of

FOREWORD

the Shoe – Sports Outreach for the World shares great insight on how to do this and leads the reader to the point of accomplishing the Great Commission in their own lives and ministry; what the author terms: Evangelistic-Disciplemaking.

My wife and I are the parents of 19 children, including 14 adopted from four nations. Additionally, I have been blessed with 18 grandchildren. All of our children and grandchildren have followed in my footsteps and have been involved in sports, recreation and fitness in some way. I hope and pray that they might one day get involved in the kind of Sports Ministry that is explained in this book.

You will find the principles shared in this book to be very applicable to Sports Ministry, certainly, but also valuable for anyone who is ministry minded. The examples that are shared from around the world will challenge your heart and expand your vision. I strongly endorse The Life of the Shoe – Sports Outreach for the World as a book to empower any believer and church who wants to grow in their understanding of God and His plan for their life and ministry. I believe that it is especially pertinent for the coach, player, church sports ministry leaders, manager and anyone involved in using sports to make this world a better place. My prayer is that this book inspires you to action that will have results in eternity.

— **Pat Williams**

ENDORSEMENTS

"I grew up in poverty in rural Mississippi. One of my dreams was to get out of poverty and basketball became a way of getting out. At the age of 17, I became a Christian under the ministry of Voice of Calvary, led by Dr. John Perkins. In 1967, I got a basketball scholarship to attend L.A. Baptist College, now Masters College, in California. After graduating from the seminary there, my wife and I returned to Mississippi to work to make a difference in the lives of others.

In developing one of our ministries, we built a gymnasium. The gymnasium gave us the platform to start a Sports Ministry that would help us reach out to the young people in that community. P.F. Myers was one of the key figures who helped us develop that Sports Ministry for a numbers of years. P. F. learned a few things from us as he served our youth in Mendenhall. During that time, he gained a passion for Sports Ministry that continued after he left. Today, God is using him to do Sports Ministry internationally and it is my joy to endorse his book: The Life of The Shoe because I know it will be a blessing to so many who will read it."

— **Dr. Dolphus Weary**
Former President/Executive Director of Mission Mississippi;
Purpose Prize Fellow
4 Honorary Doctorates

"As both a classical concert pianist and piano professor at the 3rd largest collegiate school of music in the United States, I can honestly say that mentoring (the art of engaging, inspiring and empowering) is the greatest privilege of my professional career. Each day I invest in the lives of my students, much in the same way that a committed sports coach invests in his players. P. F. Myer's vision for Sports Outreach and its impact, through relationship investments over time, is an inspiration that mentors in many fields can follow. I tell my students not to play to the contest or audition, but to play beyond it, reminding them that there is nothing to prove but everything to give. Readers around the world will be challenged and equipped by the life-changing principles thoughtfully and powerfully delivered in P. F. Myer's *The Life of the Shoe!*"

— **Dr. Heidi Louise Williams**
Associate Professor of Piano
Florida State University College of Music

ENDORSEMENTS

"This author of this book, P. F. Myers is the most authentic and effective Sports Minister who leads a *Dedicated-Discipled* life to fulfil the Great commission. Just like the life of a shoe that can go thousands of miles no matter the weight, the author, P. F. Myers has travelled hundreds of thousands of miles like a modern day apostle to equip leaders globally in Sport Ministry. I believe this book will shape all readers to strive to live a dedicated and effective discipled life through their local church and community. It certainly has challenged, changed and shaped my life in Sport Ministry in the past 11 years knowing P. F. Myers and applying the principles I have learned from him."

— **Bradley Barnes**
South Africa
Former professional soccer player
CSRM Africa Continental Director

"The best books offering advice are written by those who have experienced … who have lived and practiced the topic being written about. P.F. Myers began working in a Sports Ministry in rural Mississippi and then led a community wide church Sports Ministry in California. He then served on the staff of Church Sports International (CSI), which led to his globe-trotting ministry to help churches understand how to use sports and recreation as an *Evangelistic-Disciplemaking* tool. Those experiences empowered him to become a valuable missionary with a large international para-ministry in the Netherlands and actually got that para-ministry to focus on the local church! More recently, P.F. Myers has become known as the Apostle Paul of Sports Ministry as he serves around the world through CSRM and other ministries. In other words, P.F. Myers knows what he is talking about. I highly recommend you sit under his teaching through this book."

— **Rodger Oswald**
CSRM/CSI Staff Emeritus
Founder & Former Executive Director CSI
Former Sports Ministry Professor
Founding Board Member - Church Sports and Recreation Ministers (CSRM)
Former local Church Sports Minister

ENDORSEMENTS

"I have known P.F. Myers for 12 years now and have worked closely with him while he served me and our teams in Liberia and as we worked together on projects around the world. P.F. Myers is a man with great integrity. I can recall our 2009 and 2011 projects in both Liberia and Sierra Leone (nations that have been ravished by war) where his selfless leadership and service to humanity were able to transform the lives and leaders of those nations. His many years of mentorship in my life have helped me to be a global agent of change and by the grace of God, I am grateful to say that I have become a culturally competent servant leader, enthusiastic, engaged trainer, strategic thinker, people-focused and problem-solver. It is my privilege to endorse this great book: The Life of the Shoe as I believe it will make a great impact across the globe. As a former Liberia national soccer team goalie who has played several years as a professional soccer player and chaplain at the 2010 World Cup in South Africa and 2012 London Olympics, I believe the principles from this book will be tremendously useful for the reader and will also serve as a resource to mentor many fatherless youths who are struggling with identity and true purpose of life across the continent of Africa and the world at large."

— **George Festus Blamoh**
Country Director of Association for Life of Africa-Liberia
Oscar Johnson Award For Excellence in Scholarship and Service.

"Some people are thinkers and some people are doers. Some people theorize and some people actualize. Few do both. P.F Myers is an Apostolic leader with worldwide experience in athletic ministries and is one of those rare servants who do both. This work is the result of a keen mind, a love for people, a devotion to Christ, and a wealth of experience substantiated by years of perseverance. All of which is confirmed by "fruit that lasts." I heartily recommend The Life of the Shoe."

— **Pastor Brad Stephenson, DMIN**
Deltona Alliance Church, Deltona, FL

"Sports, especially team sports, helped prepare me to be a pastor. I highly value team and how teamwork is such a big part of a healthy church staff. Being a team player is critical to working successfully on a staff. Sports also teach self-discipline through rigorous training and conditioning. Sports Ministry, specifically

ENDORSEMENTS

through a Soccer outreach is the strategic and highly valued methodology that enables us to reach kids in Cambodia and bring them into the Kingdom."

— **Pastor Kurt Langstraat, M.A.**
Lead pastor at North County Christ The King (NCCTK) in Lynden, WA
Former Collegiate Athlete; Former High School Basketball Coach

---

"Myers has a love for God and a passionate dedication for bringing the Gospel to the entire world. His many years of experience in equipping and training leaders and congregations combine to bring both Biblically-based integrity and pragmatic-functionality. While reading I felt the joy again of the privilege of ministering side-by-side with P.F. for many beautiful years. This book will move you to greater effectiveness of sharing the Gospel in a world that so needs it. It's a treasure!"

— **Theo van den Heuvel**
Senior Pastor, City Church, Groningen, The Netherlands.
Former Short Term International and National Director of Athletes in Action
Co-founder of 4M Global, Men's Ministry

"It's my privilege and honor to endorse such a beautiful book: "The Life of the Shoe" by P.F. Myers. "Beautiful are the feet of those who bring good news" comes to mind when I read a few passages from this book. P.F. is a most unique person. Engaging in even a brief conversation with him makes you see, feel and think differently. So imagine what you will experience when you read his book! P.F. has a gift to inspire you through his wisdom, knowledge and experiences. His passion about the power of the Sports & Recreation Ministry is inspirational and contagious. This book is a testimony to his many years of faithfully traveling and teaching the Good News through the Sports Ministry strategy. As you read this book, you will be blessed, inspired, more knowledgeable and refreshed to pursue Sports & Recreation Ministry."

— **Alfredo Whitaker**
President - Cayman Islands Football Association
Former FIFA Referee & Assessor
Former Professional Soccer Player, Costa Rica

ACKNOWLEDGEMENTS

Honestly I never imagined that I would write a book. I am not anyone special and I never really thought I had much of a story to tell… so guess you can call me an "accidental author"… it just kind of happened.

First and foremost I give praise and honor to God who has allowed me to serve Him through all my brokenness and imperfections. This book is a testimony to the faithfulness, joy, hope, peace, grace, forgiveness, purpose, and passion He has brought to my life through Jesus. To Him be all the glory!

I want to thank all my former and current staff and Sports Ministry partners and colleagues around the world for your friendships, examples, support, encouragement, faith, and perseverance. I wish I could list each one of you here, but I am afraid I might forget someone. Plus if I listed everyone, your names would fill these pages and more. This is also your story.

I want to thank Rodger Oswald, my mentor and friend who has knowingly in many ways and unknowingly in many others, shaped a lot of my thinking. I speak for many who thank you for graciously letting us "steal" your ideas and make them our own in our own context.

I want to thank Dr. Greg Linville who has taught me much through the "competition of ideas" and who always supports and encourages me to keep shaping church Sports Ministry for the world.

I want to thank my friend Debra S. who inspired me to go for it and who edited the first version of this book.

I want to thank Firefly. Your sacrifices did not go unnoticed.

I want to thank all of you who have prayed for, supported, and encouraged me through the years. This book is a celebration of all that God has done because of you. May you find joy and inspiration in these pages.

Throughout this book I have tried to give credit where it is due. I apologize to anyone who may feel slighted for some reason. It was not intentional. Please contact me so that I can give you proper credit in the future and in any future editions of this book.

In many cases where it was deemed necessary, many names, locations, and specific details of events have been changed in order to maintain the safety and security of those involved. I pray that my brothers and sisters around the world who are living under persecution will be blessed as I share some of their story.

All proceeds from this book will be invested in the development of local church Sports Ministries, to equip indigenous church Sports Minsters around the world to change lives through sports outreach.

PREFACE

Isaiah 52:7-10
⁷ How beautiful upon the mountains
are **the feet of him who brings good news**,
who publishes peace, who brings good news of happiness,
who publishes salvation,
who says to Zion, "Your God reigns."
⁸ The voice of your watchmen—they lift up their voice;
together they sing for joy;
for eye to eye they see
the return of the Lord to Zion.
⁹ Break forth together into singing,
you waste places of Jerusalem,
for the Lord has comforted his people;
he has redeemed Jerusalem.
¹⁰ The Lord has bared his holy arm
before the eyes of all the nations,
and all the ends of the earth shall see
the salvation of our God.

While this book's focus is local church Sports Ministry, I believe it will help any believer grow in their calling, vision, and ministry. The key Biblical principles apply in any *Evangelistic-Disciplemaking* setting. As I have taught these truths around the world, God has proved faithful again and again as leaders' eyes have been opened to new strategies and concepts. Many have said: "Wow! This changes my ministry and focus;" or "We see now that we need to multiply ourselves and truly make disciples!" One young leader in Africa proclaimed: "I come from a tribe of hunters. I used to hunt animals. Now I am going to change my focus and use these principles to hunt people (make disciples) for Jesus!"

Much of what is found in this book comes out of a training manual and workbook I had written and is based on my many years of personally leading a Sports Ministry. In 2012 I compiled the key principles for the first time after being encouraged to do so by colleagues to make the concepts transferable. Since then the manual and workbook have been used in over 80 countries to train thousands of pastors, church leaders, and sports people for church-based Sports Ministry. These concepts emerge out of my experiences of leading sports ministries in very diverse settings. Over the past couple of decades these transferable concepts have

PREFACE

proven to be *Strategically-Relevant* and *Efficiently-Effective* in rural & urban; rich & poor; congregational & para-ministry; and domestic & international settings. Many leaders around the world are now leading effective Sports Ministries and equipping future generations of Sports Ministers to go and make disciples mobilized, equipped and empowered by the training they received. God has used it to inspire leaders to engage in closer walks with Jesus and expand the vision of congregations even beyond the tool of Sports Ministry.

I've often encountered pastors and other church leaders who say they have a Sports Ministry. Upon further inquiry, what they call Sports Ministry amounts to: "We have some guys who play soccer together every Sunday after church." That is the full extent of what they call their congregation's Sports Ministry. Now I ask: "is that Sports Ministry?"

The Foundation of This Book

The mission we're called to, living for Jesus and fulfilling the Great Commission, doesn't happen by accident. Effective *Evangelistic-Disciplemaking* is founded on the clear *Theological-Truths* which inform and shape *Philosophical-Principles* out of which emerge *Methodological-Models* of ministry.[1]

Our Theology, or what we think about God, is the first tier of an effective foundation. It provides the basis for how we think, what we believe and how we envision our philosophy of ministry. It also determines how we live and what goals we pursue. Because God is immutable and never changes, *Level #1 Theological-Truths* remain the same across all cultures, countries and time periods. He is the same for all people of all languages and cultures worldwide.

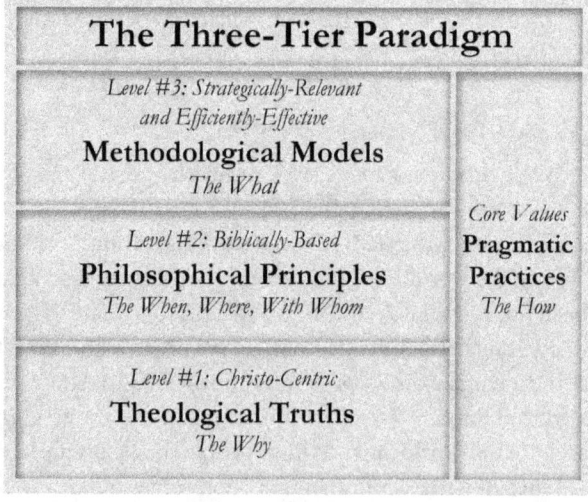

Then the second tier, *Level #2 Philosophical-Principles*, are informed and

---

1 What CSRM calls *The 3-Tier Paradigm: Level #1* - Christo-centric, *Theological-Truths; Level #2* Biblically-based *Philosophical-Principles; Level #3 Methodological-Models*. Sports Outreach Fundamentals – Chapter 3. OVP. See Diagram on page 31

PREFACE

shaped by our Theology. This set of Biblically-based principles enables us to envision a ministry structure that truly reaches those who are far from Jesus and His Church. Such informed ministry structures help us identify *Who* we are to reach and *When & Where* it is most strategic to reach them. These principles guide our actions, and shape the answers to the various issues and questions that are relevant in any given context. Therefore a philosophy of Sports Ministry is similar but not 100% the same across various cultures, countries and time periods because it is determined by what questions are being asked in each time and place.

For example, big questions such as: what exactly is salvation; what does it mean to say someone has been saved through a ministry; what is the church; or what defines a *Dedicated-Disciple*; should be asked in every country and context. The answers will be informed by Theology and will shape our philosophy of, or principles of, life and ministry. Yet specific Sports Ministry questions can be different from country to country. For example in America and many other countries in the west a current question has to do with the redefinition of human sexuality and gender. In specific what's a local church Sports Minister to do when an irate parent states that their 8-year old child is too young to decide their gender and therefore the parent resents the congregation's philosophy of designating separate boys' and girls' leagues?

Regardless of the specific methodological questions that vary from country to country, how to respond to them are best addressed from the philosophies and principles that are shaped and guided by Theology.

Then the third tier (what we call *Methodological-Models*) is often very different across cultures. This is because Sports Ministry needs to be relevant to specific cultures and in order to be relevant, it needs to be contextualized in each setting according to each individual congregation's vision, mission, calling and culture. While football (soccer) is the king sport most places in the world, many other sports vary in popularity from culture to culture. For example, ministry leaders I trained in Madagascar were strategizing on how to use the national sport of cow-wrestling to reach people for Jesus. In each country and language, among different audiences and groups, the method will vary but the underlying Theology and philosophies will not. Our method is where the 'the rubber meets the road' or 'the ball meets the court.' The process of establishing one's *Theological-Truths, Philosophical-Principles, and Methodological-Models* is not necessarily linear, but nevertheless is important. Without such a solid foundation on Theology and philosophy, a *Methodological-Model* that starts out with good intentions may end up as only an activity and fall far short of anticipated Great Commission goals.

PREFACE

Sadly, all too often Sports Ministry devolves into activity rather than ministry. This is understandable, because many sports people are quick to act instead of sitting around. While this can be good, the danger is that sometimes little thought or planning is put into building a successful and lasting ministry. We might regularly take a ball to a field in order to build relationships; we might organize a sports camp, league, or clinic. But what next? Our methodology can be limited or even flawed if our Theology and philosophy of Sports Ministry have never been articulated.

The purpose of this book is to inspire people across the world in every culture to more effective practical ministry by exploring key models and tools gleaned from Scripture; what I call *Ministry Principles in a Sports Jersey* or for the sake of this book, ministry principles for the sports shoe. The Theological truths and *Philosophical-Principles* of Sports Ministry will be conveyed through stories from my personal international experiences. The book will begin with my own testimony, creatively compared to a shoe, and how I was called into (sports) ministry. From there key concepts about vision will be discussed. The next chapters will define Sports Ministry, lay a Biblical foundation for Sports Ministry, discuss how all this relates to The Church, give practical tools for effective *Evangelistic-Disciplemaking*, express the concepts of the *Person-of-Peace* from Luke 10 and (sports) parables, and introduce the concept of *Missional-Sports-Communities*, *The Mansfield Graph of Evangelism*, and *2-T-2-2 Relationships*, and much more. The ultimate goal is for you, the reader, to apply what you will learn in building your ministry and become the shoe that God has created you to be.

The author gives permission to copy and use any appendices for teaching and training purposes.

Chapter 1

The Life of the Shoe

What is it about the shoe?

The shoe is the most basic piece of athletic equipment and is essential for success in many sports. However, it has become so much more than part of an athlete's wardrobe. Today, sports shoe sales account for billions of dollars annually. Shoes are sold for thousands of dollars at huge conventions where dealers compete for new releases of the latest styles. Some individual models promoted as limited editions are worth many times the original price as soon as they are introduced into the market. Led by the legacy of Michael Jordan and his culture-setting "Air Jordans;" (which now sell for hundreds of thousands of dollars), athletes are courted with multi-million dollar endorsement contracts by the top brands. The world's most expensive shoe is marketed in Dubai for $17 million. It is made of silk, leather and gold before being encrusted with 236 diamonds!

The question must be asked: what is a shoe really worth? The materials often cost less than $10. Yet it is how these elements are brought together in form, shape, and color, and then most importantly whose name is on it, that gives it value in today's market. Yet it is just a shoe, and it often becomes nothing more than a smelly and stinky covering for a foot!

The Start of This Shoe Story

In 2000, while I was preparing to address a soccer team in Latvia and encourage a local church in their sports ministry, I asked God to give me a fresh idea for making the gospel come alive to the players (See Time Out – Shoe Beginnings). The parable of the shoe was born, as was ultimately, the idea behind this book. The parabolic analogy went something like this:

Question: Have you ever thought of what your purpose might be or why you were created?

Illustration: In almost every sport, participants must wear shoes. I asked for a few volunteers to remove one of their shoes while I removed one of my own shoes. I then set the two shoes side-by-side and asked:

"Which shoe is faster?" (To anyone wishing to recreate this in your setting it is best if you encourage responses from your audience).

TIMEOUT

Shoe Beginnings

We had 35-40 people come out for a soccer game on a Saturday morning. A devotional (the Sports Parable of The Shoe) was shared at the conclusion of the game that included a clear gospel presentation. The local church team lost, but it was still a very positive experience. Two guys from the community team gave their lives to Christ! One comes from a Muslim family. In the evening we had over 50 people come to watch a video with testimonies of famous Christian soccer players and the Jesus Film. Many relationships were started with neighbors. A church that originally seemed to have no leaders had many volunteers step forward this weekend, including five or six leaders. God is answering our prayers for workers for the harvest.

I then said: "Let's find out."

I launched into: "On your mark, get set, go!" (Again, encourage cheering from your audience for the shoes—but of course, they don't move).

To emphasize the point, I repeated: "On your mark, get set, go!"

My next question began to bring home the parabolic lesson. I asked: "What's wrong with these shoes? Why don't they move?"

Answers from the audience varied until someone said: "You have to put feet in them."

To which I responded: "Ah, ok. Now let's see."

Demonstration: I then challenged my volunteers to put the shoes back on their foot and race with me to a point and back to see which shoe was faster. At the conclusion of the race I held up the winning shoe… with the foot in it!

Spiritual Principle: I then closed with the spiritual principle and lesson. I shared how our lives are just like those shoes; created for a purpose, nice and beautiful on the outside but empty inside. Only after the shoe has been filled by a foot does it realize its purpose. Similarly, only after we allow Jesus to come into and fill our lives do we realize our purpose. I also shared how we are individually created special by God with our own unique form, shape, and color. Yet we are smelly and stinky on the inside (sinful), separated from Him, pursuing our own dreams, going our own way. After Jesus comes into our life, we bear His name and everything changes.

Supporting Verses: I closed with the following Bible passages: Proverbs 3:5-6; Psalm 139:13; Ephesians 1:4-5; Colossians 1:16; 1 Peter 2:9.

The Journey of This Shoe

So this book is about a shoe. That is, it is about the life of an individual who was empty and lost until Jesus came into his life, to fill it and bring meaning and purpose.

Growing up in rural southwestern Virginia, we lived next to my grandparents. My granddad, who had graduated from Moody Bible Institute in the early 1920s, was an itinerant tent preacher up and down the East Coast. My grandmother was a school and Sunday school teacher who often told my sister and me Bible stories using a flannel board. Living simply and frugally, they survived off the land by growing a large garden, cultivating orchards, and raising bees and cattle. They gave away much of what they grew or harvested. I loved getting off the bus at their house to the smell of fresh cornbread, which we would devour after smothering it in molasses. My grandparents were a wonderful influence for my sister and I, and I attribute my early confession of faith to them. One day when I was probably 5 years old, my grandmother told me about Jesus. I asked Him into my heart, and because I wanted to make sure that I did it right I continued to ask Him to come in again and again every day of that week. In my childish understanding my grandparents were almost perfect, following God wholeheartedly and selflessly loving people. With a more mature perspective, I now know that their lives were not perfect, and following God's calling for their lives was often a struggle. Yet they set an example of faith that I aspire to today.

While I don't often wonder if I missed my calling, I sometimes contemplate what my life would have been like if had God called me to be an actual farmer, rather than a spiritual one.

Consider the following joke:

> A young farmer, standing in his field, observes a peculiar cloud formation. The clouds form the letters G, P, and C, and he thinks them a call from God: "Go preach Christ!" The farmer rushes to the deacons of his church and insists that

he has been called to preach. Respectful of his ardor, they invite him to fill the pulpit. That Sunday, the sermon is long, tedious, and virtually incoherent. When it finally ends, the leaders sit in stunned silence. Finally, a wizened deacon mutters to the would-be preacher: "Seems to me the clouds were saying, 'Go plant corn.'"

I have never seen my calling in the clouds, but I know I am called to preach Christ in and through sports, recreation, and fitness around the world. Recently I was asked to explain my "Whys;" as in: Why am I called to serve in the ministry that I am? My response is:

- I want to see the world reached and discipled for Jesus, and thus the ministries I serve are committed to seeing lives changed through the power of the gospel in the most difficult and unreached locations of the world.
- I believe the local church to be the agency that God has ordained to shine as His light in this dark world. The para-ministries I serve are committed to this, serving the worldwide body of Christ; equipping local congregations to become all that God intends them to be in a local community.
- I believe that Sport, Recreation, and Fitness Outreach Ministry (SR&F) is the most *Strategic-Relevant* and *Efficiently-Effective* methodology God has given His Church to connect those far from Jesus and His Church with the gospel. The ministries I serve are committed to using SR&F Outreach Ministry to bring people to Jesus and to serve the Church.
- I want to personally build relationships with people who believe in the work that I am engaged in. I seek ministry partners who will stay in regular contact and communication (about both success and failure), and offer prayer, friendship, and support. I'm looking for ministry partners who will "walk in their shoes" with me as I walk in mine. Together, we can journey together so that together we can share in the eternal and earthly joy and blessings from all that God is doing around the world through this great work.

My calling did not come from the clouds, but from the One who forms them. I attempt daily to continue to stay true to my calling as His farmer in the harvest fields of Sports outreach ministry. I hope you are staying true to yours as well. I praise God for the opportunity to know and serve Him each day. He is good and faithful!

CHAPTER 1: The Life of The Shoe

Living and Dying for What Matters

It was February 1944. Brigadier General Teddy Roosevelt, Jr. (the oldest son of President Theodore Roosevelt), had been injured serving in World War I. Now at age 56, with arthritis, a heart condition and a cane, Teddy was assigned to England to help lead the invasion of Normandy. After several of his verbal requests to lead from the front were denied, Roosevelt wrote a letter to his commanding officer and was finally granted permission to join his division in the first wave that would hit Utah Beach on June 6. He would be the oldest man in the invasion and the only general to land by sea with the first wave of troops. It is well documented that his leadership on the beach that day brought calm, confidence, leadership, and even humor to the invasion which we now know as the beginning of the liberation of Europe and the end of World War II. He continued to command his men valiantly; but on July 12, just over one month after the Utah Beach landing, Roosevelt died of a heart attack—while still on the battlefield.

What would drive a man such as Teddy Roosevelt, Jr. to make such a choice? He had a good education, a good career. He came from a famous and wealthy family. Why not enjoy life and leave the fighting to younger, stronger men? Yet he didn't. Instead of sitting in the background, he took on the most dangerous task and never did he let his frailties stop him. I wonder if they actually led him to conclude: "I am going to die soon anyway, so why not give my life for what truly matters?" Like Roosevelt, thousands of young soldiers entered battle that day knowing they would likely die, and many did. Yet they were willing to pay the ultimate sacrifice. Today inscribed on the memorial at Utah Beach are the words:

> To the officers and sailors of the United States Navy whose competence, courage, and sacrifice enabled Operation Overlord, The Greatest Amphibious invasion in history. Their selfless cause was to destroy tyranny and restore freedom and self-determination.

On June 6, 2014 (70 years after that fateful invasion), I got to walk on Normandy's Utah Beach—in my shoes. I was overwhelmed and humbled reading about the competence, courage, and sacrifice of those who walked in their shoes and fought for freedom. Here I believe God gave me a vision. A vision of waves of men and women storming the beaches of spiritual darkness for Jesus, bringing His hope and spiritual freedom to this dying world. The same qualities the soldiers exhibited on D-Day are also needed to convey the gospel to the in the most difficult and unreached places today; and also to our own communities.

So are we ready?

Are we ready to go or do we need to grow in the following key qualities?

- **Competence:**
    Are we prepared and knowledgeable about the gospel and those we are called to reach?
- **Courage:**
    Are we willing to step out in the face of our own fears—fears of rejection, failure, and inadequacy—fear stemming from our own brokenness?
- **Sacrifice:**
    Are we willing to give everything—even comfort, political parties, or our own pride—for the sake of the gospel?

Jim Elliot, who was killed taking the gospel to the Waorani (also known by the less-preferred term Auca) in Ecuador, is one of my heroes of the faith. Echoing an inspired passage of Matthew,[1] Elliot wrote: "He is no fool who gives what he cannot keep to gain that which he cannot lose."[2]

Roosevelt and his men were willing to give their physical lives for physical freedom. Unfortunately, the reality often is, both cannot be kept. However, just as in 1944 many men gave their lives to fight for freedom, we can now choose to fight for ultimate freedom. I believe God calls us each to give our lives for something much greater than ourselves; something of eternal value; something that will last. Now is the time; I can see it: men and women storming 'the beaches' bringing true freedom through Jesus to a captive and broken world.

The Fifty-Year Impact

There is an immediate impact we make on others through our words, deeds, choices, and smiles each day. But there is also the lasting impact that persists through the years.

My mom recently received the following letter: "You may or may not remember me, since it's been 50 years since we last met. I was that little boy you brought to Christ in 1962 at the mission in New York City. You were my Sunday school teacher at the time. You brought me to Christ and prayed with me while you were a student in college. You were kind, caring, persistent, and even tough, even though I was mean, absolutely immature and an uncaring little child. I'll never forget that time I cussed you out, but you hung in there with great patience and brought me to know our Savior Jesus Christ. You're one of the reasons why

---

1 Matthew 16.25f.
2 Jim Elliot's personal journal. Entry on October 28, 1949.

CHAPTER 1: The Life of The Shoe

I continue to serve the Lord today. Anyway, I just wanted to thank you. It's because of you that I know Jesus Christ today." That's a fifty-year impact!

Recently on a flight, I met a Chinese man. I learned that a Christian friend had been sharing truth with him and impacting his life. He had been reading (and was stuck) in the Old Testament, and did not yet have a clear understanding of the gospel. As I spoke, he hung on every word and then accepted Jesus as his personal Lord and Savior! God had clearly prepared his heart. It was an amazing opportunity. I just happened to be the next person God brought into his life to impact his journey of faith. I hope his decision will also make a fifty-year impact!

Instead of rushing through life, I was reminded to be available to God and accessible to people. As Paul was inspired to write to the first century Christians in Colosse, I want to make the most of every opportunity He brings my way.[3]

What about you? No matter your age, it's not too late. Are you striving to make a fifty-year impact? Even if you have not before, you can start now. You can begin your own ministry of the shoe. Read on to be encouraged, challenged, and to glean some great insights for your life and ministry. Discover what your life was created for as you explore the Life of the Shoe and discover how to become the shoe God as created you to be.

Reflection

How is your life like a shoe? Have you allowed Jesus to enter your life and fill you in the same way that a foot fills a shoe? If you haven't yet, why not do so now?

Prayer

Father, as I seek to become 'the shoe' that you have created me to be, help me to grow in competence, courage, and sacrifice so that I can be a more effective follower of Jesus and make a fifty-year impact on the world around me.

---

[3] Colossians 4.5.

Chapter 2

The Impact of Godly Vision

This shoe must know where it is going.

Growing up, I had a poster on the door to my bedroom. It portrayed a basketball player at the free-throw line with a ball, preparing to shoot. The caption read: "Without a goal, there is nothing to shoot for!" The double meaning is that just as you cannot play basketball without a hoop (goal), you cannot live life well without purpose, meaning, and vision.

There is a quote often attributed to Helen Keller[1] that goes: "The only thing worse than being blind is having sight but no vision." In her essay "*Three Days to See*" published in Atlantic Monthly (January 1933), Helen gives greater insight into this thinking.

> I have often thought it would be a blessing if each human being were stricken blind and deaf for a few days at some time during his early adult life. Darkness would make him more appreciative of sight; silence would teach him the joys of sound.
>
> Now and then I have tested my seeing friends to discover what they see. Recently I was visited by a very good friend who had just returned from a long walk in the woods, and I asked her what she had observed. 'Nothing in particular,' she replied. I might have been incredulous had I not been accustomed to such responses, for long ago I became convinced that the seeing see little.
>
> How was it possible, I asked myself, to walk for an hour through the woods and see nothing worthy of note? I who cannot see find hundreds of things to interest me through mere touch. I feel the delicate symmetry of a leaf. I pass my hands lovingly about the smooth skin of a silver birch, or the rough, shaggy bark of a pine. In spring I touch the branches of trees hopefully in search of a bud, the first sign of awakening Nature after her winter's sleep. I feel the delightful, velvety texture of a flower, and discover its remarkable convolutions; and something of the miracle of Nature is revealed

---

[1] **Helen Adams Keller** (June 27, 1880 – June 1, 1968) was an American author, political activist, and lecturer. At the age of nineteen months she contracted an illness that left her deaf and blind. She was the first deafblind person to earn a Bachelor of Arts degree.

to me. Occasionally, if I am very fortunate, I place my hand gently on a small tree and feel the happy quiver of a bird in full song. I am delighted to have the cool waters of a brook rush through my open fingers. To me a lush carpet of pine needles or spongy grass is more welcome than the most luxurious Persian rug. To me the pageant of seasons is a thrilling and unending drama, the action of which streams through my finger-tips.

At times my heart cries out with longing to see all these things. If I can get so much pleasure from mere touch, how much more beauty must be revealed by sight. Yet, those who have eyes apparently see little.

We read in God's Word: "Where there is no prophetic vision the people cast off restraint."[2] To be successful in life, we need prophetic vision. Such vision inspires being able to answer the questions about where are we going and why we are going there. If we live and work without knowing where we are going and why we are going (vision), we will not likely stay focused. Vision guides us regarding which direction to go and what tasks to do as it keeps us on course. When shared, vision can also encourage others who are passionate about similar goals.

George Barna, researcher, church leader and author of many books including *The Power of Vision* says: "True vision comes from God. If you want to be a leader, (not having) vision is not an option!"[3]

As Christian leaders, our vision should start with the question: "What does God want me or us to do?" Everything starts with God. Our serving God is a response to what we have seen Him do for us. Out of love for Him we want to share his love with others. Our work must be based in, and carried out of, a God-given vision. Indeed vision is not optional.

John Maxwell's says there are four types of people in relation to vision:

1. Some people never see the vision. They are **WANDERERS**.
2. Some people see it but never pursue it on their own. They are **FOLLOWERS**.
3. Some people see it and pursue it. They are **ACHIEVERS**.
4. Some people see it and pursue it and help others to see it. They are **LEADERS**.[4]

How do you see yourself? Which ones are you, and in what settings? The tendency is to believe that being a *leader* is the best. However, I would argue that the only one you don't want to be for very long is the *wanderer*. As we live our lives, we play out each of these types of 'vision people' at different times in different ways,

---

[2] Proverbs 29.18.
[3] George Barna, *The Power of Vision*, Baker Books, 2018.
[4] John C. Maxwell, *Developing the Leader Within You*, Thomas Nelson Publishing, 2012.

CHAPTER 2: The Impact of Godly Vision

and in some way, we are all leaders. God has given each of us opportunities to influence those around us and lead them closer to Him. If we want to *lead* other people in this vision, we need to breathe the vision. How do we develop a vision? Or how do we improve our vision? Many people have a vision for something. Some visions are too big and far reaching while others are smaller and more attainable. As we work on our vision, we need to find a balance between faith and reality. We must consciously consider both. We do not want to make the vision so big that we never achieve it. On the other hand, we do not want to stop dreaming big or limit God by our small vision.

The Old Testament prophet Isaiah speaks about the servant of God as an arrow.[5] Speaking from the servant's perspective, part of the prophecy given to him by God reads: "He made me into a polished arrow…." That's exactly what we should desire for ourselves and our ministries.[6] An arrow can be:

- Dull but well-directed
  - Such an arrow may hit its target but not penetrate and therefore have little effect
  - This is like vision without substance or without good planning
- Too broad and lacking a piercing edge
  - This is like vision with too many focal points
  - Instead of sticking to the main thing, there is much distraction with irrelevant ideas
- Too thin and narrow
  - This is like vision that sticks with tradition and is not willing to change or accept new ideas
- Polished, sharp, and perfectly shaped
  - This is like a vision that is just broad enough, just sharp enough
  - It has room for new ideas and is also focused and balanced

How polished is the "arrow" of your vision? Try **the Improving Your Visions exercise in the Scoreboard #1** on page 12 as a way to challenge yourself in three ways:

1) See the limitations of your own vision
2) Appreciate other people's vision
3) Expand your and their vision as well

This exercise will help you to further understand and experience coming to grips with comprehending how to establish the vision of God's will in your life.

---

5   Isaiah 49:2
6   Ford, Leighton. "The Arrow Vision," Leighton Ford Ministries, 6 Feb. 2015
    www.leightonfordministries.org/2015/02/06/the-arrow-vision

SCOREBOARD

#1: IMPROVING YOUR VISION

1. **Take one minute to look at this photo.**

2. **Now take two minutes to jot down your observations.** What do you see?

3. **Ask a friend or two to do the same.**

4. **Compare your observations and notice that you each have different perspectives.** One person may see the flower, and another may see the different shadows and shades of gray of the flower. Maybe someone sees the bee, while another sees the bigger picture and imagines that the flower is in a field full of flowers.

5. **After some sharing, now each look at it again.** If you saw the details be challenged to look at the bigger picture. If you saw the bigger picture challenge yourself now to focus on the details. Again, write down what you see.

6. **Realize our vision for life and ministry is much the same.** We sometimes need to see the details and sometimes step back and focus on the bigger picture. Other people with different perspectives can help us do both.

CHAPTER 2: The Impact of Godly Vision

My Vision Journey

It was in the 1990s that I started using "Keep pressin' on!" as a final encouragement and challenge in my email signature. I didn't realize then in how many ways it would become a theme for my life. I was inspired by Paul's jubilant explanation in his letter to the Philippians of why he kept pressing on.[7] He was confronted with the all-surpassing beauty of knowing Jesus and the personal, individual presence of God. He was overwhelmed by the reality of becoming fully righteous (perfect before God) through faith in Jesus. He became willing to suffer and lose everything; counting everything else as rubbish or garbage—all for the sake of knowing Christ and making Him known. He was so captivated by the truth of the gospel and the power of the resurrection. I marvel at how his salvation and calling was so alive to him.

As we strive to see with spiritual eyes; keep our hearts pure; and have enormous faith; may we be captivated in the same way by the reality of God's great love for us. May our salvation be so alive that we can't help but keep pressing on for Him. Through the ups and downs of life, I pray we will keep going. May we never give up! The optimism that comes from this exhortation can be energizing, motivating, and even freeing. Yet I know it is only a statement that is true when I live it out daily with my actions and attitudes, which comes from a deeper knowing of God and His vision and purpose for my life. We will each face challenges in every day that at some point will dim our optimism and dampen the enthusiasm. After that first game of a new season or the first use of a new iPhone, the euphoria wears off; often very quickly. We come back to the humdrum rhythm of daily life. So how do we stay on track and keep pressing on with vision? There are three questions I ask myself almost daily that help me refocus and regain a proper perspective and vision to press on. They allow me keep the 'arrow' of my vision sharp: 1) What do I see?; 2) Where is my heart?; 3) How is my faith?

1. What do I see?

Personally, I understand my sight to be a very precious thing. When I was in high school, I learned I was the one of the 1 out of every 100,000 people in the world with Coats Disease.

Coats disease affects my right eye. Even after more than seven surgeries (including laser treatments, cataract surgery, and a partial cornea transplant), I do not see well with this eye. Because I still have a good left eye, I am able to adjust and compensate. On a daily basis, I hardly notice a difference; but don't ask me to play baseball or cricket!

A few years ago, I began experiencing problems with the vision in my good left

---

[7] Philippians 3:8-14.

eye. Faced with the potential that I could be losing vision in my one good eye was extremely disconcerting. I knew I needed to trust God, but in those dark moments He seemed very far away. Yet I experienced God's presence in a very real way during those days. One night God brought me to tears in both eyes with the words the Prophet Isaiah was inspired to write: "See, I have engraved you on the palms of my hands...."[8]

About this passage Charles Spurgeon wrote:

> I have graven thee. It does not say: 'Thy name.' The name is there, but that is not all: 'I have graven thee.' See the fullness of this! I have graven your person, your image, your case, your circumstances, your sins, your temptations, your weaknesses, your wants, your works; I have graven you, everything about you, all that concerns you; I have put you altogether there. Will you ever say again that God has forsaken you when he has graven you upon his own palms?[9]

What an amazing truth! I am thankful for good doctors and God's healing in my left eye. Now my sight is almost back to normal. My eye journey continues to be a great reminder for me, with many lessons in trusting God for both my physical and spiritual vision. What do I see? When challenges come, do I see the problems and the difficulties? Or do I see the potential, the opportunities for something new, and a God who will walk with me through and even overcome these obstacles? How I answer these questions reveals a lot about my life and my faith.

Consider the words the Apostle Matthew was inspired of the Holy Spirit to write about how when Peter stepped out of the boat, he could walk on the water—as long as his eyes were fixed on Jesus! Once Peter lost his focus and was distracted by the wind and the waves, he began to sink. In that moment Jesus was there to reassure him and escort him back to safety.[10]

Just like Peter, I can easily lose focus when I get overwhelmed by my circumstances. At that point, I need to look to Jesus. Let us not also forget that as Peter cried out to Jesus, the other eleven saw Him only as a ghost and were left behind, while Peter experienced an adventure. I am sure as Jesus and Peter returned to the boat there was some disappointment from the others that they did not have a proper vision of Jesus and take the risk too. We can strengthen our faith as we step out and take spiritual risks for Him.

Don't get left in the boat. Be encouraged today: God has graven *you* on the

---

8   Isaiah 49:16.
9   Charles H Spurgeon, *Morning By Morning,* New Kensington, PA: Whitaker House; 7 November 2002.
10 Matthew 14:22-33.

CHAPTER 2: The Impact of Godly Vision

palm of His hands! Look to Jesus. He is there. He is faithful. He loves you so much!

2. Where is my heart?

Our vision comes from God and flows out of our hearts. We understand the heart to be the center of our being. As God works through us, one of the most important things we can do is to guard our hearts. We are told by a passage in the book of Proverbs: "For above all things, guard your heart, for it is the wellspring of life."[11] To know where your heart is, all you need to do is look at three things:

1) Where you spend your time
2) Where you spend your money
3) Where you invest your talents

Time, money, and talents are the most precious resources in a person's life, and God should be a part of everything we do.[12] Be careful that your heart does not get corrupted or become self-focused. Neither should you allow anyone to take away the passion and calling God has given you. Let this be your heart's desire. We shape our heart as we strive to become more like Jesus each day.

A Bible translator was working in the jungles of South America, translating the gospel of Matthew into the language of a local tribe. Upon literal translation of a portion of the gospel of Mathew which reads: "Jesus replied: 'Love the Lord your God with all your heart and with all your soul and with all your mind,'"[13] the Bible translator received a quizzical look from the indigenous translators he was partnering with. The verse did not make sense in their culture. All your heart? Why heart? As hard as he tried, the translator could not get them to understand. Later, their confusion became clear. This tribe understood the center of their being to be their stomach, not their heart. When he translated the verse: "Jesus replied: 'Love the Lord your God with all your stomach and with all your soul and with all your mind,' " it made sense, and his interpreters nodded in agreement. They now understood.

Whatever is the center of your being—your heart, stomach, or something else—God calls us to love Him with it. Out of the center of our being should flow our passion for everything else, including our purpose for playing or participating in sports.

3. How is my faith?

Do I really trust God? Do I just trust Him for the things I see? Do I trust

---

11 Proverbs 4:23.
12 Matthew 22:37-38.
13 Matthew 22.37.

TIMEOUT

Faith Beyond Sports Ministry in Kenya

One afternoon we hiked into the village up in the mountains. We packed a backpack with clothes to bless people on the way, where we passed small huts, no beds, no electricity, and no water. Returning we saw how much damage the terrible drought brings to the harvest in this area. It had not rained for so long, which caused these people to have great hunger. Unfortunately, rain was something we didn't pack in our backpack, but knowing our God we decided to pray, since He always listens. That night God sent His rain! The next day the little streams were full of water, and children were drinking out of the streams. Wow, how water brings life! Wow, how faithful is God, alive and hearing all our prayers.

On the final day of our outreach in Kenya, around 600 people were attending the soccer match between two local churches. All the members of Pastor David's [our host] church were present on the playground and experienced the huge impact of evangelism through sports. Many people accepted Jesus into their lives!

God even when I do not see Him working things out the way I want or expect?[14] Furthermore, do I limit God by my lack of faith as I consider my vision and the people we want to reach?[15] Who is living in my neighborhood? Who am I called to reach (male, female, age)? What are the people in my community like (ethnic group, singles, young families, etc.)? What do they like (sport and recreation)? What are their interests? What are their needs (physical and spiritual)? What facilities do I have in my neighborhood (fields, parks, parking lots, gyms, etc.)? Why would I start a chess ministry in my neighborhood if nobody living there actually likes chess?

Besides examining your faith, it is also important to consider the people in your own church or ministry. What are the talents represented there? We are each a part of the Church, the body of Christ, which needs to partner in a communal vision. Sometimes we make excuses about the things we don't have or the

---

14 Matthew 6:25-34.
15 Matthew 9.36.

CHAPTER 2: The Impact of Godly Vision

people we work with. We say: "If only we had somebody else to partner with, or the money to do this or that." Ours should be the same attitude as Jesus as recorded by Matthew when he describes how Jesus fed the 5,000.[16] Jesus demonstrated that instead of looking to the things we do not have, we should see and believe that God is willing to bless the very things He has already given us. So what do we have, and do we have the faith to trust God to do something with us and with it?

The gospel writer Mark records the story of when Jesus returned to Nazareth.[17] He was teaching in the synagogue when someone remembered that he was one of them. To them, Jesus was a simple carpenter's son, with brothers and sisters that they knew. As a result, they asked by what right did Jesus talk to them in such terms. Mark records how the crowd became very angry and upset and Jesus had no choice but to stop and literally escape. At the end of this passage, we learn that He healed some, presumably those who recognized Him not as just one of them but as someone with more authority. Their lack of faith amazed Him. The implication is that Jesus was limited in His interactions with the people because most did not believe in Him or accept Him. Their lack of faith hindered Jesus from doing what He wanted to in their lives. How often do we limit God by not having the faith for what He wants to do?

In Albania, a predominantly Muslim and largely secular country, we were organizing sports outreaches alongside local congregations. I was overseeing three teams working in different communities. One morning as I prayed, I felt God impressing me to pray that more than 100 people would accept Jesus through our two-week project. I shared my vision with one of the team leaders and asked him to join me in praying each day. I was shocked when he answered: "We can't pray for that! How can we put a number on what God is calling us to do? No!"

Wow! I was exasperated! After some doubt but still convinced, I went to a second team leader. He had no problem joining me in this prayer. Together we prayed and fasted for the next days. By the end of the project, we saw not 100, but more than 200 people accept Jesus as Savior! Then I thought: *Why did I not pray for 500?*

The Truth that Drives Vision

From youth, I was taught to tell the truth. One day in Mrs. Lawrence's second grade class I learned this the hard way when I was accused of a crime I did not commit. There was something interesting going on outside our classroom window. My best friend had been sent to collect a rock specimen for a lesson and I decided I just had to be out there too. So when Mrs. Lawrence turned her back

---

16 Matthew 14:15-21.
17 Mark 6:1-6.

I got up from my seat, exited the classroom and the school building through a door next to our classroom. I was having a grand time until she realized I was gone. Not only was I in trouble for leaving without permission, but my classmates, even my best friend, accused me of climbing out the window! I was distraught, but no matter how much everyone insisted that I had climbed through the window, I just could not admit I had done something I hadn't. I spent the rest of the afternoon in the principal's office and was only allowed to leave once my mom arrived to pick me up at the end of the day. For a second grader, truth can be a tricky thing. Today truth is under attack. Many are asking:

- What is truth
- When can I believe someone
- What makes something true

The first truth we must hold to in order to maintain our vision is the truth about Who God is as our Father. One of my favorite chapters in the Bible is found in the Psalms where God's qualities and character are on display. He is holy, righteous, omnipotent, omnipresent, omniscient, faithful, sovereign, kind, loving, and more.[18] The truth about His love is that is so wide and high and long and deep it is beyond our understanding and even "surpasses knowledge."[19] It was demonstrated in Jesus' birth, and by it all love is defined[20] It chose us even while we were separated from God and wanted nothing to do with Him.[21]

The second truth is who we are as His children. A few passages that speak to this are:

> But as many as received him—to those who believe in his name—he gave the right to become children of God.[22]

> You are all sons [and daughters] of God through faith in Jesus Christ.[23]

> But you are a chosen people, a royal priesthood, a holy nation, a people belonging to God, that you may declare the praises of him who called you out of darkness into his wonderful light.[24]

---

18 Psalm 103. A great study is to read Psalm 103 and write down all the characteristics of God found in these verses.
19 Ephesians 3.19.
20 1 John 4.7-12.
21 Romans 5.6-8.
22 John 1.12.
23 Galatians 3.26.
24 1 Peter 2.9.

CHAPTER 2: The Impact of Godly Vision

We are children of the King. This makes us princes and princesses! He created us and we are chosen by Him, special and unique. These truths are simple yet profound. They are exemplified in the birth of Jesus, our Savior! Dr. Neil T. Anderson, founder of Freedom in Christ Ministries, writes:

> The two most important beliefs you possess are Who God is and who you are as his child.... If Satan can destroy your belief in God, you will lose hope. God is the source of all hope. If Satan can't destroy your concept of God he will seek to destroy your concept of who you are as a child of God. He can't do anything about your position in Christ, but if he can get you to believe it's not true, you will live as though it's not even though it is. Not only do we have the wrong concept of our heavenly Father, but we have the wrong concept about ourselves.[25]

May we always treasure these truths by fully embracing them, living in them, walking in them and celebrating them. They are grounded in a perfect God who loves us and accepts us as His children.

One evening my grandparents arrived home in Franklin, NC. Walking through their garage, they noticed what looked like a little clump of feathers lying on my grandfather's workbench. When my grandmother started to pick it up, she discovered it was actually a humming bird. Although it looked almost dead, it was still warm and slowly breathing. While my grandmother held the tiny bird, my grandfather ran inside and mixed up some sugar water. He then returned and used a little medicine dropper to insert it gently into the hummingbird's beak. After a few minutes the little creature rose its tiny head, shook off its tiny wings, and flew away.

My grandmother, until 93 years old, loved to tell this story to illustrate God's love and care for us. She went on to say, "Just as I held that tiny bird in the palm of my hand, God holds us in the palm of His." Matthew records Jesus' reminder to us: "Look at the birds of the air: they neither sow nor reap nor gather into barns, and yet your heavenly Father feeds them. Are you not more valuable than they?"[26]

Often I am reminded of this truth in a very real way. I was traveling to attend a Sports ministry conference in Rock Hill, SC, but upon arrival at the airport my ride did not show up. It was already past midnight and everything in the airport was already closed for the night—no car rentals, no shuttles, no cabs, no buses. I was preparing myself to sleep at the airport, but half praying, half in exasperation

---

25 Neil T. Anderson, *Bondage Breaker*, Eugene, OR; Harvest House Publishers, 2000.
26 Matthew 6.26.

I cried out: "Lord, I'm really tired. If at all possible, I really don't want to spend the night in this airport tonight." In the next moments two people came through the door and sat down next to me. As it turned out the man was from Africa. This was his first time in the US and he was in town to attend the same conference I was. The woman was from a private transport service and she was trying to assist him in getting to his host family. Incidentally my ride was also originally supposed to pick him up. So we were chauffeured in a private car and around 3 a.m. arrived at the home of our host family.

However, the story does not end here. I found out later that I was originally scheduled to stay with another family, but God placed us in this particular home for a reason. The husband in this host family is an optometrist. As previously stated, I have had no less than seven different surgeries on my right eye. Upon hearing about my struggles through the years, he offered an eye exam; the first one in more than seven years. During the exam it was discovered that the pressure in my eye was extremely high, which if left untreated could eventually cause me to go blind in that eye, so the next day he gave me a free laser treatment to lower it. No medication was needed and barring any more unexpected developments the pressure should remain at a normal level for the rest of my life. Was this more than a coincidence? Absolutely! God had His foot in this shoe all along, or in more familiar words, God had His hand all over it.

Reflection

What is the calling and vison that God has placed on your life? Ask God to reveal it to you clearly and then write it down. Display it somewhere so that you can see it and be reminded often as you begin to take steps to live it out.

Prayer

Father, thank you for creating me as a special and unique shoe. Give me more courage and faith to daily follow you. Help me to step into the vision and calling that you have placed on my life.

Chapter 3

One of The Greatest Strategies to Reach This Generation: Sports Ministry

This shoe must know its purpose.

I find it ironic that God has chosen to use a shoe, a person like me in an outreach like Sports ministry because I was never a professional, collegiate, or even highly skilled recreational athlete. Actually I was far from it. While most people get injured playing sports, my major injury in life was at age 13 when I broke three toes playing the piano... but that's another story. I always did my best in recreational sports as a child and won a number of trophies, but that was mainly because of the other players on my team. Then in middle and high school I desperately wanted to play on my school's basketball team. For five years in a row from 7th-11th grade I participated in tryouts, but was cut from the team each year. Later in university I tried playing lacrosse. Lacrosse originated with Native Americans and is a game that has a goal and uses a ball and sticks that have a basket on the end. The local club needed all the players they could get so I finally made the team only because there were no try-outs! My point is that if God can use me in sports ministry, then He can use anyone.

From Mexico to the China and beyond, I have gotten to share the vision for local church Sports ministry in more than 80 countries. Opportunities to share the gospel through sports continue to expand exponentially. There are more than 6,000 spoken languages in the world today, but another type of language rises above spoken languages—the language of sport.

Sports can bring together a community, a country, or even the world. Many people of all ages watch, read about, or participate in sports on a regular basis. Maybe you've noticed huge outdoor television screens being placed in public areas so people can join together to cheer on their team. Or perhaps you have been to a park or sports hall in your own community that is crowded with people enjoying basketball, soccer, running, exercising, skateboarding, climbing (on a climbing wall or tower), or jumping on trampolines. Sports and recreation are everywhere. Do you know the most popular sports (and thus most strategic) in your own country and community?

I lived in The Netherlands where the most popular sports are football (soccer), cycling, speed skating, and field hockey. No matter your country, you needn't go far to see someone participating in some sort of sporting or recreational activity.

The Challenges of Language

I grew up in a small town in the Appalachian Mountains of southwestern Virginia as an unlikely candidate for anything international. Thus, I continue to be humbled by the privilege God has given me to serve Him around the world. I never could have imagined God's plan for everything that has happened. In fact the only foreign language I had ever heard was "country!" I am still amazed by people who speak more than one language. As my former Dutch colleagues know all too well, learning languages is not my forte. I well understand how easy it is to make language mistakes! Consider these examples from around the world with both sympathy and humor:

- After boarding a plane to Belarus, a stewardess came by and politely told me to be careful putting down my tray because "this plane breaks very easily."
- "The manager has personally passed all the water served here." (Acapulco Hotel)
- "Ladies are requested not to have children at the bar." (Norway)
- A doctor who specializes in "women and other diseases." (Rome)
- A dentist advertised "using the latest Methodists." (Hong Kong)
- "Please do not feed the animals. If you have suitable food, give it to the guard on duty." (Budapest)
- The airport will "take your bags and send them in all directions." (Copenhagen)
- Albania's national soccer team, 37 people, traveled through Heathrow airport in London. They misunderstood the "Duty Free" sign to mean "All Is Free" and filled their bags and pockets.

Someone once asked me, "What tricks do you use to figure out the different languages and spellings when you are in another country?" My response:

1. Stay close to my interpreter.
2. Be gracious and patient.
3. Ask people to repeat things 5-10 times and then have them spell it out if necessary.

Most of the time this method (apart from being gracious and patient) still doesn't work. Different languages for the linguistically-challenged like me can be very difficult.

Yet no matter what country I am in and what languages are spoken there, the gospel transcends it all. The love and hope of Jesus breaks through to the human heart. I have seen the reality of Jesus' proclamation as recorded by John in his

TIMEOUT

Open Doors in Liberia

During a 10-day project, the sports team:

- Hosted a 2-day reconciliation and Sports ministry conference that was attended by 150 leaders representing 45 churches and organizations from 12 or the 16 tribes in Liberia

- Spoke to a select group of 70 commanders and soldiers from the new 2500-strong Liberian Army

- Spoke on a university campus to 60-65 students

- Met with the Honorable Joesph Boakai, Vice President of Liberia

- Lead a devotional for the Liberian national soccer team and coach

- Spoke to 15-20 business executives and government leaders

- Spoke at a marriage seminar for 10 couples

- Preached at an outdoor campaign for 600 people, where 20-25 people accepted Christ

- Preached in 5 churches on Sunday morning, where more accepted Christ

- Hosted a soccer tournament for 7 teams, including one from the University of Liberia, two from Liberia's 3rd Division, and the Liberian Army Team

- Participated in a live call-in television show

Gospel: "When I am lifted up from the earth, I will draw all men to Myself."[1]

As distinguished theologian Charles Ellicott wrote in his Bible commentary: "The drawing unto Himself is the assertion of His reign over the world, from which the prince of evil shall be cast out. He will Himself be the center of the new kingdom, from which none shall be shut out. These Greeks who are drawn to Him now are the first-fruits of the harvest of which the whole world is the field…."[2] The whole world is the field! As a sportsman, I love that. Jesus is the hope of and for the field of nations!

Likewise, sport transcends many barriers and cultures. Many people watch or play athletic and recreational activities every day. It is truly a language spoken around the world! Whether in Cuba playing baseball; in Romania playing chess; in Latvia playing soccer; in the USA watching or playing American football; or in the Central African Republic playing basketball; I have seen many people come to know God's love, accept Jesus, and be discipled through relationships built through sports and leisure. It is a phenomenal strategy God has given us to reach this generation with the gospel to fulfill the Great Commission and becomes the cultural bridge. It is a way to share your life with neighbors, colleagues, friends, family, and even people of other religions in the most closed, resistant and difficult countries. It becomes the practical avenue that allows people to build relationships comfortably with others who have a common interest in sports. This is our missional response.

Working in Albania shortly after it opened to the outside world, I went each evening to the neighborhood coffee shop to hang out with the locals. It was a great opportunity to learn about the culture and discuss whatever was on the minds of those present. By going often over the course of a few weeks, I met a man known locally as "The Professor." He was quite educated and because I was a foreigner I think he found me interesting and engaging. Over the next few days I began to share with him about our Christian sports work, and he continued to stay interested. During one conversation he said to me: "We are Catholic, Orthodox, Muslim, and atheists and none of us know what to believe. We need you to come help us discover what we should believe." I was a bit dumbfounded because he considered himself to be Muslim. I had never heard a Muslim encouraging me so boldly, if at all, to engage in such a conversation. For the next few years, we did come and equip the believers for athletic outreach. We saw congregations starting Sports ministries that resulted in hundreds of people coming to faith! Such is the power of Sports ministry, a language universal throughout the world.

Sports Ministry Focus Areas

Sports ministry reaches people by providing opportunities for participation in

---

1 John 12.32.
2 Charles Ellicott, *Ellicott's Bible Comentary*, Grand Rapids, MI; Zondervan Publishing House, 1979.

CHAPTER 3: One Of The Greatest Strategies To Reach This Generation: Sports Ministry

two different ways: **IN SPORT** (actually playing or otherwise actively involved athletically), and **THROUGH SPORT** (watching and following teams). Spectators often can be reached through their interest in following a specific sport or sports team. Conversely, players can be reached through another player who has publicly professed faith in Jesus and because of this, Sports ministry can involve outreach to each of these categories, but there are two basic areas of focus:

1. **COMMUNITY CHURCH-BASED FOCUS** where local congregations are encouraged to reach out in their own community. Often this is done as recreational athletes are given the opportunity to use their sporting talents to serve various programs in partnership with local churches.

2. **ATHLETE FOCUS** where highly trained and experienced elite players and coaches are converted, discipled and equipped to use their platform for the gospel.

Both are valid avenues of ministry with much to offer in planting churches and/or growing or empowering existing congregations. Increasingly these two foci are slowly overlapping as The Church universal embraces Sports ministry and as elite athletes realize their calling to use their talents to build God's Church.

While elite athletes have a great platform for sharing the gospel, recreational athletes also impact their environment through relationships. In the Bible, God used important people, those in influential positions (similar to today's professional athletes) to impact their society. Moses was raised by Pharaoh's daughter and led his people out of Egypt. Esther as queen saved her people. Paul was a religious leader and citizen of the Roman Empire.

We should not however, forget how God also used unschooled, ordinary people[3]: people without power and worldly influence, much like He can use recreational athletes today. He used: Rahab (a prostitute) to save the spies in Jericho and who became one of the members of the Messiah's own lineage; Anna the prophetess who was a childless widow and who spoke of Jesus to all those who were searching. In addition, Peter and John proclaimed Jesus to the Sanhedrin after simply spending time with Jesus.

Researcher Michael Green said:

> The key players in the extension of Christianity seem to be not those who made this (ministry) their profession, or those who committed the better part of their time to it, but men and woman who keep their daily profession and share their faith in a natural way with the people they meet.[4]

---

3 Acts 4:13.
4 Green, Michael, *Evangelieverkondiging in de Eerste Eeuwen*, Amsterdam: Buijten & Schipperheijn B.V., 1979.

TIMEOUT

Open Doors in Uganda

Our project consisted of two different components, one involving a para-ministry and the second involving two local churches. We played soccer with local teams and with the church team. We also did a lot of soccer and volleyball clinics. For the clinics we concentrated on the neighborhood around the church. Together with local indigenous pastors, leaders, and coaches we visited a lot of small villages. Again we played soccer games against local teams and served the people by sweeping houses, fumigating, and holding medical outreaches. We also camped three days in a little village in the bush. This was a very good experience.

What can be more natural than sharing Jesus after having built a relationship through playing sports? Throughout the world there are many more recreational athletes than professional athletes and as recreational athletes are trained to use their sporting talents for the gospel, the world will be turned upside-down for planting, enhancing and expanding The Church.

It is estimated that more than 4 billion people viewed parts of the 2012 Summer Olympics held in London, making it the most watched event in the history of the world at the time. There is no question that sport is a phenomenal strategy available to influence our world. Since so many people watch or are involved in sports and recreation, we must consider how to use it to share the message of Jesus and serve His Church.

In this regard, many inspirational stories are being told. We are seeing how athletes and sports people can use their influence to impact society. Anyone who makes it to the Olympics is a champion, and as such has an audience who listens to them. One of my favorite stories of an Olympian using their influence to impact their community for good is of Julian Bolling. Julian was a swimmer from Sri Lanka who first appeared in the Olympics in 1984. After a devastating tsunami hit in December 2004, many children who did not already know how to swim became more terrified of the sea. Julian started a program call "Swim-Lanka" and began taking wading pools to numerous coastal communities to overcome children's fear and teach them to swim. Julian's platform as an Olympian brought an extra level of publicity to the program, and as a result more children were reached.[5] As you read more stories like Julian's, you can share them with others as you reach out to the sporting community in your own sphere of influence. By doing so, you too can lead others to meet Jesus and serve His Church.

Is it Football or Is it Football?

Growing up in the US, I only knew one kind of football. Although it was called football, it was a game played with the hands that threw, caught and ran with a funny looking ball. It had funky rules that allowed you to wrestle, tackle or even slam opponents to the ground—all the while wearing a helmet and shoulder pads. However, early on when I started working in Sports ministry I learned that in most of the world there is another kind of football: the one played with your feet; that uses a round ball; has constant motion but almost no scoring; lots and lots of running, and tackling that is more like tripping. So in order to become culturally relevant, I had to switch my vocabulary. What I had known as football became "American football," and what I had known as soccer become "football."

When I was in Brazil a few years ago our hosts would remind us there is football and then there is everything else. It is by and large the most popular game in the world, and therefore the most strategic game to use to reach the largest number of people. It is also simple to play and requires very little equipment. Goals can be replaced by using cans or shirts as markers and a football can be made of plastic bags melted together to form a rudimentary ball. In his book *Movements That Change the World*, Steve Addison even makes the point that a movement needs easily transferable concepts like football (soccer) in order to be successful.[6] In countries like Brazil, Argentina, Malawi, Kenya, the UK, France, and Germany, just to name a few; football is a religion. Interestingly, in one country where we are working, school officials came to our office and asked if we could help them come up with a new sport to teach their students. They said that they were tired of football! In their case I think it is true that you can have too much of a good thing.

In Russia during the 2018 World Cup, it is estimated that 500 churches and 12,200 volunteers organized outreaches in 73 cities, bringing the gospel to 100,000 people! They used events including Sport Camps, Festivals, Tournaments, Sport Clinics, Match-Showing Gatherings and other creative activities.

Football is the king of sport throughout most of the world; but in the US,

---

5 Julian shares his testimony in *Struggle and Triumph*, 2007, a video produced by Athletes in Action; Xenia, OH. You can read additional stories about current Olympians at www.athletesinaction.org/olympics.
6 Steve Addison, *Movements That Changed the World*, Downers Grove, IL; IVP Books, 2011.

American football is and probably always will be number one. On February 2, 2020, the Kansas City Chiefs played the San Francisco 49ers in Super Bowl 54 (the American Football championship game) in Miami, FL. The Super Bowl is just another example of the scope and power of modern sports in our time. It was watched by more that 102 million viewers with 30-second tv commercial spots costing advertisers $5.6 million (US) each![7]

For all intents and purposes, Super Bowl Sunday has become the secular national holiday. Both casual sports fans and diehards tune in across the world to watch a sport most of the world doesn't even understand. Many congregations and ministries now recognize the phenomenal reach of sports and design a model of missional engagement around this unique strategy.

In Latvia some years ago I met Amir, a 19 year old from a Muslim family from the region of Tartarstan. His mother died when he was 17 and life for him was very hard. In the conversation leading up to his decision to follow Christ, he said he often thought about dying. What a joyous blessing it was to see Amir accept Jesus as his personal Lord and Savior after I shared the gospel with his soccer team. He found true life, not death!

One sports minister in Malawi recently shared: "After one of our soccer events at a local church, a child came crying and shouting: 'Pastor, please pray for me as the devil is after me!'" We looked back to see a little boy age around 7 or 8 years old. Pastor Chimwaza and Pastor Diya started praying for him, and afterwards the boy explained that something inside him told him to go ask for prayer. "When you do," the boy heard, "you will be free from the ancestral spirits which are leading you to steal, to be so rude to your teachers, and to influence you into very bad behavior." The boy said: "Now I know Jesus and receive Him as my Savior. I will depend on Him." This young boy found freedom and hope, not fear and bondage!

These stories make it very evident that Jesus is: The One who can heal the most-broken of hearts and give abundant life to all. Jesus is the hope of, and for, the field of nations! In the middle of this desperate world and lost generation God has placed His people to shine brightly for Him.

> ... So that you may become blameless and pure, children of God without fault in a crooked and depraved generation, in which you shine like the stars of the universe as you hold on to the word of life.[8]

Jesus is raising up a generation of people who are pure and *fully devoted* to Him in every aspect of their lives. This is a generation that does not hide its light,

---

7 Katz, Brandon. "Super Bowl LIV Ratings Show Signs of Life Amid Multi-Year Dip" (online article). Observer, 3 Feb.2020. www.observer.com/2020/02/super-bowl-tv-ratings-nfl-chiefs-49ers-viewership/
8 Philippians 2.15f.

but is willing to let it shine before this world. It is time for us to find more ways to do so. It is easy for us sit back and enjoy our salvation, but God asks us to work out our salvation.[9] We need to step out.

The world is estranged from God's language,[10] meaning we have created a "Christian-ese" way of speaking that those who do not know God find hard to understand. This separates us, creating a stumbling block to others coming to Christ. **We need to return to a simpler language universal to others to connect with hearts and be that door for the world.** [11]

Two Universal Languages

In this world, we find two languages that are "spoken" by both believers (those who know God) and the world (those who do not know God). No matter: what country or culture you grew up in; what color your skin is; what your economic situation is; what verbal language you speak; or your educational background; you will understand the language of **MUSIC** and the language of **SPORTS**! It is through these languages that we have an opportunity to shine out our light to the world in a way that can be seen, heard, and understood.

Throughout the world, sport plays an active role in the lives of many people. Wherever you go, people will kick the ball back to you if you kick it to them. Whether you are: on beautiful manicured field in Europe; a dusty back alley watching a game on a community television in Africa; or just on the street in front of a group of houses tossing a ball in the United States; sports can be used as a *tool* to share the gospel, to disciple new believers, and just build relationships.

Lowrie McCown and Valerie Gin encapsulated a rubric that categorized how people engage in sports as shown in Chart #1 on page 30.[12]

To understand Sports ministry, let's take a look at the words sport and ministry. Sport is a generic term that encompasses **almost any physical, recreational and/or leisure activity**. It can be:

- ✓ Gender inclusive (male and female, not just for boys or men)
- ✓ Age inclusive (trans-generational, not just for youth)
- ✓ Ability inclusive (elite, retired elite, skilled & conditioned, recreational, learner, special needs athletes)
- ✓ Intensity varied (highly competitive, mildly competitive, recreational, instructional)
- ✓ Activity varied (team sports, individual sports, wilderness activities, fitness, recreational games, table games)

---

9   Philippians 2.12.
10 1 Corinthians 1.23.
11 Colossians 4.4.
12 Lowrie McCown and Valerie J. Gin, *Focus on Sport in Ministry*, Marietta, GA: 360 Sports, 2003. These categories found in Chart #1 (The Sports World - page 30) are only a summary of what McCown and Gin cover in their ground breaking book.

CHART #1
THE SPORTS WORLD

Spectators	Novice	Leisure	Players	Elite	High Profile

- **Spectators** – the largest group, this group is vicariously involved in sports
- **Novice** – very basic skills, introductory level of experience
- **Leisure** – recreational with emphasis on fun, fitness, and enjoyment
- **Players** – performance based (training and winning) with some personal identity based on their sport, also includes officials and referees
- **Elite** – all the characteristics of the "Players" but with the addition of extra weight of expectation and greater rewards
- **High Profile** – has all the player and elite characteristics but with the addition of greater fame from being very well known not just in a team or town, but more at country and international levels

You can see that we have added activities that would be considered recreational when considering this list (See Appendix #3 for a full list). I love the word recreational because it actually communicates what we are hoping to accomplish through these activities: a "re" creation of the body, mind, and soul; a re-energizing of each person physically, emotionally, and spiritually. In its purest form, that is what a true Sports ministry activity should accomplish in the lives of the participants.

From this point I want to acknowledge that many of the following thoughts are not original to me. They are adapted from what I learned and taught as I served under Rodger Oswald, Sports ministry pioneer, coach, and pastor.[13] How do we define the word 'ministry'? From the original languages of Scripture, *Shârath* (Hebrew) and *Diakinos* (Greek) mean **"to serve."** Therefore a 'MINISTER' is **"one who serves,"** a "servant."

According to some it is impossible to combine the terms 'sports' and 'ministry' because in their minds sports are considered secular activities that are worldly, and ministry is something considered to be holy and ideally heavenly focused. However, when we combine them together and direct the focus from self, we are talking about more than just activity or playing a game. Sport is then being used

---

13   Rodger Oswald is also one of my mentors. Like many, I am greatly indebted to Rodger and thankful to God for the role he has played in my life. His vision, passion, and heart for The Church continues to influence many throughout the Sports ministry world. Rodger taught me these principles and he originally published them in a series of *sports ministry manuals* published by Church Sports International (San Jose,CA, 2002). These and all of Rodger's materials can be acquired through the CSRM website (www.csrm.org). I have shared these principles the world over; and hope my rendering of them here maintains Rodger's original purpose and intent. While all the credit should remain with Rodger, I am responsible for any errors or misinterpretations.

TIMEOUT

Open Doors in the Czech Republic

This nation is considered to be one of the most atheistic countries in the world. Still as we engaged in building relationships through sports, we learned from conversations with the teens that they are very interested in God and that is the reason we were there. The city where we served really needs God. Many people, young and old, are living in darkness and it hurts to see that. It was such an encouragement to hear at the end of the trip about one participant praying to receive Christ, after nine long years of listening to the faithful missionaries in Czech and hearing God's call. It was a blessing because it gives hope that the seeds planted in the young people from the sports camps will be nourished by Him and will one day be ready for harvest, according to His will.

---

for a serious spiritual goal (purpose-driven) that will make an impact for the Kingdom. This perspective must include the following question:

So whom do I serve through sports ministry?
1. **GOD** - Sports ministry allows people to worship God by using their sporting talents and gifts for His glory.[14]
2. **THE CHURCH** - Through fellowship and discipleship, sports can be used to build up individual congregations of the worldwide body of Christ.
3. **THE LOST** - We serve the lost by spreading the gospel through sports.

Scriptural Basis
God's calling to all believers is clear: proclaim the gospel to all people groups in all the world. *"And you will be my witnesses in Jerusalem, and in all Judea and Samaria, and to the ends of the earth."*[15]

We all have this mandate. Yet in many cultures, sports are not seen as an acceptable method for sharing the gospel. It is seen as evil or just a game. In places like the former Soviet Union where believers were often persecuted for their

---

[14] See the Exegesis of 1 Timothy 4.8 by Dr. Greg Linville in the first book of The Institutes of Sports Outreach Series: *Christmanship*, pp. 46-53.
[15] Acts 1.8.

faith, it is hard for some to reconcile sharing the gospel with sports ('playing a game'). As one pastor bluntly told me: "We were almost killed for our faith, and now you are telling us that we can use such frivolous activity to share the gospel? I don't see it!" Or because there is so much betting, immorality, and materialism associated with athletes and sporting events, some cannot accept the gospel opportunities also present. I had the opportunity to attend a professional baseball game in the Dominican Republic. During the game there was open gambling, drinking, smoking, and fighting. The local pastor I was with was embarrassed for bringing us and even spoke out against the evils of sport. Admittedly it was not a positive environment. However, if you can grasp the biblical foundation of Sports ministry, you will begin to see that it is not the sport that is wrong, but it is the motive of the person using the sport that makes it right or wrong, good or bad.[16] It is true: God loves people—people love sports—God loves sports! He even inspired the Apostle Paul to write:

> Do you not know that in a race all the runners run, but only one gets the prize? Run in such a way as to get the prize. Everyone who competes in the games goes into strict training. They do it to get a crown that will not last, but we do it to get a crown that will last forever.[17]

These verses can be considered the foundational biblical proclamation for Sports ministry. Let us consider what this means for us as we lay a biblical foundation for Sports ministry.

The Principle of Liberty

Many things in life are not good or bad. They are neutral. Often what makes something good or bad is the way it is used and/or what our attitude is when we use it. Take television, movies, the Internet, money, and yes, even sports. In 1 Corinthians 9, Paul is an advocate of liberty. He is not saying he is free to do whatever he wants or anything that is unrighteous. He is indicating that he is free from any sort of legalistic posture or man-made rules if they interfere with the proclamation of the gospel. He is inspired to communicate that in a letter to the Corinthian church stating he did "*all things for the sake of the gospel.*"[18]

The gospel was Paul's driving desire as evidenced by his willingness to be culturally relevant even if it means adapting to another culture at the expense of his own culture. If Paul were alive today, he might be an athletic musician or a

---

16   For a full discourse about the Biblical Defense of Competition and Sport see Chapters 2-4 of *Christmanship: A Theology of Competition and Sport* by Dr. Greg Linville – the first book in the Institutes of Sports Outreach Series.
17   1 Corinthians 9.24f.
18   1 Corinthians 9.23.

musical athlete because those are the two main interests of the world that would give him greatest access to people in order to proclaim Jesus Christ.

God's Character - Principle of Divine Diversity

The God of the Bible is a majestic, multi-faceted God. He is diverse in His essence (Father, Son, and Holy Spirit). He is diverse in his character. Have you ever considered how many names God has? With our finite minds we try to understand an infinite God by putting names to different aspects of his character. One theologian identified 750 names he found in the Bible, and this is surely just the beginning!

God is also diverse in His character and how He interacts with His creation. Consider how He walked and talked in the Garden with Adam and Eve. He appeared as a cloud by day and a pillar of fire by night to the Hebrews wondering in the wilderness. He appeared in a burning bush to Moses. He wrestled with Jacob. In Jesus, we know Him as the Way, the Truth, the Life, the Door, the Living Water, the Bread of Life, the Good Shepherd, the Rose of Sharon, the Lily of the Valley, and the list could go on and on. Then there is also the fact that we all have different testimonies of how we came to faith. God meets us, and called us to Himself at a time and place and in a way that is solely unique to our individual lives.

Our CREATOR created CREATION with CREATIVITY. The point is that our majestic God works in a variety of ways. In the same way, God allows us to be creative (to use sports) in reaching others for Jesus.

Principle of Silence

While Scripture nowhere clearly states we can or cannot personally engage in, or utilize sports or recreation for the gospel, the fact that the Bible is silent on this is actually an argument for using it. In dealing with the silence issue, the question must be asked, "Who wrote the Bible?"[19] Using Scripture to answer the question, the answer is, of course, God as He supernaturally inspired the men who put pen to parchment[20]. That then leads us to a second question, this one dealing with God's character. "Is God holy?" The obvious answer is "Yes." The conclusion is therefore that a holy God would not have used sports or athletics as a metaphor for the Christian life if it were wrong.[21] While the Bible is silent, the use of sporting metaphors clearly indicates that God has no problem with sports[22].

---

19 See pages 53-59 in Dr. Greg Linville's *Christmanship* about The Holy Spirit being the real author of the Bible! It was the Holy Spirit Who inspired each word penned by all earthly authors. The Institutes of Sports Outreach book series is based on this belief and consistently references each biblical passage as being inspired by The Holy Spirit.
20 2 Timothy 3:16 and 2 Peter 1:21
21 See Dr. Greg Linville's exploration of the argument From silence in *Christmanship*, pp. 25-27.
22 Consider Hebrews 12:1-3, 1 Corinthians 9:24-27, 2 Timothy 2:5

The Principle of Human Giftedness

In Psalm 139, the psalmist is praising God for the fact He is an omnipresent God—so omnipresent that He was even involved intimately in the Psalmist's birth (v. 13). The psalmist declares that God has created him as a spiritual being ("inward parts"), as a physical being ("frame"), and that God's work was thoughtful and careful ("skillfully wrought"—a literal translation is to crochet, to delicately create lace). The implication is that God has made—each person as a physical being exactly as he willed and that His creation is "fearfully and wonderfully made."

God has also blessed each person with certain physical skills and abilities, and people participate in kingdom building when using those skills to declare Jesus Christ. That means when the soloist sings, the pastor preaches, or the athlete uses his or her platform for God's purposes, each is fulfilling God's will. To fail to use what God has given us through the creation of our physical being is poor stewardship.[23]

The Principle of Stewardship or Tithing

God has gifted everyone in different ways, and He desires we use even athletic skills to bring Him glory and build His Kingdom. If we do not use them properly or effectively, we are not being good stewards of what God has given us. As followers of Jesus, we must be good managers of our skills just as of our money and material possessions. Likewise we must tithe them, that is, give them back to God for Him to use for His purposes. Consider these verses:

- Exodus 35:1-36; 36:1-7—an example of many physical talents given by God to build the Tabernacle
- Matthew 25:14-30—the Parable of the Talents
- Colossians 3:17,23—our purpose to glorify God in all that we do

The Principle of Preparation

Sports are a tool that can refine us mentally, physically, and spiritually. As followers of Jesus we are in a process of being conformed (made to be like Him)[24] to His image and this process will not be completed until we die or are raptured.[25] Other Scriptures indicate that our trials and challenges are a part of this refining process.[26] Sports puts us into a living laboratory, under a microscope that reveals our character. What we experience through them is a microcosm of life. Winning and losing; injuries; bad referee calls; or other challenging sports situations; all reveal our spiritual maturity (or lack thereof). When we see how we handle

---

23 Matthew 25.14-30.
24 Romans 8.29.
25 Philippians 1.6.
26 James 1.2-4; 1 Peter 1.6f; Romans 5.3-5.

these things in the sports arena, we can see where we need to grow overall.

The Principle of Survival or Competition

We are engaged in a spiritual battle and satan wants to destroy us[27] Like any soldier, we need to become disciplined and trained to fight effectively. Sports provide a training ground that the competitor can use to learn how to be successful in this spiritual battle. Consider the traits of being a runner or boxer that Paul compares to the Christian life.[28]

Wisdom

Wherever you go in the world, millions of people are playing, reading about, or watching sports. Doesn't it just make sense to use sports to reach these people with the gospel? It is wise because the numbers interested in sports are huge. Consider this: Soccer may be king, but on June 16, 2019 more than one half BILLION PEOPLE watched the World Cup Cricket match between India and Pakistan, and for the entire tournament there was a global cumulative audience of 1.6 BILLION PEOPLE for live coverage![29] Is there anything else in the world

TIMEOUT

Open Doors in India

A local church hosted a weekend soccer tournament for 8-10 teams. Many of the players came from Hindu families, but during the weekend 75-80% or the players accepted Jesus! Follow-up was a priority, so the church came up with a creative plan. Instead of encouraging the players to come to church, where they would struggle to adjust to the Christian culture and face sure persecution from their families, the church started weekly soccer trainings. The coach of each team in the tournament was appointed as the "pastor-shepherd" of his players. At some point during the trainings, the coach would take time to lead his players in a Bible study or discipleship topic to strengthen them in their new faith until the day when they had to take a stand among family members for Jesus.

---

27 Ephesians 6.10-20; 1 Peter 5.8.
28 1 Corinthians 9.24-27.
29 Outlook Web Bureau. "ICC Reveals Astonishing 2019 Cricket World Cup Viewership Numbers; India Vs Pakistan Broke Records" (online article). 16 Sept 2019. www.outlookindia.com/website/story/sports-news-iccreveals-astonishing-2019-cricket-world-cup-viewership-numbersincluding-figures-from-record-breaking-india-vs-paki/338795

that can bring together 1 billion people at the same time? There are some people who may never be reached any other way than through sport. In his letter to the Corinthians, Paul was inspired to emphasize the strategic wisdom of adapting to those around you in order to win them for Christ when he penned: "I have become all things to all men so that by all possible means I might save some."[30]

Many other principles could also be included in this study. These few lay a foundation for the biblical basis of Sports and Recreation Ministry. I pray that you will consider them and ask what you and your congregation or ministry might do to use sports to spread the gospel. We know that God desires that *"none should perish, but that all should come to repentance."*[31] The only way some people may ever hear about God's love is through the relationship you build with them as you watch or play sports together. When we use sports we may be using a game, but we are not playing a game. Eternity is at stake! So PLAY ON!

Here again I would like to reference Sports ministry pioneer and pastor Rodger Oswald who often posed these questions when discussing Sports ministry:[32]

Is it appropriate for a believer to be involved in sports and recreation activities?

If what you mean by appropriate is, does involvement in sports and recreation violate a principle or command of God, the answer is "no." It violates no command of God. Of course, to say that means we need to define the word "sin," and then to discover if participation in sports and recreation falls into that definition. The word "sin" in early Greek was actually an archery term; it literally meant to "miss the mark." When an archer shoots at a target, he aims at the "bull's eye"—the center of the target. When the arrow landed anywhere else, the archer "sinned"—he missed the mark. The term began to be used in Christendom when people began to miss the mark—the absolutes of God found in His character or His commands found in Scripture. In other words, when I live my life contrary to the precepts, counsel or commands of God (the center of the target for my life), I have "missed the mark, I have sinned."

When involved in a sporting or recreational event, it is not the event that will determine whether the participant has sinned—sin will be the result of the motivation for participation, actions within participation, or attitudes after participation. A game is not intrinsically sinful; however, if one participates in order to achieve self-worth, that person has denied the value God places on him through the sacrifice of His Son. That is sinful. If the participant acts out violently or speaks wrathfully during participation, it is not the game that has sinned. but the participant that has. If the participant becomes haughty and proud because of

---

30   1 Corinthians 9.22.
31   2 Peter 3.9.
32   These concepts were originally published in a series *of Sports ministry Manuals* by Church Sports International, San Jose, CA., 2002.

SCOREBOARD

#2: Relevance of Sports Ministry

Sports ministry is suitable for many purposes which you will come to understand more fully as you read on, but to start your thinking now, these purposes include:
- It provides an opportunity for fellowship among the people of the congregation as well with the people from outside the church
- It can be used for evangelism
  - You can proclaim the gospel, as well as demonstrate it very practically.
- You can use it for discipleship
  - Those people who attend the program as well as those who are working in sports ministry can be discipled.
- It brings people to your church and allows them to be assimilated into the life of your church.

---

victory, or despondent over defeat, again it is not the game that has caused this, but an ungodly response to the outcome of the game. The participant has sinned.

As long as the participant can maintain his or her witness and bring glory to God through the participation, no believer is constrained to avoid sports and recreation.

I thought the Bible said that physical exercise/activity had no value. Is that true?

There are some who incorrectly interpret I Timothy 4:8, stating that this verse indicates we should not be involved in any physical activity—including sports. However, this is not what I Timothy 4:8 says. Paul is writing to Timothy who is pastoring a church in Ephesus; Ephesus is right across the Aegean Sea in close proximity to Greece—a country that revered the body at the expense of the spirit. Paul is trying to help Timothy to understand and teach proper priorities in one's life. So, he says in verse 7, "*discipline yourself for the purpose of godliness.*" The word "discipline" also means train. In verse 8, Paul does not say that physical exercise has no value; rather he says it has some value. HOWEVER, of greater value is godliness—which also comes from discipline or training. Therefore, Paul would encourage both types of training to take place, but that godliness should always have a higher priority.

It would be inconsistent of Paul to warn someone away from physical activity here and then to challenge him to "run the Christian race" or to commit himself as an athlete, when ultimately, his entire life should glorify God.

We are using something that is of some value (sports and recreation) to pursue something of greater value (godliness)[33] as we run for "the crown that will last forever."

Bill Hybels is helpful when he says:

> What God expects, He enables. Not only does He tell us that this world of wayward people matters to Him, but He also sees to it that we have the information we need to start us on the path of effectively reaching them.[34]

Review Scoreboards #2 & #3 (pages 37 & 39) as you consider what other Sports ministry leaders say that is also helpful and relevant:

> Where most ministries have to find an entry point, Sports ministry has intrinsic bridges.[35]

> As The Church seeks to carry out the Great Commission, sports can be used as a culturally relevant and therefore strategic tool to reach the nearby community as well as resistant parts of that same community. It is a means to fulfill the global call of Christ.[36]

> Sport in ministry is in many respects more strategic now than ever because sport itself rather than ministry models and programs provides real-life experiences where change, visual stimulation, and a built in community can naturally feed intense spiritual hunger.[37]

A Church Revived and Relevant

Some years ago I lived in a neighborhood in California similar to many throughout the U.S. Once largely populated by European-descent middle-class families, it was now filled with families from throughout Latin America and Southeast Asia. Often, when out to jog, I would pass a small Presbyterian church just down the street. My interest was piqued because I could tell that there was a small gymnasium under the same roof. The church certainly seemed out of place, and I surmised that its spiritual fruitfulness and opportunity to impact the community had long passed. I began to wonder what really was happening in

---

33 1 Timothy 4:8.
34 Bill Hybels, *Becoming A Contagious Christian*, Grand Rapids, MI: Zondervan Publishers, 1994, pg. 41.
35 Steve Connor is a Sports ministry pioneer, valued colleague, ministry partner and fellow OVP author. He states this in various books and seminars.
36 Rodger Oswald: This is just one of many truths that I have gleaned from him.
37 Lowrie McCown and Valerie J. Gin, *Focus on Sport in Ministry*, Marietta, GA: 360 Sports, 2002.

SCOREBOARD

#3: Practical Opportunity Overview

Sports ministry:
- Is a **STRATEGY** for The Church in evangelism and discipleship
- Can be used in conjunction with **OTHER EVANGELISM STRATEGIES**
- Takes away **BARRIERS** for the gospel
- **BUILDS BRIDGES** between people and cultures
- Keeps people **INVOLVED** and **ENGAGED** in ministry
- Helps to prevent **BACKSLIDING**
- Makes use of both your **PHYSICAL** as well as your **SPIRITUAL** gifts and talents
- Creates easy and natural **PARABLES** to explain the gospel
- Promotes an **ACTIVE** and **APPLIED** faith

that church, so one day I dropped in to see the pastor. Indeed, they were down to a Sunday morning attendance of 35-40 mostly elderly people—the extent of their ministry. Seeing this as an opportunity, I mentioned my work and asked if the pastor thought Sports ministry could be useful for the church. He immediately and excitedly agreed that it could, but he added that there was no one available to lead such a program. I invited him to meet me for prayer monthly, to ask God to send the right person to implement this vision. We did so for six months. Finally the pastor told me he had a candidate! He asked me to meet him along with the missions committee, the most (only!) active committee of the church.

On a Thursday night, we met in the church basement. The missions committee was comprised of five people with a median age in their 70s. I started to share the Sports ministry vision, but a woman raised her hand and said: "I don't mean to be rude, but look at us; do we look like we can do Sports ministry?" I replied: "Imagine there are kids coming from the surrounding neighborhoods to play sports here at the church. We are going to need smiling people welcoming them, signing them in, and learning their names. Then during the activities they'll get hot and sweaty. We'll need a team to provide water, snacks, and drinks. Then we want to get to know these kids—where they live, their family situations, and their needs. We'll need people to pray for them and their families by name and to step into opportunities to serve them. Do you think you can do any of these things?" At the end of the meeting, they were so excited they decided to turn their missions committee into the Sports ministry committee.

As we began the Sports ministry, they stepped into these roles and served well. This church that before was not even recognized or known in the community began establishing its presence, the presence of Jesus! New people started attending the Sunday services and joining the church. People started responding to the gospel, and the congregation got involved in the lives of people in their neighborhood. That is the power of Sports ministry, the purpose of the shoe and the language of the world!

Reflection

What are the sports, recreation, and fitness interests of the people living in your community? What are your sporting interests? Where do the two intersect? Do the exercise in Appendix #3. How might God want to use you in such a ministry?

Prayer

Father, thank you that you are such a creative and diverse God! Help me to understand more how to "think outside the box" so that you can use me to reach those around me who don't know you yet.

Chapter 4

The Church and Sports Ministry

This shoe cannot run alone.

For a shoe to realize its purpose, as previously discussed, it obviously needs to be put on a foot. In the same way the empty vessels of our lives must be filled with the Holy Spirit in order to be effective. This is the first realization that comes as we understand that we cannot live this life alone.

The second realization is that we also need other people. Just as shoes should function as a pair and also often as part of a larger team (the body), we need each other to accomplish greater things and to fulfill the purposes God has called us to. Without our team, we can easily become isolated, lonely, lost, and maybe even useless and forgotten. These "other people" or team we know as The Church: the "called out ones;" [1] those who have been united under the banner of Christ to shine as His light into this world's darkness.

So how is The Church still relevant for this day and age? What is God's view of The Church, as expressed through its individual congregations, and why is the Church so important?

First let us consider this obvious reality that is often forgotten... the fact that God indeed still loves The Church.

I asked one pastor: "Is it always easy to love your church?" His response? "It would be if it wasn't for the people in it." Sometimes we make the mistake of thinking that churches should be perfect. After all, they should reflect a perfect and holy God. The truth is, The Church is made up of broken and hurting people who bring their brokenness with them into God's family. They are being transformed into the likeness of Jesus, but they are not there yet. If we are expecting to find a perfect local church, we will always be left lacking and never satisfied or content. Somehow we must learn to love The Church and its individual congregations. After all, Jesus did and still does! We must see her as the central agent that God has chosen to redeem and has ordained to reach this world with His love.

---

1 The word Church comes from the Greek word *Ecclesia*. As a background to this discussion I refer you to the 3rd book in this Institute of Sports Outreach Book Series by Dr. Greg Linville entitled: *Putting The Church Back In The Game: The Ecclesiology of Sports Outreach*. As stated in that book any reference to the universal Body of Christ the words "The Church" will both be capitalized and whenever a localized assembly of Christ's Body is referenced it will be written in the lower case with words such as: local church; congregation or assembly.

TIMEOUT

Beginnings in South Africa

In Pretoria the local church grasped the vision. Especially the pastor is keen to go on with the work. This mainly happened because of his involvement in the whole project which included sports camps, organizing teams, and service projects. He saw that his congregation was joining the team and became very enthusiastic about serving their neighborhood. He now understands that sports can be used to fulfill Matthew 28.

Some years ago at a church-planting conference, a pastor from the Middle East (name withheld for safety reasons) shared many Bible verses to show much how Jesus loves The Church (see points 1-8 below). Keep in mind that in the Middle East, congregations are under a lot of pressure because they exist in countries where Christians are the minority. In addition, relationships between local congregations are often contentious, and differences are magnified because of these pressures. The pastor's points are good reminders of Jesus's unconditional love for His Body, but they also set an example for how we all should view and love The Church.

1. Jesus gives value and prefers it over His own family.[2] In this passage, Jesus is laying the foundation for The Church.[3] The Body of Christ is our true eternal family, and therefore we should prioritize it over our own families.

2. Jesus served The Church.[4] Likewise, we are to be learners and have a servant attitude towards other believers.

3. He intimately knows The Church. "I know your works."[5] He knows everything, the good, the bad and the ugly about The Church, yet He still loves it anyway. So should we.

4. He redeemed The Church with His own life and death.[6] Of course Jesus paid the ultimate price and in the same we should be willing to sacrifice greatly for our church family.

---

2 Matthew 12.46-49.
3 John 1.12.
4 Mark 10.45.
5 Revelation 2 & 3.
6 Ephesians 5.25-27.

CHAPTER 4: The Church and Sports Ministry

5. He prayed for and is praying for The Church.[7] We should be praying for our brothers and sisters regularly; even those we disagree with.

6. He brings victory to The Church.[8] Gates are not offensive weapons. They are defensive barriers. The Church is God's concern for the world today and it will be (is) victorious in Christ.

7. He loves it as His flock.[9] As a shepherd cares and protects his sheep so does Jesus care and protect His Sheep.

8. He has compassion for The Church. "Saul, Saul, why are you persecuting Me?"[10] When we injure The Church, we are hurting Jesus. When we help The Church, we are helping Jesus.

Some of these points are easier for us to accept and commit to than others. If you have been part of a congregation for any length of time, your church experience has surely not been all positive. Many reasons keep us from loving The Church such as are found in Scoreboard #4 on page 44.

While most of these may be valid concerns, often they are used as excuses that keep us away and too critical to get involved. However, based on how we see Jesus loving His Church we must be active participants in and supporters of His Church. Whether we want to admit it or not, we are just as broken as the next person; and the Church is made up of broken people.

Consider this anthropomorphic illustration. Once upon a time there were two clay pots. They were hung by ropes on the opposite ends of a pole that was daily carried by a human to fetch water. One pot was impeccable with no cracks or blemishes. The other was quite the opposite end of a pole that was daily carried by a human to fetch water. One pot was impeccable with no cracks or blemishes. The other was quite the opposite, cracked and well worn. One night as the clay pots were talking among themselves, the imperfect pot said to the other: "I wish I were perfect like you. Every morning we are taken down to the creek to be filled with water. By the time we make it back to the house, all my water leaks out and I am empty." In response the impeccable pot responded: "I understand your desire to be like me, but tomorrow morning as we are coming back from the creek look at what is below you and I think you will change your mind." As the sun rose brightly and the pots were filled, the cracked pot looked down as they begin their journey back to the house. He was amazed at what he saw. In the exact line where his water was dripping was a glorious row of flowers of all colors. Unbeknownst to him, his cracks had been watering them each morning.

We, The Church, are all cracked pots. Through those cracks God wants His

---

7   John 17.20f.
8   Matthew 16.18.
9   John 21.15-17.
10 Acts 9.1-5.

SCOREBOARD

#4: The Unlovable Church

- We think The Church, as it represents a perfect God, should be closer to "perfect" than it is
- We have been hurt or disappointed by people and/or by God because of unmet expectations
- We see the weaknesses of the people and "the organization" of the church
- We feel let down and unloved
- We don't like the style of music, preaching, or the people, whom we consider hypocrites
- We have been the victims of failed church or congregational leadership
- We don't want people to tell us what to do, or we consider those in leadership to be just about rules
- We don't feel holy or good enough
- We have theological differences that we cannot surpass

living water to drip through us. When it does it will produce a beautiful bouquet of flowers!

Real Church

The Church is not a building.[11] It is people. Each year many congregations close the doors of their buildings. Some are converted to community centers. One in the Netherlands was converted into a tea house and another into a mosque. Over time many become neglected and collapse around their foundations. Buildings do not last, but The Church as the Body of Believers will last for eternity. The Bible makes it clear that many things will not last in this world, but The Church will withstand all. Matthew recorded Jesus on this point: "*And I tell you that you are Peter, and on this rock I will build my church, and the gates of Hades will not overcome it.*"[12]

Nobody wants to invest energy in something that will not last. We want to

---

11   Greg Linville, *Putting The Church Back in the Game: The Ecclesiology of Sports Outreach*, p. 51, and *The Saving of Sports ministry: The Soteriology of Sports Outreach*, Chapter 5.
12   Matthew 16.18.

CHAPTER 4: The Church and Sports Ministry

work, not in vain, but as Paul was inspired to write: *"for the crown that will last forever."*[13] This eternal crown we must pursue includes most importantly God who is eternal, His Word because those are His promises which reveal His character that does not change, and the souls of men who once they accept Jesus form The Church. So it starts with The Church.[14] As we consider how to move together I want to propose as our goal building spiritual movements that become communities, not just planning nice activities or programs. Then in order to think big and reach the world we must first think small, that God wants to use us to touch one person at a time. Spiritual movements start with individual people who, as the Body of Christ, are following Jesus and making a difference where they live. Our impact will be measured by the lives we touch.

The Church as the Body of Christ is directed by Christ Himself who is the head. If we want to build into something that will continue, even after we are long gone, we need to work as members of The Church through one or more of its local congregations. God protects His Church and He cares about her as His bride as Paul wrote to the Ephesians: "…just as Christ loved the church and gave Himself up for her to make her holy, cleansing her by the washing with water through the word, and to present her to Himself as a radiant church, without stain or wrinkle or any other blemish, but holy and blameless."[15]

All people who love to win, and to be on the eternally winning side must become part of The Church. Local congregations are the ones directly winning, building, and sending people and developing movements of spiritual multiplication that result in new local assemblies of The Church. If we are able to work adequately in partnership with our local church, we are serving an organization that has the longest history: past, present, and future!

When God enables us to lead people to Christ, how are we going to actually make disciples of them?[16] Who is taking care of these new believers who can only drink spiritual milk?[17] Who is going to Baptize them?[18] Who is going to "teach them to observe all that" Jesus commanded?[19] Who is going to help them to grow and stand firm in the midst of this generation to become a star shining in the universe?[20] This is best done by bringing them into the safety and fellowship of a local church—better yet, it is best and most easily done when the evangelistic

---

13   1 Corinthians 9.25.
14   Consult Chapter 5 of *The Saving of Sports ministry: The Soteriology of Sports Outreach* by Dr. Greg Linville the 4th book in the Institutes of Sports Outreach book series which explores in detail spiritual movements and people who plant and grow local congregations.
15   Ephesians 5.25-27.
16   Matthew 28.19f. Consult *The Saving of Sports ministry: The Soteriology of Sports Outreach* which discusses this concern in great length.
17   1Corinthians 3.1-3; 1 Peter 2.2.
18   Matthew 28.19.
19   Matthew 28.20.
20   Philippians 2.15f.

TIMEOUT

Changed Life, Changed Community in Malawi

It was last month when we had a follow up in one district, where congregational leaders had organized Sports Outreaches. After completing all sports activities (soccer and netball, the most loved sports here), all people came together to listen to the Word of God; and after the pastor shared, one man stood and cried loudly. He said he has one thing to confess. That man confessed that he has killed albino people in the country. He went on to receive Jesus Christ before he surrendered himself into the police's hands. It was a very shocking and amazing confession as many albino people have been killed for ritual beliefs in my country and surrounding countries. Police intelligence fails to trace the killers but through sports outreach ministry a dangerous criminal surrendered to Christ. Right now he is in the hands of police but preaching the Word of God in prison... from criminal to preacher. It was at the same program that 15 people others also confessed their sins and accepted Jesus Christ.

---

part of *Evangelistic-Disciplemaking* is done by and through a local congregation! The greatest impact anyone can make in this world will be done as a member of a local congregation of The world-wide Church. Consider the testimony of changed lives from a Sports Minister who is working in Africa as a part of our network (see the Time Out above).

Yet there is great ineffectiveness and dysfunction of The Church worldwide because it is often paralyzed by greed, pride, lack of vision, or misplaced resources.[21] Everywhere pastors and church leaders say they lack resources and need more people to help. Paul reminds the Corinthian church that the resources we receive from God are directly tied in with a heart of giving and generosity.

> Remember this: whoever sows sparingly will also reap sparingly, and whoever sows generously will also reap generously. Each of you should give what you have decided in your heart to give, not

---

21 Consult Chapter #2 of Linville's *Sports Outreach Fundamentals* for an expanded understanding of the two "dysfunctions" of local church Sports Outreach.

CHAPTER 4: The Church and Sports Ministry

reluctantly or under compulsion, for God loves a cheerful giver. And God is able to bless you abundantly, so that in all things at all times, having all that you need, you will abound in every good work. As it is written: 'They have freely scattered their gifts to the poor; their righteousness endures forever.' Now he who supplies seed to the sower and bread for food will also supply and increase your store of seed and will enlarge the harvest of your righteousness. You will be enriched in every way so that you can be generous on every occasion, and through us your generosity will result in thanksgiving to God.[22]

Ideally if The Church had fulfilled its potential there would be no better network, and it would be: a) well-organized; b) have the best connections in the community; c) have great influence; and therefore d) have the **MOST AND BEST RESOURCES.** God Himself is the Provider for His church.

Relevant Church

So what do you think? How is The Universal Church doing today? Unfortunately the previous description of The Church is not true in most countries. Many denominations and congregations are struggling. Some local churches have shrunk as their congregation has aged or as the cultural dynamic in their neighborhood has changed. The Church is no longer seen as relevant as many congregations have broken apart and split over various issues. Many have closed their doors. Many seem more dead than alive. Young people commonly think that to attend a church is boring or old-fashioned and has no connection to their lives. Fewer and fewer congregations are making a significant impact in their neighborhoods. I frequently meet pastors who ask: "What can I do? My church has few men, few youth, and limited resources."

How can The Church wake up? What is The Church's mission?[23]

From Scripture we can extract these three simple purposes for The Church (See Appendix #2). As we do, we will also explore how Sports ministry can uniquely fulfill each stated purpose. Everything starts with God and a relationship with Him, so The Church must reach up, in and out.

First, Reach Upward in **WORSHIP** (Action: May I invite you to practice your worship right now before your read on by spreading your arms and reaching them up heavenward in praiseful worship of your Heavenly Father).

Worship is not spending an hour or two in church on Sunday singing songs

---

22 2 Corinthians 9:6-11.
23 Once again it is advised to read the 3rd book in CSRM's Institutes of Sports Outreach book series entitled: *Putting The Church Back in the Game: The Ecclesiology of Sports Outreach*, for a full comprehension of this topic.

and listening to a preacher. Paul was inspired to write that true worship equates to: "offering our bodies as a living sacrifice."[24] We are called to live for Him. In a sense, showing God how much He is "worth" (the word "worship" comes from the same root word) to us by giving Him everything we have and all that we are 24 hours a day, 7 days a week!

Maybe you have heard it said: "The problem with a living sacrifice is that it can crawl off the altar!" Yes, unfortunately that is what all too often happens in life, but also when many people play sports! They don't allow God into that area of their life and leave Jesus on the sideline. That has to change. To learn how to worship God through sports in one of the greatest, yet most difficult, things for any athlete to do.

Consider the story of Eric Liddell. Eric was a rugby player and track star from the U.K. who lived from 1902-1945 and was immortalized by the movie *Chariots of Fire*. The writer of the movie script quoted Liddell saying: "God made me for the (mission field) but He also made fast, and when I run I feel God's pleasure."[25] Eric understood that when he was using his physical gift to run at the highest level for God's glory, not for himself, he was worshipping and honoring God. This is exactly what Paul is inspired to write to the Corinthians and Colossians.[26] Christian athletes are to run "for the crown that will last forever," and play for the audience of One!

For comparison you could call Eric the original "Usain Bolt." Now retired, the Jamaican runner holds many world records for short distances. Eric was one of the fastest, if not the fastest, man in the world. In the 1924 Olympics in Paris, Eric won the bronze medal in the 200m and gold in the 400m. His best event was the 100m, but when he found out that the preliminary heats were to be run on Sunday, he chose not to compete in that event. He also chose not to compete in the 4 x 100m and the 4 x 400m events because the finals would be run on Sunday. For Eric this was a firm decision. As a *Dedicated-Disciple* of Jesus, Eric had decided at his career's beginning never to compete on the Lord's Day which was to be a day set aside for rest (Sabbath) and also for spiritual formation (worship, Christian education, fellowship, witness). Even the opportunity to win gold medals in the Olympics was not a reason for him to waiver and break his commitment.[27]

Many believe that Eric's victory in the 400m was God's way of honoring Eric for his commitment to keep the Sabbath. His commitment to follow God

---

24   Romans 12.1-3.
25   In the movie *Chariots of Fire* there is a scene in which Liddell makes this statement to his sister. However, Dr. Greg Linville (based on his interviews with Liddell family members and fellow prison camp members) claims Liddell never said these exact words in real life. However, Linville affirms that everyone he interviewed agreed these words accurately described Liddell's Theology. He truly believed he worshipped God when he ran.
26   1 Corinthians 9.24f & Colossians 3.17 & 23.
27   www.ericliddell.org

CHAPTER 4: The Church and Sports Ministry

continued after his athletic career was over as he moved with his family to be a missionary to China. Eric later died in a Japanese concentration camp in China in 1945.[28] Will we now choose to follow Liddell's example in everything we do? We can choose to run for God's pleasure and His glory, not ours. We can choose to 'run' in worship to Him, not for ourselves. A Christian's highest purpose and calling is to glorify God.[29]

Second, the Church must reach inward in EDIFICATION and LOVE to build other disciples up. (Action: I would invite you to practice this right now by giving yourself or someone else a hug).

Some languages have many different words for love, but English has only one, which limits our meaning when we use it for multiple situations. For example, a husband might say: "I love pizza;" but he might also say: "I love my wife." Does that mean he loves pizza in the same way he loves his wife? If so, he would certainly be in trouble.

The disciple John shared the following message he received from the Holy Spirit: "This is love, not that we loved God but that He loved us and sent His Son as an atoning sacrifice for our sins."[30] Jesus not only demonstrated but was the full embodiment of love. In short, true love is being willing to give your life for that which you love. This is the definition by which all other love must be defined. God loved us so much that He sent His Son who gave His life for us. Now, you may not be called to give your life for someone else, but each day you are called to give up your own selfish desires for the good of others as an act of obedience to God. This is no different in sports.

In the sports culture often idolatry and selfishness reign; by comparison, love for others shouts out like a megaphone. An incredible example happened in Grapevine, Texas. Grapevine Faith High School's American football team played Gainesville State School, which is a maximum-security correctional facility 75 miles north of Dallas. Many players from Gainesville came from broken homes and broken lives, having been sent to prison for any number of crimes. Their team had no fans to follow their games and played with substandard equipment.

Before the game Faith's head coach, Kris Hogan, asked that half of Faith High School's fans cheer for the Gainesville team. Not only did they cheer, but they sat on the visitor's side of the bleachers (many cheering against their own kids) and made banners and a human tunnel for the Gainesville team to run through at the start of the game. Then afterward, each Gainesville player received a bag

---

28   Ibid.
29   I am not advocating that sports can never be played on Sunday, however there are many things to be considered in this matter. The reader is encouraged to contemplate this topic by studying the scores of Bible verses and passages relevant to Sabbath and Lord's Days and also by reading how it is discussed in other books in CSRM's Institute of Sports Outreach book series (*Christmanship*, Chapter 7; *Putting The Church Back in the Game*, Chapter 6; "*The Saving of Sports Ministry*," pp. 62-66.
30   1 John 4.7-12.

TIMEOUT

Open Doors in Sierra Leone

Over the course of the 10-day project the church missions sports team:

- Led three different sports ministry training seminars: one for 35-40 pastors; another for 50-60 sportsmen, pastors, and community leaders; and another for 15-20 top level soccer coaches and administrators

- Spoke to 10-15 of the country's top soccer clubs

- Spoke at 7-10 schools

- Met with the mayor of Freetown, the head of the Parliamentary Oversight Committee for Youth and Sports, and the Olympic Committee

- Spoke with many of the Sierra Leone national teams (boxing, track and field, basketball, volleyball, a team of retired national team soccer players, among others)

- Preached in 3 churches

- Spoke on two national radio programs and conducted various interviews with reporters

- Saw hundreds of people accept Christ through many of these opportunities!

for the ride home that included a burger, fries, a drink, candy, a Bible and an encouraging letter from a Faith player.

The Gainesville coach saw Hogan, grabbed him hard by the shoulders and said: "You'll never know what your people did for these kids tonight. You'll never, ever know." As the bus pulled away, all the Gainesville players crammed to one side and pressed their hands to the window, staring at these people they'd never met before, watching their waves and smiles disappearing into the night.[31]

Sport is one of the best tools to build up and love others with the hope of drawing them closer to Jesus.

Third, The Church must reach Outward in *Evangelistic-Disciplemaking*,[32] becoming like Jesus. (Action: I invite you to actively practice this right now by spreading your arms out as wide as you can to symbolically indicate your desire to reach those far from Jesus and His Church). We are all familiar with the Great Commission as recorded by the disciple Matthew, when after His death Jesue appeared to His disciples with final instructions.[33] However, there is an important element within this passage that is often overlooked. Unbelievably, verse 17 says that even as Jesus was standing before them, some doubted! It's as if Jesus knew what they were thinking because He began His instructions by reassuring them. When He said: "all authority in heaven and earth has been given to me," He insinuated: "Remember guys! I Am the one who calmed the storm, walked on the water, raised Lazarus from the dead and healed the blind, the lame, and the leper. I rule and reign over this universe, over all elements of nature, death and life." Then He concludes His instructions with a second encouraging word; that they are not alone. He is with them "to the very end of the age." Because we have not yet reached the end of the age, this is a promise for us today and all those who come after us.

Great Commission Church

Okay, so in the middle of all of this God does not tell His disciples to make converts, but instead to make disciples! Those He called to be a disciple understood they needed to be both a learner (head knowledge) and a follower (first a watcher, then a doer, putting what they had seen into practice). Then the Disciples were challenged to go do the same. "Teaching them to obey all I have commanded" covered the head knowledge. Baptism was the visible requirement that symbolized a willingness to die to the old life and commit to the new life. Evangelism and discipleship were to be accomplished as one activity, not to be

---

31 www.sports.espn.go.com/espnmag/story?section=magazine&id=3789373
32 This concept of *Evangelistic-Disciplemaking* is expanded and explored in depth in chapter 5 of this book and also in the fourth book in CSRM's Institute of Sports Outreach series: *The Saving of Sports ministry*.
33 Matthew 28.16-20.

separated. They cannot be separated and must always go together; there must be a plan for discipleship when we begin to evangelize.

So let us consider what role The Church, though broken and filled with broken people, has in this in relation to our society today. The condition of religion within the US, while characteristically different then much of the world, is a good starting point for comparison. Many things happening in our communities give cause for concern. This may be becoming obvious to you, but in his book *Christians in the Age of Outrage*, Dr. Ed Stetzer suggests that the USA is shifting from a country of cultural Christianity to one with a more secular world view. When you divide up the US into four religious categories, Stetzer reasons that it might be something like this: 25% non-Christian, 25% cultural Christians, 25% congregational Christians, and 25% convictional Christians. He says that the population of people identifying themselves as non-Christian is growing, while at the same time the U.S. moves further and further away from Christian values.[34] As a result, I strongly believe in our postmodern society the distance (in relevance and relationship) between The Church and the world is growing. In his book *The Present Future*, Reggie McNeal discusses the growing phenomenon of what he calls post-congregational Christians, people who choose to pursue their spiritual journey outside the routines and rhythms of the congregational model of church that has dominated religious activity for centuries.[35] It used to be that the attractional church model, where people come to us, was effective and could draw people in. All we had to do was sit in our comfortable churches. Today many people don't see their need for God or The Church, so in most cases no matter what program is organized, they will not come.

With this in mind, we can classify people into four general categories in relation to The Church. If we can understand our audience then we can better understand how The Church can reach them. Above it all, consider the fact that each of these four groups of people can all be reached effectively through Sports ministry!

Four Categories of Non-Churched People[36]
1. Never Churched
This group has never been to church and has a limited to no understanding of a Christian world-view or a faith in Jesus. They have no religious underpinnings that give them any reference for a discussion about God and faith.

---

34   Ed Stetzer, *Christians in the Age of Outrage*, Tyndale House Publishers, 2018.
35   Reggie McNeal, *The Present Future*, Jossey-Bass, 2009.
36   See an expanded exploration of the first three categories of non-churched people in *Christmanship: A Theology of Competition and Sport*. The fourth category originated with me but would compare somewhat with one segment of Dr. Greg Linville's "Churched" category—those who have a relationship with a local church but not with Jesus.

2. De - Churched

This group has had a negative experience with church. Whether they have been hurt by someone in church, seen church as just a bunch of rules that take away their freedom, or had a negative experience in church as a child, these people need healing and a fresh experience with someone who is following Jesus.[37]

3. Other Churched

This group has been exposed to some other faith or religion and has not accepted Christ as their savior and does not hold a Christian world-view. These people are spiritually minded and are following other religions. They often don't want to rely on someone or something else for their "salvation." For them, salvation is about doing good deeds, achieving a higher level of consciousness, being a good person, and living a good life while following a religious code. It can also be that they are practicing other religious rituals or traditions.

4. Dumb Churched (Cultural Churched)

The term "dumb" is not used to describe the intelligence or mental capacities of a person, but rather it is used to describe a person who lacks a basic comprehension of, and/or application of foundational biblical truths. Each person within this sub-category has an affiliation and/or familiarity with church but not a personal relationship with Jesus. Some may identify themselves as Christians simply because they were born into a Christian family or attended a Christian school. Others may attend a local church on a regular or limited basis, but they remain uninformed, or possibly even misinformed, about Christ and Christianity and would not be considered to be a Christian. If they do have a faith, it is very shallow and ineffectual or very new. The *Dumb-Churched (Cultural-Churched)* range from to being what is called a "CEO" (Christmas-Easter Only) Christian, to being more seriously religious (attending services once or more each month). Regardless of their participation in a local congregation, they do not have a growing relationship with God. Those who make up the very religious segment are the "white-washed tombs" that Jesus refers to in Matthew 23:27. They look pretty good on the outside, but inside from their heart they do not know Jesus.

The *Sports Ministry Pyramid*

Ultimately ministry is about people, and The Church should work tirelessly and selflessly to reach each of these four categories. We must remember that Jesus developed relationships and worked with individuals, not programs.

---

[37] Joshua Packard calls this group the "Dones." He gives a fuller explanation along with strategy to reach them in this article: www.christianitytoday.com/pastors/2015/summer-2015/meet-dones.

SPORTS MINISTRY PYRAMID

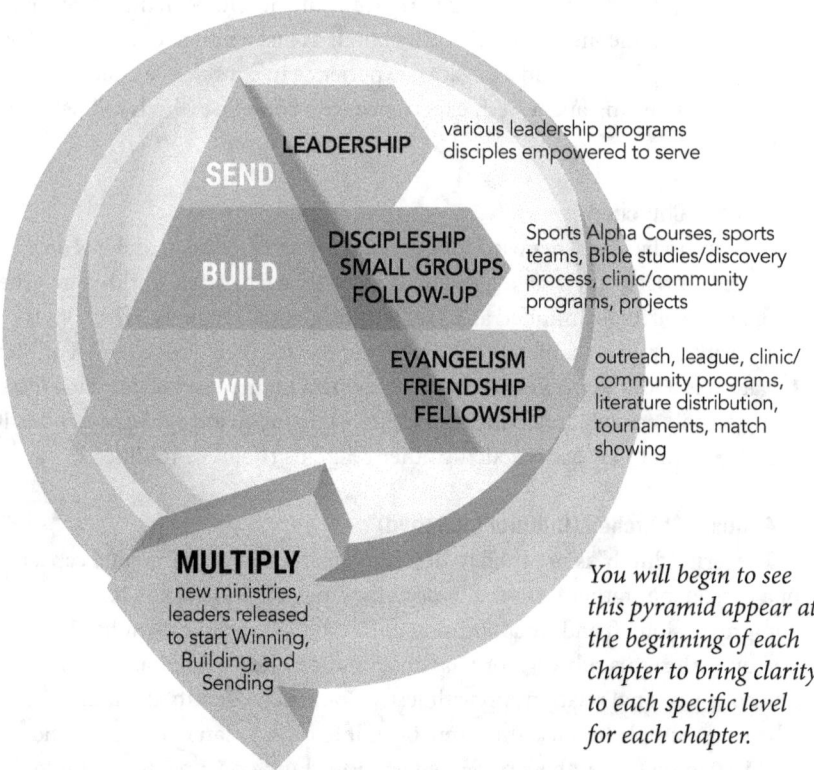

You will begin to see this pyramid appear at the beginning of each chapter to bring clarity to each specific level for each chapter.

Years ago when I started in ministry in Mississippi, I was busy running lots of Sports ministry programs. We were running leagues, tournaments, afterschool programs, fitness programs, special sporting events, and more. My stated goal was to fulfill the Great Commission and make disciples. So after more than a year of great activity, when I had a chance to slow down, I sadly realized that there were no disciples. My initial reaction was to be angry at God. I thought: "Here I am through my blood, sweat and tears working for You, and You, God, are not holding up Your end of this bargain!" Upon further reflection and a clear rebuke from God, I realized that the problem was with me and not with Him. I had gotten off track. I had lost focus. I was working so hard *for* God that I had missed the relationship *with* God and left out the necessity to build relationships with others. I had forgotten that our impact will be measured by the lives we build into, not by doing nice programs. I was missing what Howard Hendricks eloquently summarizes:

> What am I doing today that will guarantee my impact for Jesus in the next generation? If I understand the New Testament

correctly, there are two things God is going to take off this planet. One is His Word, and the other is His people. If you are building into people, you can be confident that will last forever... Mentoring is a ministry of multiplication. Every time you build into the life of another man (or woman), you launch a process that ideally will never end. [38]

After further evaluation, God brought me back to a model that I had been first introduced to me by a youth leader when I was working in youth ministry in college in 1987. I took this pyramid and adapted it to our Sports ministry. Years later when I joined a larger Sports ministry and moved overseas to serve internationally, I adopted their common language for the different levels. This ministry pyramid has proven to be timeless and culturally transcendent while clearly bringing into focus people and relationships. It also shows how and where sports fits in.

As I experienced doing Sports ministry, it is possible to lose focus and not accomplish all that God intends for us. Sports ministry events can easily become just nice, fun activities unless we stay focused on our goal and have a plan to make disciples as we expect God to work and incorporate those who come to Christ into the life of The Church. This Sports ministry Pyramid shows how Sports ministry fulfills the mission of The Church and helps us to stay on target through the planning and implementation of any program. As an initial contact is made with a person at an entry level sports ministry program or event, it should be the desire of the Sports ministry leadership for that person to progress up the pyramid to become a mature follower of Jesus, and a leader, and a multiplier. There is no set timeframe for each person to move from one level to another. After all, we are on individual spiritual journeys of faith. Throughout the ups and downs, opportunities and challenges in our lives we are constantly being molded, growing to become more like Jesus Christ.[39]

This can be summed up in one verse: "And these things you have heard me say in the presence of many witnesses entrust to reliable men who will also be qualified to teach others."[40] As Paul admonished Timothy in the movement of spiritual multiplication, this Sports ministry Pyramid is the foundational core of 2 Timothy 2:2. We will identify the relationships from this verse as *2-T-2-2 Relationships* and discuss them at length in chapter 7. This cyclical model perpetuates itself as leaders are trained, developed, and then released to their own callings and ministries as trainers themselves. A brief overview of the levels of the pyramid and a brief summary of each follows.

---

38   Howard Hendricks, *Promise2: A Man and His Friends, A Mandate for Mentoring*; Al Janssen and Larry K. Weeden, *Seven Promises of a Promise Keeper*, Colorado Springs, CO: Focus on the Family Publishing, 1994.
39   Philippians 1.6.
40   2 Timothy 2.2.

The WIN Level

This level is geared toward the mass of humanity as a whole, anyone who is under our geographic, demographic or digital sphere of influence in our neighborhood, community, country, even the world. Programs, activities, and outreaches strive for numbers. Yes the numbers game is acceptable here! The only commitment required by those who come is participation in the activity being attended, or acceptance of the literature being distributed. The desire of the ministry at this level is to establish a presence in the community. Fellowship/Friendship and Evangelism takes place here as a person has an opportunity to make a first-time decision for Christ or make a commitment to go deeper with God in their own spiritual journey. The key is to create an environment that facilitates building relationships and where Christian values can be displayed; verbally and non-verbally when appropriate. Growth of individuals is encouraged and facilitated through general, open (to the group) or closed (one on one) devotional times and prayer times, as relationships develop between the believers and unbelievers, and by maintaining a Christlike atmosphere and witness.[41]

Some program examples for this level include the following: organizing sports teams, recreational activities, outreach leagues, sports camps, sports clinics, match-showing videos, literature distribution, and clubs, etc.

The BUILD Level

This level is geared toward those who have committed their lives to Christ as well as those who are open and searching (*Persons of Peace*)[42] but who are also willing to take initiative and responsibility for their own spiritual growth. Commitment and discipline are now required to participate in any program at this level. Follow-up with individuals identified at the WIN LEVEL begins here. Numbers are not important. In order to participate, a person must be what has been called a "FAT learner"—Faithful, Available, and Teachable—in order to gain the understanding of what it means to be a disciple. Facilitating spiritual growth and discipleship is the goal. All disciples are encouraged to seek to discover God and enter a process to be equipped for life and ministry. This is also the beginning of a process to train local leaders to continue the Sports ministry vision.

Some program examples for this level include following: Sports Alpha Course, sports clinics/community programs, sports small groups or teams, affinity Bible study groups/discovery process, etc.

---

41 For a deeper consideration of the Win Level concepts I strongly recommend studying previous books in CSRM's Institute of Sports Outreach book series: especially *Sports Outreach Fundamentals*; *Putting The Church Back in the Game*; *The Saving of Sports ministry*; and *The Mission of Sports ministry*.
42 See Chapter 8 for a full description and explanation of *Person of Peace*.

SCOREBOARD
#5: The Sports Ministry Truths

As you reflect on your ministry and evaluate it with the perspective of this Sports ministry Pyramid consider that this WIN-BUILD-SEND-MULTIPLY model:
1. Works together with your **CHURCH MISSION** of worship, love and edification, and *Evangelistic-Disciplemaking*.
2. Is the key to **BIBLE-BASED MINISTRY** which should be the foundation for all that we do.
3. Enables the **START OF A MOVEMENT** of ongoing, reproducible ministry.

The SEND Level

This level is all about leadership and seeks to expand the spiritual development within the disciple by giving them a vision for serving others and by providing hands-on opportunities for practical application. In order to reach this level the person has been and continues to be trained and is serving in a leadership capacity, even at a basic level. At this level, leaders are being effectively discipled and a*ssimilated* (brought in) into the body life of The Church.

Some program examples for this level include the following: various leadership programs, individuals trained and empowered to serve in various leadership capacities, ministry partnerships developed, etc.[43]

MULTIPLICATION (the Cyclical Arrow)

Once a leader has been trained, it is important to release them as a *Reproducing-Reproducer* into the calling that God has place on their life. As they have reached a significant level of maturity, they are now given the opportunity to WIN-BUILD-SEND as they reach out to serve through Sports (or other) Ministry. One of the tendencies here is to hold on to those we train or begin to feel jealous and concerned that they might develop a ministry that competes with or is greater than our own. Of course, this is a wrong perspective. Instead, we need to celebrate what the disciple has become and give them permission to fulfill their calling to reach out to their target audience. The fruit of any leader

---

[43] Sending actually begins at the Build Level and elements of sending continue as the person grows on their faith journey.

SCOREBOARD
#6: Sports Ministry Pyramid Keys

- This model is cyclical and repeatable as represented by the large circular arrow.
  — When a Sports ministry is functioning effectively then Winning, Building, and Sending results in the empowerment and Multiplication of new disciples who are being raised up and released as leaders.
- Use this pyramid to evaluate your ministry programs often.
  — At some point you may be focusing on one level more than another and need to readjust your programing to raise up and produce, reproducing reproducers. Or maybe you are, like I was, skipping a level all together. Now is your opportunity to refocus.
- *Evangelistic-Disciplemaking* (2 Timothy 2:2) is your goal with the goal of creating a spiritual movement that develops *Missional Sports Communities* and potentially should be used to even plant new churches.
- Some programs will have elements of multiple levels.
  — Be sure to keep your goals clear and measurable and fulfilling the *4-Fold Evaluative Rubric* – **Strategically-Relevant** and *Efficiently-Effective*
- Look for leaders who are FAT
  — Faithful, Available, and Teachable—and build into them
- Pray, pray, pray

who has been released is also the fruit of the one who has released them. In this way, we need to hold people and things with open hands, and when the time comes, we should be confident that we have done our job. Releasing leaders who we have trained should be one of the greatest joys of ministry! This is when a movement has truly begun to take place.

A relevant quote from John Perkins, an author, speaker and community leader from Mississippi is appropriate here. He writes:

> We need leaders. Leaders with the faith that sees the depth of our need, yet persists in believing in the power of the gospel. Leaders with a hope which can see the future and move others toward it. Leaders with a love that will sacrifice self in order to serve others. If we are to have that kind of leader we dare not leave leadership

development to chance. We must make the discipling of new
leaders the very center of our missionary strategy. [44]

This is it: seeing the need; working in the power of the gospel; hoping for the future; moving others; sacrificial love; serving; intentional about leadership development (discipleship)—the center of our strategy!
In my situation, I realized as a ministry that we were skipping the BUILD LEVEL of the pyramid. We were doing a lot of great programs with a lot of activity. We were boldly sharing the gospel, but we were not intentionally building relationships with those who were responding. We were just moving on from one activity, to the next event, to the next program. After this period of evaluation, I saw the need to pioneer BUILD LEVEL programs which we did. Almost immediately, I began to see people growing in their faith and leaders being raised up and released as multipliers.
Sometimes in ministry, as an example, we focus on winning people through one-time *Mega-Events*. We like big events, we like projects, and we put a lot of energy in them; but I ask you: is this a biblical model? No! Instead we need to **PLAN** to make *Dedicated-Disciples* and that needs to become apparent in our way of working. We don't just want to do engage in nice projects. We want to develop **movements** and **ongoing ministry**. This is truly accomplishing the Great Commission and putting 2 Timothy 2:2 into practice.

The *Sports Ministry Pyramid* in Practice

We cannot function effectively apart from our team, The Church. Our thinking must change from *Project-Thinking* to *Movement-Building* (developing on-going ministry). That is winning people to Christ, building them up to become disciples, and sending them out to win others.
A great example of the role of Sports ministry in The Church as worked out through the Sports ministry Pyramid model comes from a partnering church in Uganda. Every week a pastor meets around 10 guys, mostly soccer players, from his congregation. Each of these 10 guys is considered a 'coach' and works in a particular neighborhood or village. Every Saturday these coaches are sent out to serve their area, and even before they arrive dozens of kids are waiting for him at the field. Many of these kids are orphans, do not go to school, and do not have good prospects for their future, but come Saturday, they are always excited because it is their sports day. As soon as their coach comes, they start training. The kids learn skills, enjoy themselves, and develop their personalities as they discipline their bodies. During break-times their coach sits them down and starts conversations with his players. Since he is there every Saturday, the

---

[44] John Perkins, *With Justice For All*, Ventura, Cal.: Regal Books, 1982, pp.74-75.

coach knows the kids. The kids really start to love and respect their coach. Soon the break times are used to talk about spiritual subjects and scripture. Over time, the conversations grow deeper and the kids get an opportunity to share their life, the problems they face, the despair the feel, and the things they need. As they open up, their coach shares his life, parables from the Bible, Sports Parables, and his personal story about how he met Jesus. Many are led to Christ (WIN). As time goes by many of the teenagers come to visit the church or if there is no church in their community, they form one. Discipleship takes place (BUILD) and that the kids grow in their new faith. On another level, the ministry also provides opportunity for leadership development. Slowly the kids are given their own responsibilities. One player may lead a warm-up exercise; another teaches the week's Bible lesson. After a while, one of the players can even run the whole training (SEND). Eventually the players have enough experience and maturity that some become coaches themselves, and then they are sent out to another neighborhood to start their own team (MULTIPLY). The ministry multiplies and disciples are being sent on their way to go share their faith in new regions of the country.

Reflection

Consider the points mentioned in Scoreboard 5 (see page 57) and 6 (see page 58). What could it look like if you adopted The Sports ministry Pyramid in your church and ministry?

Prayer

Father, thank you that I am a part of Your Church. Forgive me for having unrealistic expectations. Help me to love it the way that you do and to truly be committed to it as I strive to follow Jesus. Thank You for using me to make disciples who will impact their communities and build your Kingdom!

Chapter 5

Evangelistic-Disciplemaking: The True Measure of Our Success

This shoe wants to be truly successful.

Some years ago I was in Rwanda with a small sports team. I remember vividly going to a prison and sharing the gospel with the inmates. More than 600 prisoners indicated their decisions to follow Jesus that day! For us it was a great response. However afterward, the prison's volunteer chaplain expressed deep regret that it would be impossible for him to follow up on each decision. He did not have the time or the resources to disciple each individual, and he knew that many of those prisoners would be unable to keep their new faith without the encouragement or input from mature believers. With tears in his eyes he said: "How many of these new believers do you think I can follow up on? Maybe 10; but 600? What am I going to do?"

Still, I dutifully reported the truth that we had seen 600 confess Jesus—but I often wonder if I was just playing the numbers game. Had I reported how many would be involved in a discipleship process, the much smaller number would probably more accurately reflect how many would still be following Jesus. In our world, more is better: on the scoreboard, regarding a salary, in church size or event attendance numbers. The larger the number, the better we feel about ourselves and our results.

Unfortunately, those of us from the West have demonstrated and passed on an example we call *Counting-Conversions,* otherwise known as the "numbers game," rather than making *Dedicated-Disciples* to our brothers and sisters around the world, and this has encouraged the development of a church that is a mile long and an inch shallow. There is no depth, and discipleship is often non-existent. This is an evangelism-only focus that allows for a *Day's-Decision* by asking people to "pray a prayer and raise their hand" if they want to accept Jesus. The process and relationship, if you can call it that, ends there.[1]

We need to take a hard look and re-evaluate the true measure of our effectiveness for the gospel. We need to re-assess what we call our *Success-Statistics.* Maybe it's time for a change in our thinking?

---

1 The italicized words and phrases used here and elsewhere have been coined, defined and explained throughout CSRM's Institute of Sports Outreach book series. In specific I would refer you to the Glossary of this book and the following books by Greg Linville: *Christmanship: A Theology of Competition and Sport*; *Sports Outreach Fundamentals*; *Putting The Church Back In The Game: The Ecclesiology of Sports Outreach*; and *The Saving of Sports ministry: The Soteriology of Sports Outreach*.

A common method of evangelism has been to share the gospel-based testimony through a *Platform-Proclamation* at a *Mega-Event*. This often occurs at the end of a game or during the halftime break by a member of a mission-based sports team or at the end of a season banquet or festival. This model works on the premise of asking people to raise their hands to make a commitment to follow Jesus.[2] While this has been a way for many to start their personal relationship with God, it is just that: a beginning point of conversion. Just as a math student first learns the timetables and does not yet understand what is coming such as algebra and calculus, the convert does not yet understand what it truly means to know and follow Jesus at conversion. They certainly must make Jesus the Lord of their life and give everything to Him, but knowing and following Jesus is a process, not a one-time, one-day appreciation with passing warm and cozy feeling about Jesus. Please don't misunderstand this. Throughout Scripture we see people commit to Christ upon a verbal proclamation of the gospel. However, that commitment must continue for a lifetime. Yes, it is true that people will not come to know Jesus unless someone tells them,[3] but what they tell them must include accepting Jesus as Savior is a lifelong commitment to becoming His disciple. We see the examples of Jesus with His disciples (only 12!); Paul with Timothy; Timothy and Titus with those in their churches and many other biblical examples of disciplemaking; and we see that true follower-ship comes over time as new believers are discipled through the words and actions of the spiritual parent.

However, we do need to focus intentionally on a combined strategy that we call *EVANGELISTIC- DICIPLEMAKING* because evangelism and discipleship really cannot and should not be separated. By merging the two terms in one, we are deliberately striving to emphasize this principle and bring it into the spotlight. I will be so bold as to say that unless we have a plan to disciple, we must not evangelize! Whereas some call discipleship the "follow up," I would say evangelism is the preliminary stages of disciplemaking. Otherwise we birth spiritual orphans who at best will never become more than immature followers.[4]

Maybe you have heard this quote attributed to Plato: "You can discover more about a person in an hour of play than in a year of conversation." While this truth is what often makes Sports ministry effective, it also has a downside because the sports and recreation part of Sports ministry is often better executed than the ministry part! Sports and recreational activities are led by active people for active people where the game can easily become more important than

---

2 This *Level #3 Methodological Model* has been described as the *Blow In; Blow Up; and Blow Out;* model of Sports Outreach. See Chapter 9 of *The Saving of Sports ministry: The Soteriology of Sports Outreach*

3 Romans 10.14.

4 For a more in depth consideration of *Evangelistic-Disciplemaking* I refer the reader to the fourth book in the Institute of Sports Outreach book series: *The Saving of Sports ministry: The Soteriology of Sports Outreach*.

TIMEOUT

Open Doors in The Central African Republic

We stayed in a Catholic mission where the facilities were basic but good. My days were full and long and the vision for church Sports ministry was very well received. The local church leaders see it as a great tool for reaching the people and beginning to transform their country. Here are some highlights:

- While waiting for my visa in the border town of Garouaboulai (Cameroon), a small city with a large Muslim population, God literally brought a local youth soccer coach to our doorstep. We shared the gospel, he accepted Jesus, and we gave him Sports ministry resources.

- We preached twice and participated in other smaller sports outreaches in two other villages.

- We met with the president of an Evangelical Bible Seminary, the president of the National Olympic Committee, and many other ministry leaders and groups.

- We met one of the national basketball team's coaches and the 1st Division team he is coaching. Six players accepted Jesus and were discipled!

- We spoke two other times, once on discipleship to 50 people from 8-10 churches and once on why loving The Church is important to 350-400 people from about 75 churches.

the relationships. It's fun to play, compete and recreate, but it takes time and intentional effort to share the gospel and develop disciples. The combination of emphasizing "the numbers game" (*Counting-Conversions*) and a lack of focus on making *Dedicated-Disciples* results in sucking the very life and resources out of many congregations. Therefore I believe that *The Sports ministry Community* has largely failed at making disciples. It is time for a change.

Application to a Lesson Learned

After my experience in Rwanda I learned my lesson and was able to implement it in another African country. In many ways, the Central African Republic has been forgotten by the rest of the world. Elections have been held in the past, but the international community does not recognize the results. In protest of what they perceived to be unfair elections, most of the international community has pulled out of the country. In Bangui, the capital city where one would expect embassies from around the world, there were only 11 still operating when I was there.

The central government is very weak and does not control all of the country. Rebel groups continue to fight in the northeast and southeast. The trade corridor in the east is mostly secure, although the following story will give you cause to wonder about that.

To enter the country, we traveled by bus from neighboring Cameroon. When we arrived at the border, they would not issue my visa. The head of immigration was apparently the only person who could sign it, and we learned he was off "visiting his fifth wife." The entire day passed with us waiting, and I was getting impatient. I was starting to ask: "Lord, what are You doing? Come on! We need to get going. We are going to serve You there." Finally a day and a half after arrival, on a Wednesday afternoon, I received my visa. We quickly entered and continued traveling overnight, arriving in Bangui early Thursday morning. Then we heard the news and understood why God had not granted my visa sooner. On Wednesday morning thieves had fired guns at a public bus, injuring four people, but the bus driver refused to stop. Then they fired at a passenger car, which did stop. The passengers were robbed at gunpoint and released. Had we obtained my visa at our intended time we would have been in the area of the robbery. Sometimes when things don't go the way we want, we need to be patient and keep trusting. God's plan is good and we never know what danger or difficulty He might be keeping us from.

While some neighborhoods in Bangui bustle with people and business, in general Bangui is uncrowded and poor. Streets are unpaved and utilities are unreliable. There are relatively few cars on the street, and once you get out of the city you might be passed by no more than 10 cars in an hour.

The life expectancy for men and women is 40+. Of the 1,000 children who begin elementary school, only 200 will enter high school. Of those 200, only 50 will graduate. Then opportunities are limited inside the country. Yet the Central African Republic is rich in natural resources, lush and green, covered by rolling hills. It is a beautiful country full of brokenness but also limitless opportunities for ministry.

A church-based Sports ministry training conference was organized for 86 pastors and church leaders representing 56 different congregations. The conference included a practical Sports Outreach day in a local schoolyard. All leaders were divided into the following strategic outreach groups which included opportunities for non-sports persons:

- A soccer team—to play and minister to other neighborhood players
- A basketball team—to play and minister to other neighborhood players
- A children's ministry team—to play games and activities with children
- A prayer team—to prayer-walk around the field and interact with people whenever the opportunity came
- A fellowship team—to share the gospel with anyone watching the event

By the day's end, the names of more than 200 people who had professed faith in Jesus had been collected. The local churches then contacted each person and arranged follow-up plans with various ongoing Sports ministry activities in order to develop *2-T-2-2 Relationships*[5]. The purpose was intentional disciplemaking so new converts could learn how to follow Jesus.[6]

Then consider this example from Ecuador. A local church planter started a soccer team in a neighbourhood where he wanted to plant a church. The team played in a local league and practiced 4-5 times each week. Through the practices relationships were built, the gospel was shared, and many players came to faith. Also activities such as picnics, Bible studies, and children's activities where organized that served the players' families. Eventually entire families came to know Jesus. The following season some of the players started their own teams and began to reach out. The teams gathered monthly for activities, and eventually a church was formed that grew to more than 600 committed members. The soccer teams functioned similarly to small groups, and many lives were changed.

In the end, it's not about the number of people who attend an event or the program. It's about developing relationships and ongoing ministry that leads to discipleship. This must become the focus, whether serving in open or closed countries, no matter how easy or difficult the circumstances.

---

5   *2-T-2-2 Relationships* are discussed at length in Chapter 7.
6   This *Level #3 Methodological Model* is what we call the Win-Build-Send-Multiply Model of *Evangelistic-Disciplemaking*. The evangelism wins people to Jesus and the disciplemaking builds the new converts up and prepares them to be sent out to win/build/send others.

Reflection

In what areas of life and ministry have you been playing the numbers game (*Counting Conversions*)? What is the true measure of your success? How should your expectations and your definition of success begin to change after reading this chapter?

Prayer

Father, forgive me for playing the "numbers game". Give me the discipline and willingness to set aside time to build deep relationships with others. Help me to be willing to pay the price by investing myself, my treasure and my talents in what truly matters—*Evangelistic-Discipleship*.

Chapter 6

Evangelism Through Sports Ministry

This shoe has a wonderful message to carry.

The story of Jesus is still the greatest news the world has ever heard, and it continues to be the center of all I do. It is such an unbelievable reality. Does it make sense that God would offer His Son to die and come back to life for a people who mostly curse and reject Him? Yet that is exactly what He did. On top of this it is hard to imagine why God has entrusted this perfect Good News to us frail, fickle, sinful, and imperfect humans. Yet He has and does.

In their Gospels, Matthew and Mark record Jesus providing another metaphor focused on our calling to be engaged in evangelism through the familiar parable of the sower.[1] We are confronted with difficult observation about evangelism as we consider the farmer's unusual sowing strategy. Usually a farmer tills the soil and prepares it. Then he places the seeds carefully and strategically as to ensure the most success for the plant's growth and maximum harvest. This farmer, instead, wildly throws seeds everywhere, even where it was not likely to germinate and where three out of four seeds were wasted. Most of the seeds do not land in good soil or produce fruit, but this does not stop the him. In the same way we must not judge where we share the gospel or to whom based on our own stereotypes or expectations. We must share it with everyone in the most difficult and unlikely places.

Playing the American sport of baseball is the only "job" I know of, wherein a 25% success rate is rewarded. If a player maintains a batting average of .250-.300, he will have a long career in the major leagues. However, if you are producing a product and only 25% percent of your goods are not defective, you are not likely to stay in business long. Being a farmer in God's Kingdom is arduous work that sometimes appears wasted. Yet as followers of Jesus, we are each called to spread gospel seeds.

Evangelism is often considered something that only religious fanatics or super-spiritual people do. Many Christians look for reasons not to share the gospel. I like to contrast these excuses with Moses's experience when God called him to go back to Egypt.[2] He tried every excuse to get out of following God's directive: fear; busyness; pride; ego; ignorance; and ineffectiveness. He argued with God that he didn't know what to say, and that even if he did say something

---

1 Matthew 13 and Mark 3:4-9
2 Exodus 4.1-17.

TIMEOUT

A Modern Parable

A missionary moved to a remote village to bring the gospel through a missional sports outreach. He organized all kinds of activities that served widows and the orphans. He was kind and compassionate and everyone got along well with him. For many years he was faithful in service, but he never opened his mouth to tell the people about Jesus. He thought they will see Jesus in me and through me and that will be enough. This missionary became old and died. He had left instructions to be buried on a hill outside of the village. According to his wishes he was, and the entire population came to show their respects. Some months later a second missionary moved into the same village. He also organized all kinds of activities that served widows and the orphans. He also was kind and compassionate and everyone got along well with him. However, this missionary was not only committed to being faithful in service but he also verbally shared with the people about Jesus. The first time he was telling them, the villagers' eyes got big and they got excited. They said: "Wait! We know where he is buried" and they lead the second missionary to the hill where the first missionary was buried. The first one had lived his life well and represented Jesus, but he had never told them about Jesus. When they finally heard they thought he was Jesus. Evangelism is both living the gospel and sharing the gospel!

they wouldn't listen to him, but in the end Moses could not deflect his calling any more as God provided him with what he needed (Aaron included), to do the task!

Those of us in the *Sports Outreach Community* frequently recite a quote regarding evangelism that is attributed to St Francis of Assisi: "Preach the gospel always and if necessary, use words."[3] While I fully support the core essence that is communicated by this quote, I believe it is often misrepresented to imply that preaching the gospel by how we live our daily lives is enough, and thus becomes the excuse for not verbally sharing the gospel. When coupled with a rationale that verbal proclamations are left for those who have the "gift of evangelism," many believers feel released from ever engaging in conversations about faith in Christ. That is not what we read in Scripture. Sharing your faith is a spiritual discipline that must be practiced by all followers of Jesus.

Consider these general evangelism truths:

- Sharing the good news is not an option. It is a necessity[4] (Read Timeout: A Modern Parable on page 68)
- We should sow the Word pervasively, not in a limited way, because we cannot see with spiritual eyes. It must be purposeful, even if it seems to be haphazard[5]
- Sowing the Word can be discouraging, as the obstacles represented by the birds, sun, and weeds illustrate. Many seeds are wasted and we should push through the fear and discouragement[6]
- Don't let excuses stop you;[7] especially fear[8]
- Sowing the Word is fruitful, not a waste of time[9]
- The seed is powerful[10] and the only thing that will fill and change the human heart[11]
- Prayer is vital as we boldly share the good news[12]
- We should be humble and good listeners. Ask questions including: observation questions; open-ended questions; and response-related questions; all which will help you get to know people.[13]

---

3 There is no specific evidence that St. Francis ever uttered these exact words, thus no specific citation for this is available. However, it is widely believed these words accurately portrayed his life and the subsequent Franciscan movement.
4 2 Corinthians 5; Acts 1.8.
5 Mark 4.
6 Psalm 126.5.
7 Roman 1.20.
8 2 Timothy 1.7.
9 Isaiah 55.11.
10 Romans 1.16.
11 1 Corinthians 15.
12 Ephesians 6.18-20.
13 Colossians 4:5-6.

- Show gentleness and respect[14]
- Make the message clear! The good news never changes. It transcends time and culture[15]
- Sharing the good news takes place one person at a time. See each person as God's individual creation and communicate: "Jesus died for you!"[16]
- Lack of gifting does not exempt you from this responsibility. Jesus' first commandment[17] and last commandment[18] call us to share the good news.
- Sharing the good news is a process, moving each person up the "steps" from unbelief to belief. Consider the Engle Scale of Evangelism which explains this process and its steps.[19]
- The results are not up to us! It is God who must open the doors of an individual heart to understand the mystery of the gospel.[20] (This should be a relief and give us more freedom to share).

The bottom line is: If Jesus is truly good news for you, be sure to share Him.

So now the question becomes, how do we do evangelize through Sports ministry?[21] I am encouraging us to use a game, but not to simply play a game. We are called to share the gospel and make an impact for Jesus. We are not called to administrate sports. We do not want our *Evangelistic-Disciplemaking* efforts to be in vain. They are to be effective.

There are five main elements to effective *Evangelistic-Disciplemaking* that I would like to explore briefly.

1. Availability
2. Accessibility
3. Prayer
4. Clarity
5. Boldness

The first two deal with our relationship with God and those we are trying to reach. The third is most important and deals with the overall task. The final two deal with the message we are trying to bring and how we present it. An explanation is needed.

---

14 1 Peter 3.15.
15 Colossians 4.3-5.
16 John 3.16.
17 Mark 1.17; Matthew 4.19.
18 Acts 1.8.
19 www.en.wikipedia.org/wiki/Engel_scale
20 Colossians 4:3.
21 Keeping in mind what I've shared earlier that evangelism is best understood in the transferable concept of *Evangelistic-Disciplemaking*.

CHAPTER 6: Evangelism Through Sports Ministry

To share the gospel, we must first be **AVAILABLE** to God. Ultimately this means we want to be used by Him. Generally if we don't want to be used we won't be. Even though God wants to use us, He won't make us tell others about Himself. If we are willing, this is where **ACCESSIBILITY** comes in. We have to make ourselves accessible to people. That is, to put ourselves in places where we can interact with others and they with us. Let me share an example of how to become accessible to others after, with both their heart and their attitude, someone has made themselves available to be used by God.

In the Netherlands, train travel is common. The seats are arranged in pairs, and the normal procedure is to board looking for an empty pair. Next you take your bag and lay it in the seat next to you. Then you pull out a book, computer, or smart phone and noticeably occupy yourself. When someone boards and comes down the aisle, you don't acknowledge their presence or look them in the eye. Usually because you are not friendly, they move on. In this scenario you are certainly not being available to God or accessible to people. God convicted me that I needed to use my time on the train to be available and accessible. I would board and find an empty pair of seats. Then I would put my bag in my lap and smile at people as they came down the aisle. Very often God would bring someone to sit next to me who I could share truth with. I think it is easy to contrast the difference between the two scenarios.

The third and final two come from beautiful verses about evangelism found in Colossians and Ephesians.[22] Paul reminds us that **PRAYER** should be our beginning point. Evangelistic outreach is a spiritual exercise, so we need to have our spiritual antennas up by watchfully looking and having a heart attitude of thankfulness for opportunities to share Christ. It is God who will open the doors, so we can have confidence and not fear as we join Him in what He is already doing in the situation. It is also interesting that in the letter to the Colossians Paul asks for prayer to proclaim the gospel **CLEARLY**. This indicates to me that he struggled with being clear some of the time. Otherwise why would he ask for prayer for clarity? Paul is definitely one of my heroes of the faith. In my reverence for him, I can easily think he was the perfect evangelist. He never struggled with where to go or what to say; right? Wrong! In Scripture we see an entirely human man who did struggle with many of the same things we do. When I realize that Paul may not have always been clear, I feel released to struggle with being clear. However an important distinction is that he did not let that challenge stop him.

Clarity involves how we live out our testimony for Jesus. This is where sports people can run into trouble. Intensity runs high in competitive people, and the desire to represent Jesus can be superseded by a "win at all costs" mentality. When this happens, we need to repent quickly and seek forgiveness. That process can also honor God as unbelievers see that God works through imperfect people.

---

22 Colossians 4.2-6; Ephesians 6.18-20.

Paul goes on to admonish us to: "Be wise in the way you act toward outsiders. Make the most of every opportunity."[23] It's hard to see and respond to every opportunity. I am thankful that often God gives us multiple chances. Still our "conversation must be full of grace seasoned with salt."[24] I believe being full of grace means becoming a listener. Show interest in people and ask questions about them and their lives. Then steer the conversation toward spiritual things. Have you ever considered that your conversations have a flavor? Now that's an interesting concept. They do, and what Paul is saying is that we need to make Jesus taste good to people. Just as when your food does not have enough salt, there is little or no flavor and yet too much salt makes the food taste awful so that you spit it out. Just enough salt makes people want more!

Then Paul finishes up this section with another interesting statement. "…so that you will know how to answer everyone."[25] Is this even possible? Is there anyone who can know ever answer to every question? I believe you can, but only if you are able to say these three words: I don't know! In this way, you show yourself to be human. This often opens further opportunities to talk with people and acknowledges, like them, that you are also normal..

In Ephesians, after his well-known description of the spiritual battle we face and the armor of God that is available to us, Paul also reminds us that prayer is most important.[26] He again asks for prayer for himself, but this time to **BOLDLY** and fearlessly make known the mystery of the gospel. This indicates to me that he struggled with being afraid some of the time. Otherwise why would he ask for prayer to overcome fear? When I realize that Paul may have been afraid, I feel released to struggle with my own fear. However, an important distinction is that he did not let the challenges paralyze him. He pushed through. In the same way we need to push through our fear and share the gospel fearlessly, with boldness.

Some may theologically disagree with equating boldness with fearlessness; I believe that the biblical definition of boldness can include doing the bold thing with fear but doing it anyway! The exact point is that the task of evangelistic outreach takes courage which must overcome fear to act boldly, but herein lies the exact reason why sports ministry is so strategic. It provides opportunity for believers to engage with non-believers in an environment that removes barriers and makes sharing the gospel easier.

So then, evangelistic outreach necessitates an attitude of prayer and a balance between boldness and clarity are essential. Sometimes we can have boldness without clarity. In New York City on 7th Avenue I once saw a man carrying a sign that read: "I'm a fool for Jesus." That takes boldness, but that's not very clear and perhaps not wise. For the person walking by on the street their thought process

---

23 Colossians 4:5.
24 Colossians 4:6.
25 Colossians 4:6.
26 Ephesians 6:18.

could go something like: "Who is Jesus and yes, you are a fool!"

Other times we can have clarity without boldness. Church programs that are organized as evangelistic outreaches when there are no unbelievers invited to hear the message would fit this description. The gospel may be preached and made very clear, but the congregation is not bold enough to meet in a location where there are unbelievers or to invite their unbelieving friends. In both scenarios the goal of sharing the gospel fails.

How Effective Are You?

Don Mansfield of Campus Crusade for Christ (known now as Cru) who was one of the first group of believers to share the gospel in Albania after the fall of communism in 1992, introduced me to a graph using Boldness and Clarity, (Paul's prayer points), as the parameters to evaluate our efforts in evangelism. (See graph on page 74)

On the *Mansfield Graph of Evangelism*, take a moment to rate yourself on a scale of 1-10 regarding Clarity and Boldness. The number 1 is low or ineffective and 10 is high or most effective. Ask: How Bold am I in sharing the gospel? How Clear am I when I do share the gospel? Give yourself a rating for each between 1-10. After you have done this, record your ratings on Scoreboard 7 on page 74 and then place an X on the graph where the two numbers intersect to identify where you stand.

Now take a moment and do the same for your church or ministry. This time place a C on the graph where the numbers intersect to identify where your church or ministry stands on the diagram.

The ultimate goal is 'The Star' to be both **Bold** enough and **Clear** enough with the gospel so the message is both heard and received. Keep in mind that the boldness and clarity lines often move with culture. In some countries because of security and risk issues you cannot be as bold as in others.

As I came to understand these principles and saw where I needed to grow in evangelism, God took me from being shy, unclear, and insecure to having faith and boldly stepping out with courage. It's hard to put into words how much my heart now burns for sharing the gospel, but maybe Jeremiah sums it up best when he writes: "Your word is like a fire in my bones. I just can't keep it in."[27]

Don Whitney compares evangelism to other spiritual disciplines such as Bible reading, prayer, worship, Scripture meditation, serving, stewardship of time and money, Bible application, fasting, silence and solitude, journaling, and learning. All must be pursued and practiced in order to pursue holiness and live a full Christian life.[28]

---

27   Jeremiah 20:9.
28   Donald S. Whitney, *Spiritual Disciplines for the Christian Life*, Colorado Springs: NavPress, 1997.

74 THE LIFE OF THE SHOE: Sports Outreach for the World

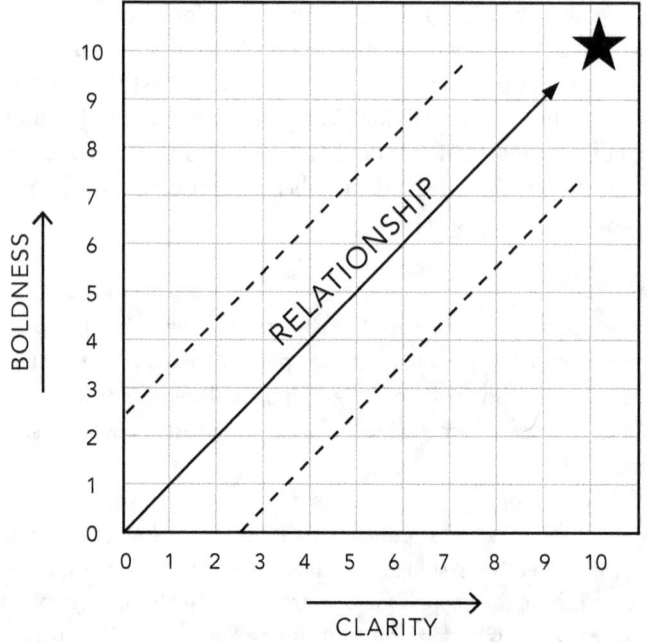

The Mansfield Graph of Evangelism
Ephesians 6:18-20 and Colossians 4:3,4

SCOREBOARD

#7: Write in your rating from the mark you placed on The Mansfield Graph of Evangelism. How much do you need to grow?

	You	Church/Ministry
Boldness	_____	_____
Clarity	_____	_____

SCOREBOARD

#8: Steps to Take Action to Grow in Evangelism

- ✔ How do I move my X / C to become more bold?
  Answer: **PRAY** and **TRUST** God to be faithful to His Word, then step out and go for it.

- ✔ How do I move my X / C to become more clear?
  Answer: **LEARN** the following or other evangelism models:
  - ✔ The Romans Road (Romans 3:23, 6:23, 5:8, 10:9-10)
  - ✔ The Bridge Illustration
  - ✔ The Four Spiritual Laws
    www.greatcom.org/laws/languages.html
  - ✔ Personal Testimony (see Chapter 9)
  - ✔ There are others to consider that may work better in your culture and context.

When I was growing up my mom made me take piano lessons. I was forced to practice every day for at least 20 minutes. I fought her! I smashed timers! I hated it! I did not see the benefits of practicing because I wanted only what would give me immediate satisfaction, like playing outside with my friends. For me the discipline of practicing became drudgery as I often went through the motions just so I could move on to what I really wanted to do. Needless to say, I did not improve very quickly as my drudgery produced little fruit and even less joy. If I was to become good at playing the piano, I needed to see beyond the practice to the great musician I could be. Instead I was unwilling to commit to the discipline that was required. Growing in the spiritual discipline of evangelism and others is no different. For many (maybe even you?) it is drudgery. We fail to see past the process to the Godly, Christlike person we will become. Whitney writes, "Think of the spiritual disciplines as spiritual exercise. To go to our favourite spot for prayer for example, is like going to a gym and using a weight machine. As physical disciplines like this promote strength, so the spiritual disciplines promote Godliness." Whitney goes on to give the following example:

Tom Landry, coach of the Dallas Cowboys American football team said, 'The job of a football coach is to make men do what they don't want to do in order to achieve what they've always wanted to be.' In much the same way, Christians are called to make them do something they would not naturally do—pursue the spiritual disciplines—in order to become what they've always wanted to be, that is, like Jesus Christ. 'Discipline yourself,' says the scripture 'for the purpose of godliness.'[29][30]

Now that you see where you are in your own evangelistic efforts, you have a responsibility to take intentional steps of growth. Consider the suggestions in Scoreboard 8 on page 75 to begin moving more towards the STAR and more effective evangelism in your life, church, and ministry.

In addition to the biblical truths about effective *Evangelistic-Disciplemaking*, we also should take into consideration local cultural keys for effective ministry. No doubt, prayer and building relationships are important anywhere. More specifically it is necessary to understand the general make-up of the community. What do most of the people believe? What are their sporting interests? What are their physical and spiritual needs? Answering these types of questions gives insight into how to be strategic while boldly and clearly sharing the gospel.

Ways to Share the Gospel Through Sports

There are many programs and strategies. The ideal one for any situation is not determined by the organizer's preferences but by the ministry recipients' needs. Prayer and caution will guide leaders in choosing a strategy and shaping it to maximize the impact. Consider:

- **Demonstration**

During sport activities, the gospel can be demonstrated through attitude and behavior towards the players, the referees, the participants, the supporters, etc. The challenge is often that Christians leave Jesus on the sideline when they play sport and turn others away from Jesus instead of towards Him. Their witness is tainted by their over pursuit of winning at all costs.

- **Proclamation**

Sharing one's life story can help build relationships that prepare the way for people to hear the gospel receptively. You can also be more-bold and engage people in spiritual discussions. During break times in large groups you can more formally share the gospel.

---

29 1 Timothy 4:7.
30 Donald S. Whitney, op. cit.

TIMEOUT

Open Doors in a Middle Eastern Country

We were organizing sports camps and Acts of Service at three different locations. Throughout the 10 days we could share the gospel freely. Our team was made up of many new believers who were dealing with their own issues and struggles relating to life and faith. This project was a good learning and stretching process for many of them. During our closing program 70 people, including many Muslims, indicated decisions to follow Jesus!

SCOREBOARD

#9: Acts of Service

- Offer a free meal to all players and fans
- Clean public toilets at a local restaurant or pump station
- Wash car windshields as the driver fills up with fuel at a local pump station
- Organize a free car wash
- Organize a neighborhood cleanup
- Organize a Matthew Party based on Luke 5:29 for those who have not yet found Jesus
- Go door to door and offer to pray for people
- Set up a car repair service for single moms or needy families
- Organize a recreational outing for kids in your neighbourhood
- Visit a prison, a hospital, or the elderly in your community
- Present religious themed gifts to your opponents / Bible text on t-shirts

- **Sport Parables**

Relate something in sport that your audience is familiar with to a spiritual truth (read on to chapter #9 to discover more about this strategic cultural tool).

- **Literature Distribution**

Distribute sport-specific literature to people playing or attending sporting events. People will naturally be interested in reading a tract with a testimony of a soccer player while they are attending a soccer game.

- **Drama**

The use of drama or skits is a very effective, creative, interesting, and acceptable way to present the gospel.

- **Acts of Service**

Paul writes to the Romans: "...God's kindness leads to repentance"[31] and to the Thessalonians : "We cared so deeply that we were delighted to share with you not only the gospel of God but our lives as well."[32] When others are shown love unconditionally, they see Jesus. In this way it can be kindness and compassion which leads them to a personal relationship with God. A few examples might include what appears in Scoreboard 9 on page 77.

We can see the need for sharing the gospel and maybe we are willing to do so, but in real life often it seems hard to actually share. Sports ministry allows us to make the most of every opportunity and makes Jesus "taste good" to people as sports becomes the tool which makes sharing easier and allows us to be clear and bold with the gospel. Consider the account from Cana in modern-day Israel, the site of Jesus' first miracle, as told by a Sports ministry team leader. The village is now predominately Muslim with only a small number of believers.

"There was joy and jubilation as we were able to help out at a children's sports camp for 130 adorable children between 5-14 years of age. We really had such a good time as we had fun together, were able to share testimonies, stories, games, songs, crafts and especially short dramas, which God used in mighty ways. Together with the pastor, 90 of the children, (basically everyone above 9 years of age), invited Jesus into their lives. Hallelujah!! It was amazing. The pastor said it has been many years since they had seen so much love and joy in these camps. Glory to God.

It was decided to organize a party after the camp and invite the children's parents, so we also could share the gospel with them. The same evening the team was going through a tough time of frustration as we were faced with spiritual battles, words and actions of brothers and sisters in Christ who just hurt us so much. We came together, prayed and cried into the night sensing God's spirit move in an awesome way within us, strengthening and uniting us as a team. What seemed

---

31 Romans 2.4.
32 1 Thessalonians 2.8.

like a defeat earlier that evening God took and turned into a true victory.

As the parents came to the party, the children did some performances and we performed a drama about how God can mend and renew broken hearts. A personal testimony about how God saved a whole family in an amazing way was shared. The gospel was presented and 40 of the parents responded to this challenge, stood up and prayed the prayer for their salvation. Some of them were interested to join the church services, attend Bible study groups and send their children to the Sunday school in this church. Praise the Lord! Continue to pray for the seeds that have been planted, that it will be watered effectively, fasten roots and grow strong and beautiful to God's glory. The local believers are now organizing a youth group for the children and specific ministry to serve the parents as follow-up."

Reflection

What practical steps will you take to become more effective in Evangelism? Make an intentional plan using Appendix #5: Evangelistic Event Planning & Programming as your guide.

Prayer

Father, forgive me for my apathy towards telling others about You. Help me not to be afraid but to step into the opportunities and doors you will open. Give me more faith, courage, clarity, and boldness to share your Good News as I make myself more available to You and more accessible to those around me.

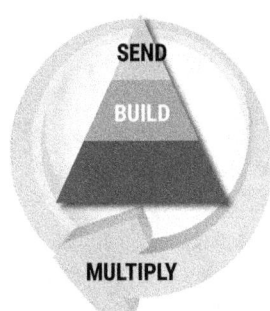

Chapter 7

Discipleship Through Sports Ministry

The shoe has a choice to mature and grow and to help others do the same.

Perhaps it's obvious that having and knowing God's Word is key to discipleship. How many Bibles do you have in your house? Most Americans own three or four. Imagine not having one. I was in Colombia ministering through soccer (of course) to the Wayuu people, who don't yet have a complete Bible in their language. So even if they want to own or read one, they can't. It's not even possible!

As we walked through the cactus and brush of the hot desert to a rancheria (rural settlement), I wrestled with how to share the truth of the gospel without words in a way that was easily understood. Our translator reminded us that we had to use simple illustrations because many of our Christianese words and expressions don't exist in their language. We came upon a hut with three women and eight kids sitting in hammocks in the shade. Their structure was made of big sticks, not logs and covered by smaller branches. They welcomed us with curious smiles, but a baby started crying as he was startled by our white faces. Through our translator, we introduced ourselves and explained what brought us to this place. After some initial conversation the translator and I shared the gospel as simply as we could using a stick to draw the Bridge Illustration, a simple way to visually explain the good news about Jesus, in the sand. All listened intently, and after further explanation, one woman indicated she would like to accept Jesus. In that moment she prayed and asked Him to be her Savior. It was a moment to celebrate!

This leads me to more thoughts. I knew that for our new Wayuu sister, her decision was just the beginning of her journey. An even greater and necessary challenge will be how to disciple her, especially without having a complete Bible in her own language. I trusted the local church leaders to invest in her life to help her grow in her new faith.

We need to be intentional about discipleship, about building into the lives of others to make an impact for Christ's Kingdom. Discipleship does not, and will not, happen by accident.

By definition, a disciple is a follower. As Jesus called the disciples, He simply commanded them to "Follow Me." Yet there was more to it than just words as they would discover. As the twelve disciples followed Jesus they not only listened to His words, but they also put His teachings into practice. It was the "head knowledge" that fed their passion, which was then lived out through the actions of their hands and feet as a "do-er." Jesus taught that what is produced in our lives flows out of the heart, out of who we are.[1] Becoming a disciple is all about becoming more like Jesus and allowing our hearts to be transformed. In the same way, discipleship is helping others to become learners and followers of Jesus.

Discipleship as the Beginning of Follow-up

The beginning of discipleship is what is often referred to as "follow-up." Yes, discipleship flows out of effective follow-up and follow-up flows out of effective discipleship and yet unlike what most think follow-up is, discipleship is not short term, nor is it ever finished. Follow-up is the short-term building into the lives of people of foundational discipleship concepts but discipleship consists of on-going and ever deepening spiritual disciplines.

Often in ministry, as has been discussed in previous chapters, we focus on getting everything ready for the programs, but we forget the most important part: the follow-up and the commitment to discipleship. In the article *Three Reasons Why*, David Bok writes, "Follow-up is an action word, an attempt to translate some theological imperatives of the scriptures into something we can actually do."[2] Bok goes on to explore three basic reasons for follow-up and discipleship, centering around:

1) A Command
2) A Responsibility
3) A Need

First, it flows out of **A Command**, the command to be good shepherds. When Jesus first called His disciples, he called them to become fishers of men to reconcile people to God.[3] Then as recorded in the Gospel of John His call deepens into a commission and His metaphor changes from fish (non-Christians) to sheep (Christians).[4] His followers must not only reconcile non-Christian men and women to God, but must then spiritually build up these new believers. John then tells the story of how Simon Peter's threefold denial of Christ demanded the threefold acknowledgement of his love.[5] In this encounter, Jesus could probably have asked almost anything of Peter, but most importantly the practical proof of this love, Jesus told him, was to "feed my sheep." Peter later wrote about his

---

1 Matthew 7.16-20.
2 (*Discipleship Journal*, Issue 4, July 1981).
3 Matthew 4.19.
4 John 21.15-17.
5 John 21.

concern for this task in the first epistle he was inspired to write. He teaches shepherds of The Church that they are to serve willingly and to set good examples in their follow-up.[6] In addition in His Great Commission, Jesus commands all Christians to "make disciples of all nations;" not only winning them to Christ, but also to help them become committed and effective followers of Christ.[7]

Second, the **Responsibility** comes as we realize that we are the spiritual parents of those we introduce to Christ. "Paul told the Corinthians that he cared for them because *"in Christ Jesus I became your father through the gospel."* [8] In this passage Paul distinguished between spiritual guardians and a spiritual father, indicating that a spiritual father has the greater concern for the children. Like the relationship between an earthly parent and child, it takes a healthy relationship between the spiritual parent and the spiritual babe for the baby to grow to full maturity. Paul is emphatic. He is inspired to say: "Imitate me!" or in other words: Follow me as I follow Christ![9] He accepted both the responsibility for leading and for making sure that they were following, and he exhibited the traits and responsibilities of a Good Shepherd that can be found in the Old[10] and New Testament[11].

Finally, the third obvious **Need** should compel us. Babes in Christ must be fed, and fed with the "spiritual milk" of the faith first.[12] That is the simple basics of the faith. Then as they mature and grow they can be fed "the steak" of the faith, that is, the more complex deeper things. Similarly in sports a player must learn the fundamentals before they can be taught the complex offensive or defensive plays. This concept was very clear to Paul who well understood sports. His ministry in Corinth and Ephesus are perfect examples of the principle of both the short term follow-up and long term disciplemaking. Paul went to both places for the first time on his second missionary journey.[13] His third missionary journey was then all about discipling the new churches that had been established.[14] Paul began his third journey by travelling from place to place "strengthening all the disciples."[15] Then, when he arrived back in Ephesus where he stayed for nearly three years, he continued to disciple his spiritual children by entrusting their discipleship to the work of his mentee Timothy.[16] Paul did not want people to only believe (make a *Day's-Decision)*, but desired that all become mature in Christ

---

6   1 Peter 5.2-4.
7   Matthew 28.19f.
8   1 Corinthians 4.15.
9   I Corinthians 4.16.
10 Ezekiel 34:7-16.
11 John 10:11-16.
12 1 Corinthians 3.1f.
13 Acts 18.
14 Acts 19 & 20.
15 Acts 18.23.
16 I Corinthians 4.17; 1 Timothy 1.3.

(Dedicated-Disciples). One of the best summaries of Paul and Timothy's work is found in Paul's inspired epistle to the Colossians:

> We proclaim Him, admonishing and teaching everyone with all wisdom, so that we may present everyone perfect in Christ. To this end I labor, struggling with all His energy, which so powerfully works in me.[17]

These are strong words. Catch these phrases of the verse just quoted: "admonishing and teaching everyone; and "to this end I labor, struggling with all His (Christ's) energy." Paul did not want to make converts but desired that all become mature in Christ. Presenting everyone "perfect in Christ" speaks to the spiritual maturity that Paul wanted to help his disciples obtain. He wanted all to become adult Christians and not to stay infants in the faith. This was his ultimate measure of success and was accomplished only through relationships.

Shouldn't this also be our aim and our desire in all we do? If it is not, then it should be! What will you do with your new contacts? What will you do with those who are interested in learning more about God? How will you help those to grow who have given their hearts to Jesus?

If you are going to host an event that has evangelism as its goal, you must have a follow-up and disciplemaking plan with those who have been impacted by the message of life in Jesus Christ. To have a follow-up plan that initiates a long term disciplemaking process that includes connecting them with a local church. This is a mandatory requirement of all evangelistic outreaches. This would include specific components in your outreach event that will assist you with it and make it easier for you at the conclusion of your outreach.

This initial follow-up can take a variety of forms, but please note such planning and implementation takes time and commitment by the congregation and the event leadership. However, the most important thing to remember is that the best the initial follow-up flows out of relationships.

The Struggle of Discipleship

We know discipleship should be central to all that we do as followers of Jesus. It is a term we hear referred to often in our churches and Bible studies, but it is often dismissed because we have created an expectation that makes it nearly impossible for the ordinary person to achieve or participate in. In reality discipleship should be simple. It comes down to relationships that every person needs in their life and if we can begin to leverage these relationships in the right way then discipleship will take places simply because we are living the gospel.[18]

---

17 Colossians 1.28f.
18 I fully recommend you consult with another book published by Overwhelming Victory Press written by my good friend and colleague Steve Connor entitled: *Rugged Discipleship* (To be released jointly with this this book in

Relationships are key. Your success and failure will hinge upon how quickly you facilitate opportunities for the participant to build significant relationships with others. For anyone to want to stay involved with your local church, they must develop relationships with congregants who will walk with them through their spiritual journey and interact with them in their daily lives. This model of discipling being done in and through relationships is found in the biblical model of Barnabas, Paul, and Timothy.

2-T-2-2 Relationships

Howard Hendricks, who was a longtime and well-loved professor at Dallas Theological Seminary, described in the devotional book *Men of Integrity* the necessity of every believer having three key relationships:

> Every person should seek to have three individuals in their life: a Paul, a Barnabas, and a Timothy.
>
> A Paul is an older person who is willing to mentor you, to build into your life. Not someone who's smarter or more gifted than you, but somebody who's been down the road. Somebody willing to share their strengths and weaknesses—everything they have learned in the laboratory of life. Somebody whose faith you'll want to imitate.
>
> A Barnabas is a soul friend, somebody who loves you but is not impressed by you. Somebody to whom you can be accountable. Somebody who's willing to keep you honest, who's willing to say, "Hey, you're neglecting your spouse, and don't give me any guff!"
>
> A Timothy is a younger person into whose life you are building. For a model, read 1st and 2nd Timothy. Here was Paul, the quintessential mentor, building into the life of his protégé— affirming, encouraging, teaching, correcting, directing, praying. [19]

Not to disparage Hendricks, but in order to more accurately depict the relationship between Barnabas and Paul, I have chosen to switch the two and build on his descriptions and rename them as *2-T-2-2 Relationships* (See Scoreboard 10 on page 87). For the sake of our discussion:[20]

A **BARNABAS RELATIONSHIP** is one that involves an older person in the faith (not necessarily in age). Someone who loves you but is not impressed by

---

2020) by CSRM's Overwhelming Victory Press—OVP). In it Steve shares timeless key principles that will greatly challenge and encourage all about how to disciple.
19 Howard Hendricks in *Men of Integrity*, Nashville, TN; Thomas Nelson, 1999; Vol. 1, no. 1.
20 Influenced by Hendricks and others I will build on his definitions and descriptions.

you. A Barnabas is willing to mentor you, to build into your life, and to hold you accountable. A Barnabas is willing to share his or her strengths and weaknesses—everything learned in the laboratory of life. This is someone whose faith you want to imitate. Barnabas was this for Paul. When Paul returned to Jerusalem after his conversion experience, it was Barnabas who encouraged the other church leaders to give him a chance despite their fears. It was Barnabas who mentored Paul for a few years before he embarked on his ministry.

> Remember your leaders, who spoke the word of God to you. Consider the outcome of their way of life and imitate their faith.[21]

A **PAUL RELATIONSHIP** is one that involves a soul brother, a peer. Not someone who's smarter or more gifted than you, but someone who is your peer in life and ministry. A Paul is willing to keep you honest and to say, "Hey, you're neglecting your spouse, and don't give me any guff!" Paul was this type of peer for Silas, John Mark, and Luke; and they were for him as well. Especially as leaders we need to be accountable to those around us. We also need others to pray for us and push us forward into the vision that God has called us for.

> When Peter came to Antioch, I opposed him to his face, because he was clearly in the wrong.[22]

A **TIMOTHY RELATIONSHIP** is one that involves a younger person (in faith, not necessarily age) and someone into whose life you are building. For a model, read 1 and 2 Timothy. Here was Paul, the quintessential mentor, building into the life of his protégé—affirming, encouraging, teaching, correcting, directing, and praying. Facing the end of his life and ministry, Paul recognized that the continuation of his work and legacy now rests with Timothy and the next generation in the faith.

If we follow this spiritual tree of discipleship based on these relationships from 2 Timothy 2.2, we can track five generations: Barnabas—Paul—Timothy—Reliable Men—Others. As followers of Jesus, most Christians already have or have had similar relationships in their life. Now that they are identified and named, each can be pursued with purpose and focus.

I was struck by the testimony of a leader who was brought by her "Paul" to a sports ministry training in Madagascar. She initially did not want to come but came anyway. She was a national basketball team player. When she got married she stopped playing and became busy raising four daughters. For her, basketball was something from her past that she had left behind. Then last year her hus-

---

21 Hebrews 13.7.
22 Galatians 2.11.

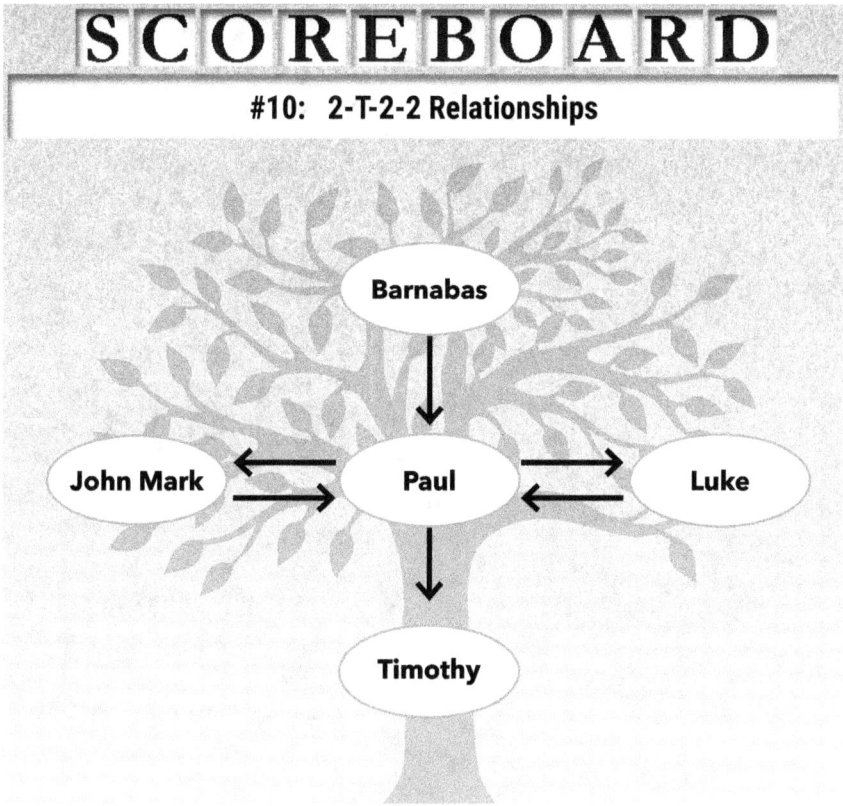

band was tragically murdered. She is still in a grief journey that has been very difficult for her and her girls. Through the discipleship training God touched her and she tearfully shared: "This entire experience has helped me move beyond my grief. Knowing I can play basketball again but this time to worship and serve God is an amazing revelation for me. I feel like I have a renewed purpose as I can now use this game I love to reach others for Him!" What a beautiful picture of how God used this relationship to encourage, restore, and redirect this leader's life.

So how will you measure success? Will it be in playing 'the numbers game" or will it be through the quality of your *2-T-2-2 Relationships*? Is it your desire to see your friends and family become all that God created them to be as they are made perfect in Christ? Allow God to use you and strive to become more intentional in the relationships He has given you! You can be the change person.

How do you see this in your own life? Can you identify one or more of these relationships in your own life? Place their names in the appropriate space in Scoreboard 11 above. Can you think of any potential candidates for each of the blank spaces that you do not yet have a name?

What can you do to facilitate the establishment of these types of relationships in your personal life? In your ministry, which of these three roles will be the most difficult for you? Why? One of the great aspects of Sports ministry is that many activities are already set up to facilitate these types of relationships. They just need to be intentionally utilized. (See Scoreboard 12 on page 89.)

Personal and Program Discipleship

As you connect with individuals who are interested in discipleship, consider what programs you will plan that can involve your new contacts. You must plan to make disciples and move the person up the sports ministry Pyramid from the WIN level where they began to the BUILD and SEND levels as they become a MULTIPLIER.

See Scoreboard 13 on page 91 for a few ideas how to incorporate personal and program follow-up within the Sports ministry Pyramid.

SCOREBOARD

#12: Example of 2-T-2-2 Relationships in Sports Ministry

IN SPORTS

League Director
Camp/Activity Director
↓
Coach ← Coach → Coach
↓
Player

Robert Tamasy wrote,

> It always warms our hearts to see people follow the call of God in their lives. But why do many who indicate decisions for Christ at a crusade meeting, or in their homes, never make it to the sanctuary? And why, not even a year after rededicating her life to the Lord, does that person in your church again approach the altar in an attitude of surrender—as if the first time didn't "take"? Years ago, a highly publicized national evangelistic campaign excitedly reported that thousands of people had given their hearts to Christ during the year-long effort. Follow-up research showed that less than five percent of those who professed faith in Christ had become part of a local church. What's going on? Why do so many people seem to slip through the evangelical cracks? I believe the problem lies in our failure to properly understand and implement the Great Commission.[23]

---

23   Robert Tamasy, "Out of the Nursery," *Discipleship Journal*, Issue 53, Sept/Oct 1989.

Hopefully through the intentional recognition of these three relationships, it is easy to see that all Christians can "do discipleship." Follow-up as the beginning of **DISCIPLESHIP (DISIPLEMAKING)** is simply acting out the Great Commission as Jesus intended it to be carried out, simply being obedient to what God has commanded us to do. Such disciplemaking does not take place by accident. We must plan for it because it is the only way that any program we do will bear lasting fruit! The truth is that a program without follow-up including connecting the new believer to a local church is only an activity. Let us not settle for just doing activity. Let us be about our Father's business.

Flying Elephants and Making Disciples

I first met Theo two weeks after we arrived in the Netherlands in 2003. We were attending our first ministry conference and he was preparing to go to the Middle East for our upcoming outreach project. He jumped in the car with me as we were driving to a sports hall for sporting activities. His introduction to me went something like this: "Hi, I'm Theo. 'Little birdy in the sky, you just let a poopy in my eye. But I don't care and I don't cry, I just thank God that elephants don't fly.'"

At the time, Theo could not speak English very well so I think this was his way of trying to impress me. I don't remember much else from that first meetings, but I do recall thinking, "Wow this guy is something. He has so much enthusiasm. Let's see how God is going to use him." Theo was a simple carpenter from a small village in Friesland and by his own admission an "unschooled, ordinary man."[24] Yet he had received a calling from God to go to the Middle East, and in obedience to following Jesus he gave up everything and went.

I subsequently became the leader of our Middle East project and thus Theo's boss. I had the privilege of mentoring and coaching him in ministry and also personally during some of the most challenging times in his life. We worked very closely together and became not only colleagues but close friends. Eventually, Theo became like a brother to me. Then the very month I wrote this chapter, I had the privilege of seeing Theo launch his own ministry that allows him to continue to fulfill God's calling on him to bring the gospel to other parts of the world. Theo has asked me to be an adviser to his board of directors, so I am excited to stay involved with him not only on a personal level, but also on a ministry level. Discipling takes on many different forms.

As I reflect on the past and consider the leader Theo has become, I am reminded that:

- God will use anyone if they are willing to step out and follow Him. He will take ordinary people like Theo, you, and me to do extraordinary things when we trust Him.

24 Acts 4.13.

SCOREBOARD

#13: Personal and Program Follow-up

1. Plan another WIN LEVEL *Mega-Event* sports-based activity that is open for everyone such as a tournament, games fair, sports day, sports camp, clinic, club, etc. Plan events that are not "churchy" and will appeal to unbelievers.
2. Provide an opportunity for the participant to join a BUILD LEVEL activity that will put them in a small group setting. This might be a Sports Alpha Course, a cell group, joining a sports team, a Discovery Bible study, or a specific leadership training program, preferably all through a local church. Meet them where they are, not overwhelming them, but connecting them with a group that meets regularly (i.e. a group of guys who play basketball together once every two weeks).
3. Plan ways to network with other ministries within the church. Don't be territorial. Instead, look for ways to work together. Partnerships within a congregation are key to getting the person assimilated and serving in the local body. For example, give the names of children to the Sunday school department, men to the men's ministry and women to the women's ministry to invite them for their activities. If you know a participant likes to sing or play an instrument, pass his or her name along to the appropriate worship leaders.

- God has given us the responsibility to work together (*Paul-Relationships*) to build into the lives of others. We need older brothers or sisters in the faith who can walk with us as we follow Jesus (*Barnabas-Relationships*). We also need younger brothers or sisters in the faith (*Timothy-Relationships*) who we can mentor and coach along their own journeys of following Jesus.
- I am so thankful for those who played the role of Barnabas who have built into my life through the years. Likewise I am also thankful for the many Paul's who minister along side me and all the Timothys (most recently, Theos) around the world I have been able to mentor as they have pursued becoming more like Jesus and following Him.

Reflection

Consider the *2-T-2-2 Relationships* in your own life. Who is your Barnabas? Who are your Timothys? Are you neglecting your Pauls? Are you making disciples who are being released to multiply? If not, why not?

Prayer

Father, help me to be intentional about the relationships you have placed in my life. Just as Paul did, help me to struggle with all the energy that comes from knowing Jesus so that I can play a part in making adult followers of Him.

Chapter 8

Persons of Peace:
A Long-Forgotten Strategy

This shoe has longing for eternity and a role to play to bring others there.

On a flight from San Jose to Paris, I sat next to a man named Ryo (pronounced the same as "Rio") who is from Tokyo, Japan. As we talked I discovered that his personal email address translated from Japanese literally means "God's not dead!" Sadly however, he knew nothing about God. I was able to share the Gospel with him and he was very excited to learn about Jesus. We exchanged email addresses and have since stayed in touch.

Obviously before I met Ryo, God was working on his heart. This encounter reminded me of a passage in the Old Testament book of Ecclesiastes: "He has made everything beautiful in its time. He has also set eternity in the human heart; yet no one can fathom what God has done from beginning to end."[1] So many people are searching for something of real meaning. God has placed this desire to know Him in their hearts and it's exciting He uses us to tell them!

Over the last few years I have been learning about a growing discipleship movement that is relevant for what God wants to do through each of us as we seek to impact our communities for Him. It focuses on an ancient principle that is newly re-popularized. The Gospel writer Luke describes how Jesus sends out the 70 disciples.[2] This number (70) is symbolic because it represents the same number as the "Table of Nations" found in Genesis and shows intent to reach the entire world with the gospel.[3] It is a good model for us and informative to break down Jesus' instructions to the 70 into three *Theological-Truths*:

1. **The Preparation**
    a. Jesus' instructions were, first of all, to pray. "Ask (pray) the Lord of the Harvest to send out laborers."[4] Incidentally, these laborers will come from the harvest just as seeds when planted will ultimately produce more seeds. Before modern agricultural methods, a percentage of each harvest was kept as seed for the next season so that another crop could be grown in the future.

---

1   Ecclesiastes 3.11.
2   Luke 10.1-12.
3   Genesis 10.
4   Luke 10:4.

b. The 70 were organized by twos.[5] This was probably for their protection and so they could encourage, pray for, and support one another.

2. **The Going**
   a. They were to go as forerunners ahead of where He (Jesus) was about to go.[6] This was important for follow-up and ongoing discipleship of all new believers.
   b. They could expect difficulties and opposition because they were going out like "lambs among wolves."[7]
   c. They were instructed not to take anything but to depend entirely on God.[8] Jesus understood that with possessions, freedom of movement is restricted.
   d. They were instructed not to greet anyone, which would require them to submit to the expectations of cultural hospitality, but to stay focused on their important and urgent task.[9]

3. **The Ministry**
   a. They were to proclaim peace and find the *Person of Peace*.[10]
   b. They were to remain at that person's house and were not to move from house to house.[11] That is, that their role in the community as it related to doing evangelism was not limited to what they themselves could accomplish, but more about building a relationship and empowering the person who was already rooted in the community. I believe this can be extrapolated out to find freedom in not trying to "save" everyone, but rather join in with what God is already doing in the heart of the *Person of Peace*.
   c. They could expect God to work miraculously. This was demonstrated as they healed the sick and proclaimed peace through Jesus.[12]

What I seemed to always miss and what has recently struck me is the importance of this *Person of Peace* and the role that they play in the disciples' mission. In many ways they were to act contrary to traditional evangelists (consider specifically points 2.d and 3.b above). The success or failure of the 70 was dependent on finding this *Person of Peace*.[13] Without this person, the message would never

---

5   Luke 10:1.
6   Luke 10:1.
7   Luke 10:3.
8   Luke 10:4.
9   Luke 10:4.
10 Luke 10:5-6.
11 Luke 10:7.
12 Luke 10:9.
13 I first heard this term used by Disciple-Making Movements (DMM) as a part of their ministry strategy. I do not know if they were the first, but it has now become a familiar term in many ministry circles. Read more in the Glossary of this book and learn more about DMM at www.dmmsfrontiermissions.com/disciple-making-movement-what-defined.

CHAPTER 8: *Persons of Peace: A Long-Forgotten Strategy*

reach its target audience. God was already working so it is just a matter of them joining Him there in this way. As I looked again at Luke 10 and explored other examples in Scripture I found many similar passages many key insights about this *Person of Peace*.

First, the *Person of Peace* is waiting for someone to help them find God. They are the insider in the community who is spiritually open, spiritually searching. God has ordained them for this role and is already calling them to Himself.

We read about Lydia who was an extremely rich gentile who owned houses in Thyatira and Philippi.[14] Her business dealt in purple goods which were only enjoyed by the wealthy. Lydia like Cornelius had chosen to become a disciple of the God of Judaism and follow His teachings as found in the Scriptures. In their encounter with Lydia, Paul, Silas, Timothy, and Luke went to her "turf," so to speak—at the place of prayer outside the city. Lydia had probably not yet heard the Gospel or had the opportunity to respond to it, but "The Lord opened her heart in response to Paul's message (Jesus)."[15] Lydia was the first convert in what would become a thriving church in Philippi and her house became central to church activity including the place Paul and Silas first went when miraculously released from prison. It was in fact, where the believers met to pray for their release.

Second, the disciples, as the ones sent out with the gospel, actively looked for the *Person of Peace*. Jesus demonstrated this Himself with Zacchaeus the tax collector, who went to extraordinary lengths to see Him.[16] Jesus acknowledged Zacchaeus, took a personal interest in him, and wanted to be with him. Jesus encouraged Zacchaeus to serve Him and show Him hospitality in spite of what others were probably saying or thinking. The result? We know that Zacchaeus' life was changed as he pledged to give back many times over all that he had swindled out of those he had been taxing. Now imagine him going house to house paying people back. I am sure that he initially was met by many slammed doors and hateful comments until they realized why he had come. Then, I am sure as word got out many would have wondered: "What has changed Zacchaeus?" His response was: "I met Jesus!" Seeing the change, I can only assume that many questioned him further and even began to believe themselves. Zacchaeus' neighborhood was changed as his life was changed and he began to tell others about Jesus.

Third, as time is spent with the *Person of Peace* and truth is spoken into their life, he or she believes more and more truth and God will use them to reach their own community. This may be why the disciples are instructed not to go from house to house. The work will be much more successful and effective when the

---

14 Acts 16.13.
15 Acts 16:14.
16 Luke 19.1-10.

Person of Peace is empowered to reach their own neighborhood. We see this demonstrated by the Samaritan woman whom Jesus met at the well as she proclaims to her town's people: "Come, see a man who told me everything I ever did. Could this be the Messiah?"[17] As a result, the whole village came to accept Jesus.

If we are open and live in such a way that others see Jesus in us, the *Person of Peace* will often find us. From my own experience finding this person can begin with a simple conversation.

Throughout Scripture, there are many more examples of God using *Persons of Peace* as a part of his strategy. Consider Rehab,[18] Cornelius,[19] and the Ethiopian eunuch[20] just to name a few. When I learned about and began to apply this strategy that God seemingly has given us many examples of, it revolutionized my approach to evangelism. Instead of feeling like I must save everyone, and everything depends on me, I now find peace and joy by joining in with God in what He is already doing and where He is already working. Of course, I still want to tell everyone, but now I try to work smarter, not harder, as God introduces me to persons or peace.

The Relevance for Sports ministry

Having been involved in sports ministry now for nearly three decades I have seen God do many things in many countries and in the lives of many people. In most cases we have always done the "sports stuff" sometimes to the detriment of the ministry stuff. That's because in many countries it is difficult to share the gospel. Understanding how God is working through a *Person of Peace* in these situations can be very strategic.

Some years ago in South Asia I met with church leaders to learn about their Sports ministries. They had purchased a piece of land that was developed into a soccer pitch. The spiritual ground in their country is very hard and antagonistic toward the gospel, but the people love soccer. Each week a team of Christians would play teams from the community made up of players from other religions. I asked them how much discipleship they were doing and they responded "None, because no one is coming to faith." They were waiting until the person wanted to "pray the prayer," so to speak, before they could follow-up with them. As I began to share with them about the *Person of Peace* they realized that their strategy needed to change. Certainly as the Christian team was interacting with the other players there were those who were struggling with different issues related to family, finances, or health, maybe open to prayer, maybe disenchanted with their own religion. These may be the *Persons of Peace* in whose hearts God is already

---

17   John 4.29.
18   Joshua 2.
19   Acts 10.
20   Ats 8:26-40.

TIMEOUT

Person of Peace in The Netherlands

A sports team from Turkey working with Turkish immigrants reported:

"One day a group of Turkish youngsters invited one of our teammates to go to a mosque with them to pray. He then told them about his Christian identity but because he has a Muslim name and background they were so surprised to hear his testimony. They were affected by it so much that they told their parents and many others in their town about him and his group. Thus, their concerned parents and many others came to see if the team was distributing Bibles or otherwise trying to convert their children. Yet when they saw that all they did was play sports with them and perform dramas for them, they relaxed and even became glad. Then some of them invited team members to their homes to get to know them better. Four of these families were especially interested in knowing more after they listened to testimonies from members of the team. They excitedly asked many questions such as: 'How could Jesus be God?' After long and nice conversations about God and Christianity, they asked for New Testaments."

working. Once they opened their eyes to see that people were searching, they began to help those players discover God, which eventually led to a discipleship process.

Ironically in this same country a high-level soccer team of Christian players came to compete against the national team. At their first match more than 10,000 spectators came out to watch. Being from the West, the team members engaged in traditional methods of evangelism: handing out tracts and sharing testimonies at half time. The FIFA president become incensed when he observed this. At first, he canceled the team's remaining games altogether, but in the end the games could go on only without fans! Imagine if the team had adopted a more sensitive method of evangelism such as sending local believers into the crowd to build relationships and share with other fans as they watched the match. In this way, they could have identified *Persons of Peace* to connect with and follow-up on afterwards. The results would have been much different.

On the Sports ministry Pyramid (see below), the *Person of Peace* fits in at both the top of the WIN and the bottom of the BUILD Levels. It must be understood that because the *Person of Peace* had not yet accepted Christ, they have not been "won" and therefore cannot yet be "built." This however, does not mean that we should dismiss them as my friends in South Asia unintentionally did. God is still at work in their lives, and we need to be open to being used to help them discover him.

Everything begins with prayers. Then after God uses a community engagement strategy such as sports, recreation and fitness ministry (SR&F) to reveal a *Person of Peace* there must be intentional followup. Disciple-Making Movements (DMM) has created a good outline to follow for next steps that I will summarize here.[21]

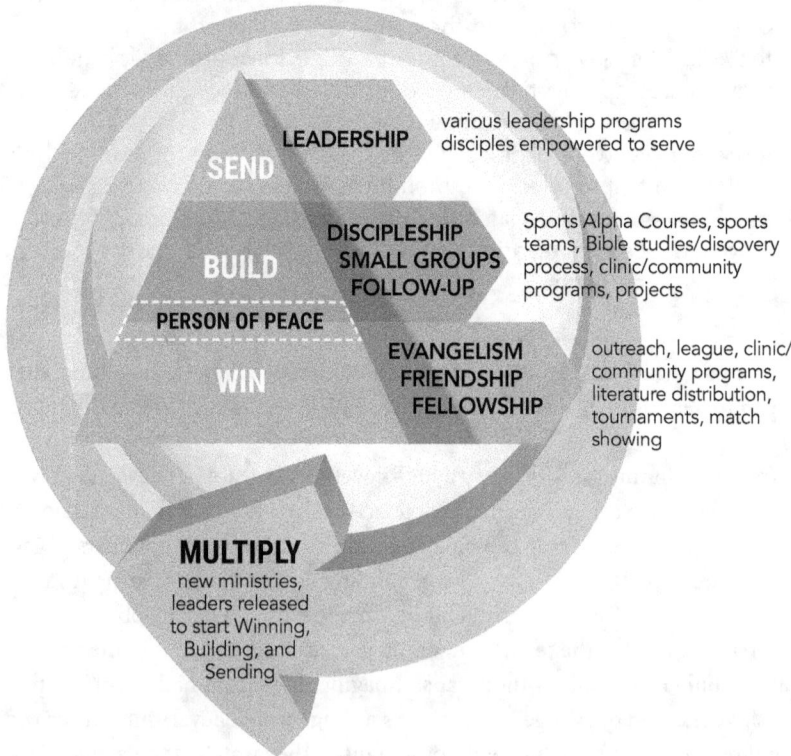

---

21 Learn more about Disciple-Making Movements (DMM) at www.dmmsfrontiermissions.com/disciple-making-movement-what-defined.

Can you see how this perfectly follows the *Sports ministry Pyramid*? The *Person of Peace* is won, built, and sent as a multiplier, and the movement develops.

God is preparing the hearts of people to receive Him in even the most unreached places. The following example shared by a friend and colleague about how this transferable concept of the *Person of Peace* works within the context of

> ## Chart #2
> ## Disciple-Making Movements (DMM)
>
> 1. **Starts with focused prayer.**
>
> 2. **Building a relationship is the first step.** Often this is best done informally by meeting regularly with the *Person of Peace* for coffee or tea or playing sports together (sports ministry).
>
> 3. **Next, after trust has been built, the *Person of Peace* is invited to meet** to discuss spiritual things in a more formal setting. This can be done using the Inductive Bible Study or Bible Discovery Method. In this way they can be introduced to God, fall in love with Jesus, and practically apply what they are learning.
>
> 4. **A small group forms** as the *Person of Peace* invites their family, friends, and neighbors to join as they are obedient to share what the Holy Spirit is revealing to them through their study of God's Word.
>
> 5. **As God works, the *Person of Peace* and family and friends accept Jesus and are baptized.**
>
> 6. **A house church forms, and reproduction takes place** as the initial *Person of Peace* and others begin the process all over again through a new community engagement activity.

Sports ministry. He and his leadership team dream by faith that sports disciple-makers will be prepared to serve in every city, town, and village in Eurasia. In one new location, a Sports ministry team met a widow with a son who asked them to stay in their house. Being poor, they bluntly told the team not to expect breakfast in the morning. Surprisingly, when the team got up there was good smells coming out of the kitchen and breakfast was set on the table. The widow testified that miraculously that morning her only cow gave three times more milk than usual. Through this, her heart was softened. She has opened a new door into the community and invited neighbors to begin the Bible discovery and discipleship process.

He or she, the *Person of Peace*, is only a sports, recreation, and fitness conversation away.

Reflection

Who are the *Persons of Peace* in your community? Are you looking for them in your neighborhood, at your work, in the gym, at your schools, and on your teams? Make a list of potential *Persons of Peace*. Keep your spiritual eyes and ears open as you spend time with them.

Prayer

Father, thank You that You have placed eternity in the hearts of men. Thank You that You are already working in their lives. Open my eyes to notice those who are seeking You and give me the wisdom to know how to be used in their lives to share Jesus!

Chapter 9

"Tell Me A Story!":
The Modern-Day Tool of *Sports Parables*

This shoe has a uniquely beautiful story to share.

No matter what country I am in, people love to talk about sports; more specifically about their favorite sports team and players. Last second goals, championship wins, dramatic losses, come from behind victories and clutch shots are celebrated and lamented. I've found people love to debate, hear, and share these stories and because my heart's desire is to introduce the people of sport to Jesus, I've come to understand how sharing and chatting about sport stories can be used to further the gospel.

Often the people I meet ask me about my faith. Many people question how I can believe in, and follow something, that in their mind cannot be proven true. At these times, I have found that most people respond well when I share stories about experiencing God's faithfulness in direct answer to prayer from my own life. After all, they cannot argue with examples of my practical application of life, faith, and prayer! It would seem that most people are primarily oral learners and stories are easy to remember and relate to. Compare communicating faith through stories with most sermons. While sermons are presented orally and contain stories that are used to illustrate a point the speaker wishes to make, stories in and of themselves can be either oral or written as opposed to an oral didactic (teaching) sermon. Through either method the receiver of a story is left to wrestle with their own interpretation.

Once when working in South Africa with the San people (also referred to as the Bushmen), I was having a hard time explaining the didactic truths of the gospel until we shared the parables (stories) that Jesus told. From Jesus' example, we then taught them how to share the gospel using indigenous parables from their own lives. It was amazing to see them become animated as spiritual truths became real and practical to them through relevant narratives.

Jesus used parables throughout His ministry. His simple stories created word pictures to capture the attention of His listeners. Through parables, His listeners could clearly visualize and understand the gospel and its basic principles. Surprisingly enough His parables ended up teaching them didactic truths! His parables often included circumstances or cultural elements that would have surprised or even offended those listening and yet they were accepted. I like to call these the "*Wow Moments*" of the parable because Jesus' audience would have gone "Wow!" when they caught His specific point. The *Wow Moments* were connected to the spiritual truth that Jesus was illustrating and were vital to communicating what He was teaching.

Consider the parable of the prodigal son.[1] This is an amazing story that communicates a picture of God's unconditional love for his children. The "*Wow Moments*" include all the points made in Scoreboard 14 on page 103.

Whenever the gospel or biblical truths or presented in various Sports ministry outreaches, it would be wise to follow Jesus' method. One of the reasons I love sports is because of the stories it creates; stories of perseverance, heartbreak, victory, defeat, joy and sorrow. Using sports stories and analogies (sports parables) today to share the gospel is a great tool to open the hearts and minds of athletes or anyone who loves sports. You may recall how Brazilian soccer star, Kaka, after scoring a goal would remove his jersey to boldly display a T-shirt underneath with the exclamation: "I belong to Jesus." On numerous occasions as I met soccer fans and players throughout the world, I would start the conversation by asking if they had seen Kaka's shirt. This story would inevitably lead to an open discussion about faith.

Creativity and Sports Parables

We can use many things from within a particular sport that the audience is familiar with to communicate your message of a spiritual truth. Usually this can be done effectively in less than 15 minutes. You are only limited by your own creativity. Some ideas for Sports Parables can include:

- Skills—receiving a pass, dribbling, defense, shooting, rebounding, heading, etc.
- Positions—forward, goalie, striker, coach, center, blocker, pitcher, catcher, etc.
- Attitudes—perseverance, teamwork, potential, humility, self-control, effort, submission, losing, competition, etc.
- Situations—winning, losing, defense, offense, scoring, missing shots
- Rules—hands, fouls, red card, substitutions, strikes, balls, outs, etc.
- Incidents and exploits involving a favorite local team or player

One of my favorite experiences using Sports Parables as a part of sports outreach involved a team that we took to the country of Turkey. We organized a sports camp for 120 youth on an Islamic sports university campus. Using the

---

1 Luke 15.11-31.

SCOREBOARD

#14: WOW Moments From The Parable of The Prodigal Son

1. The younger son had disrespected his father by asking for his inheritance. In essence he was wishing that his father was dead. In the culture of that day, the father had the right to beat his son but instead, he granted his request.

2. The story goes on to relate when the younger son had spent the entire inheritance on riotous living and had fallen to the despised job of feeding pigs, he was as low socially as he could go. To the Jews, pigs are unclean, and on top of this, he even longed to eat the food being fed to the pigs!

3. Yet, when the prodigal son came to his senses and returned home, the father ran to meet him with open arms. What a contrast this was from what would have been the father's right, which would have been to beat him. Instead he ran to him, threw his arms around his prodigal, and kissed him. Running was considered undignified and socially unacceptable because wearing a robe, he would have had to lift it above his knees and expose them in order to run. Yet his love for his son exceeded all social expectations.

4. The story continues by relating how the father put a ring on his son's finger, sandals on his feet, and a robe around his shoulders: all indications the father was fully restoring his son's rights. He was not just a hired hand, he was his son.

5. Finally, the father throws a party and orders that the fattened calf be killed to demonstrate just how extraordinarily joyous of an occasion this is and how lavish the celebration will be.

SCOREBOARD

#15: Sports Parable Outline for Writing Your Own

Title
_____

Sports Example – Skill, position, attitude, story
_____

Spiritual Principle to be Taught
_____

Explanation of Illustration/Demonstration
_____

Supporting Verse
_____

(See Appendix #6 & #7)

story of Joseph which is told in both the Qur'an[2] and the Bible[3], we created *Sports Parables* from the major events in his life to teach about spiritual principles such as betrayal, injustice, integrity, and forgiveness. Then we made the connection to the story of Jesus. Most of you can recall many of the events that happen in Joseph's life. We can see him as a Christ-figure because what happens to him parallels what happens to Jesus. He is betrayed by those he trusted. He was sold for a price and falsely accused. He was tempted to sin against God. Later he is imprisoned, then freed, and exalted to rule over all of Egypt. Given the opportunity to meet his brothers again, instead of seeking revenge, he demonstrates grace, mercy, and forgiveness. What you also may not know is that the Qur'an not only tells Joseph's story but speaks about him and it with revering words. It reads: "We do relate to you the most beautiful of stories."[4] and "Truly in Joseph and his brothers there are signs for the seeker."[5] Using Joseph and sports as cultural bridges we were able to reach the children, and even their parents, with the gospel in a relevant and effective way!

Refer to Appendix #7 to read examples of sports parables, and then use Scoreboard 15 above as an outline to write your own. Be sure to include *"Wow Moments"*. You should recognize Example #5 as the inspiration for this book.

---

2   Surah 12; The Qur'an
3   Genesis 37-50
4   Surah 12:3; The Qur'an
5   Surah 12:7; The Qur'an

Your Parable

Your best story/parable is always your own testimony. The great thing about using sports in your testimony is that sport empowers and enables anyone to be able to connect and build relationships with people who may be far from Jesus but have a common interest of sports.

We worship an amazing God. He is omnipotent (all-powerful), omniscient (all-knowing), and omnipresent (everywhere present). He is creator of the universe and above all things in authority and position. Yet, amazingly enough, He has chosen each one of us to be His children. He wants to know us, and He wants us to know Him. Paul was inspired to write to the Ephesians about this:

> Praise be to the God and Father of our Lord Jesus Christ, who has blessed us in the heavenly realms with every spiritual blessing in Christ. For He chose us in Him before the creation of the world to be holy and blameless in His sight. In love He predestined us to be adopted as His sons through Jesus Christ, in accordance with His pleasure and will – to the praise of His glorious grace, which He has freely given us in the One He loves.[6]

John also was so inspired and wrote in his Gospel:

> Yet to all who received Him, to those who believed in His name, He gave the right to become the children of God – children born not of natural descent nor of human will, but born of God.[7]

If you have accepted Jesus as your Savior then you are a child of God, and you have a unique story about how you met God. No one else has the same story. Your story is a "once-in-a-lifetime" event. Maybe you were a drug addict and God immediately saved you from that addiction when you cried out to Him. Maybe you grew up in a Christian home and accepted Jesus at a young age. Maybe you were into philosophy or science and God revealed Himself to you through reason or nature. Maybe you were in an accident or going through a deep depression and Jesus met you in your darkest moments. I don't know your story. It is an intimate story that is between you and your Heavenly Father Who has indeed chosen you as His child and it can be used to communicate the gospel to those who are far from Jesus.

---

6   Ephesians 1.3-6.
7   John 1.12.

Why is sharing your testimony so important?

1. Sharing your testimony will **draw others** closer to Jesus. While God has given you your own story, it is not to keep it for yourself. He wants you to share it freely with others so that they, too, can be challenged, encouraged, and come to know Him. Reading the following paraphrase[8] from the second letter Paul was inspired to write to the Corinthians will prove to be a good insight into the importance of our testimony.

> Now we look inside, and what we see is that anyone united with the Messiah gets a fresh start, is created new. The old life is gone; a new life burgeons! Look at it! All this comes from the God who settled the relationship between us and Him, and then called us to settle our relationships with each other. God put the world square with Himself through the Messiah, giving the world a fresh start by offering forgiveness of sins. **God has given us the task of telling everyone what He is doing. We're Christ's representatives. God uses us to persuade men and women** to drop their differences and enter into God's work of making things right between them. We're speaking for Christ himself now: Become friends with God; He's already a friend with you.[9]

This is the calling that God has given each one of us, to tell others what He is doing in our lives so that they can "become friends with God."

2. Sharing your testimony is a way to be **culturally relevant**. In this increasingly postmodern world, your testimony is the most acceptable way to share your faith. While modernity was all about reason and logic with the mind, postmodernity is about experience and action through the heart. Relationships and personal experience are the keys. As you start conversations and just talk with people, you are sharing your life with them. In his article *An Introduction to Postmodernism (and Why It's Not a Bad Word)*, Matt Kelley writes:

> Postmodernism calls into question our subjective assumptions. To postmodern Christians, evangelism doesn't begin with the assertion of certain facts, but a reflection upon **how an indi-**

---

8 Eugene H. Peterson, *The Message: The Bible in Contemporary Language*. Colorado Springs, CO: Navpress, 2002. The Message is a paraphrase of the Bible and should not be confused with being a translation of the original words of the Scripture but rather be received as a bit of a commentary on, and explanation of, the message of the verses being paraphrased.

9 2 Corinthians 5.17-20.

vidual has experienced the Holy in her own life. She then searches for points of connection in someone else's life. Postmodernism seriously questions whether or not true evangelism happens on street corners or brief encounters on the beach. It suggests that true evangelism happens in homes, coffee houses, and late-night talks in dorm rooms. Postmodern evangelism is the **sharing of souls** rather than the imparting of doctrine.[10]

As we explored in this chapter, Jesus often taught in parables. These word pictures allowed people to grasp the spiritual principles that Jesus was teaching. Your testimony is your **parable** about your life. The stories you share will reflect God's love to others through you and encourage, challenge, convict, and bless your listeners. In this way they can picture God working in their own lives.

3. Preparing and sharing your testimony allows you a "**stop moment**" to reflect deeply on what God has done in your life. Often life gets so busy that we do not take enough time to pause to remember God's faithfulness. In these moments you can look back and see how God has used the ups and downs of your life to draw you closer to Him, and you can look ahead with expectation for the future plans He has for you. Each day we follow Jesus, our lives are still "under construction" and being formed to become more like Him. Paul reminds us through what he was inspired to write to the Philippians: 1:6 reminds us, "Being confident of this, that He who began a good work in you will carry it on to completion."[11]

Now it's your turn. As you consider Paul's Example (in Scoreboard 16 on page 108) and the following, write out your own testimony using the outline in Scoreboard 17 on page 109 and also Appendix 8.

A Testimony consists of three main parts: 1) What your life was like before you accepted Jesus as Lord and Savior; 2) How you came to Jesus; and 3) How your life has changed since Jesus became your Lord and Savior. Now you may be saying to yourself: "I can only tell my testimony one time. So what am I to share in the other post-game devotionals over the next nine weeks of our outreach league?" The amazing thing about the strategy of basing our gospel "affirmations"[12] in testimonies is how many areas in our lives God needs to get a hold of.

It's true, a testimony of initially coming to faith in Jesus will get old if repeatedly shared with the same person, but each of us, if we are continuing to grow in our faith, will have a myriad of testimonies to share. Consider things like, what

---

10   Matt Kelley, *An Introduction to Postmodernism (and Why It's Not a Bad Word)*, Youth Specialties, 2004.
11   Philippians 1.6.
12   The transferable concept of Proclamation-Affirmation is explained in The second book of The Institutes of Sports Outreach Book Series – *Sports Outreach Fundamentals*. In specific see Chapter 5 and pages 58ff.

SCOREBOARD
#16: Paul's Example

Acts 22:3-5   His life before Christ
Acts 22:6-13   His experience receiving Christ
Acts 22:14-15   His life after Christ

was your language like before Jesus convicted you to "clean it up;" or about when The Holy Spirit encouraged you to stop telling lies; or your Heavenly Father challenged you to be a better father or mother! For me the list goes on and on. I need the gospel applied to my life daily, and these experiences can form the basis for my ongoing testimony. What they all share in common has to do with the three aspects of a testimony: 1) what was this area of my life like before God convicted me; 2) how did God get through to me and finally; 3) how has Jesus redeemed and changed my life in these specific areas. So to repeat the outline for a gospel testimony...

- Tell about your life before you were a believer in Christ, where you were born, grew up, and when you began thinking about your need for Christ (or what specific area of your life was like before Jesus got a hold of it).
- Tell about when you received Christ. What led up to it? Where were you? How did you feel? What did you think? What did you ask Christ to do? (or how The Holy Spirit convicted you to change or grow in a specific area of your life)
- How has Christ changed your life since you received Him—at home, at work, at school, in the problems you face, in your plans, in your feelings towards yourself and others?
- Close your testimony with a verse from the Bible that has meant something to you as a life verse or as a recent encouragement in your daily walk with Christ. If God leads you, you may also want to give your audience a challenge to accept Christ or to make a deeper commitment to follow Jesus.

Some keys:
- Remember, do not dwell on the "old creature" but speak of the "new creature" you are becoming in Christ. The Bridge Illustration may be appropriate to use if you include personal stories and relate it to your own journey of faith.
- Keep your presentation to 7-10 minutes, not longer.
- Use words and ideas that people can understand. Keep away from jargon or Christian-sounding phrases.

SCOREBOARD

#17: Your Testimony - Your Turn

Your life before accepting Jesus as Lord & Savior
_____

How you came to Jesus
_____

How your life has changed
_____

Life Verse/Challenge
_____

(See Appendix # 8)

- Be specific. Mention a real detail, incident, place, thought, feeling or statement. Wherever possible, avoid vague generalities.
- Be honest. Don't exaggerate. Don't cover up difficulties; they usually help people identify with you and add credibility.
- Don't mention church denominations, especially in a negative way and be cautious of talking about church. People are likely to have caricatures about that topic, and anyway, your aim should be to point people to Christ, not institutional Christianity.

Be encouraged and encouraging. Even if you are not that into sports, don't be afraid to share your sports stories and watch as people exclaim "Wow" for Jesus!

Only you can tell your story! Only Jesus can use it to draw others to Himself! But don't forget that the greatest story to tell is still about Jesus. I was reminded of this again in South Africa. After our sports outreach we stopped at a grocery store. While I was waiting in the car a man came up to the window. He was carrying a backpack and showed me a card in his hand. He was making kind of a grunting sound, and as I read the card I came to understand that his name was Kerwin. He was deaf and mute. We had not yet eaten all of our bag lunches for the day so I gladly gave most of our fruit, chips, a sandwich, and water to him. Then as is my custom I handed him a tract and indicated that he should read it. He nodded and went on his way. Less than 10 minutes later as I was still waiting and praying for Kerwin, a loud knock on the window startled me. It was Kerwin again. He had already read the tract and with a huge grin on his face was wildly pointing at the last page with the clear message of salvation. As best as he could he explained that he had just accepted Jesus into his heart! He also wanted me to pray for him, which I happily did. After the prayer he skipped away with a new sparkle in his eyes. The story of Jesus and a simple act of kindness made a difference for eternity.

Reflection

Who can you share Jesus' story with today? Who can you share your Jesus story with today? What *Sports Parables* do you know that you can share as you play your sport for Jesus?

Prayer

Father, thank You that I am your child. Thank You for meeting me personally in a way that I could understand You. Thank You that You are working in my life daily. As I share my story, may I truly reflect Jesus and be used by You to draw others to Yourself.

Chapter 10

Sports Ministry, the Unreached, and Persecution— The Present Reality

This shoe will face adversity but come away victorious.

The book entitled *The Insanity of God* by Nik Ripken has impacted and greatly challenged me. In the book, Nik tells of being taught by believers in persecution how to follow Jesus, how to love Jesus, and how to walk with Him day by day. He writes"

> Believers in persecution taught us ... the freedom to believe and witness has nothing to do with the government or political system or with civil or political rights that might or might not be present.... They are just as free to share Jesus today in Islamic, Hindu, Buddhist, Communist countries as you and I are in America. It isn't a matter of political freedom. It is simply a matter of obedience. The price for obedience might be different in different places—but it is always possible to obey Christ's call to make disciples. Every believer—in every place—is always free to make that choice.[1]

I had the privilege of meeting and hearing Nik teach at meetings for church and ministry leaders working in North Africa and the Middle East. He asked those of us in attendance: "What does your church preach about persecution?" He continued by stating: "I ran away from what I thought was persecution. My church told me that my God does not ask these things of us." He then shared what he has discovered in his own life and also from interviewing more than 800 persecuted believers around the world. His findings include:

1) In places where people are coming to Jesus, persecution is normal. Chinese pastors say prison is their seminary. Forty percent have been in prison for at least three years.
2) The causes of persecution ranked from the most frequent abusers are: Governments, Islam, Communism, and The Church.

---

[1] Nik Ripken, *The Insanity of God*, Nashville, TN; B&H Books, 2013, p. 307.

3) Seventy percent of those who faithfully practice their faith live in persecution (See Scoreboard 18 below).
4) Thirty thousand Christians around the world will be arrested today.
5) Obedience in sharing the Good News leads to suffering and greater persecution.
6) No matter what country you live in, you can share Jesus, but Satan desires us to keep Jesus to ourselves and to keep people from having access to Him.
7) Today 2.8 billion people in the world have no access to Jesus, and 95% of Christians will never share Jesus with another person before they die![2]

SCOREBOARD

#18: The Present Reality

According to Open Doors 2020 Watch List, their annual ranking of the top 50 countries where it's most dangerous to be a Christian, more than 260 million believers are now living under persecution. That is 1 out of every 8 worldwide!

For more information check out:
www.opendoorsusa.org/christian-persecution/world-watch-list/

Ripken continued in his book and said: "Our hope is that believers around the world will get close enough to the heart of God that the first images that come to mind when we hear the word Muslim are ... to see and think of each and every individual Muslim as a lost person who is loved by God. We need to see each Muslim as a person in need of God's grace and forgiveness. We need to see each Muslim as someone for whom Christ died"[3]

Now consider that of the 7.5 billion people living in our world today, an estimated 40%, or 3.15 billion, have little or no access to the gospel.[4] They certainly don't have the opportunities I have had, and in most cases they don't have even one person to tell them about Jesus. Most are living in countries that are hostile to the gospel.

---

2   The conference was held in Spring 2017. More specific details, including name and location, cannot be made public due to the sensitive security risks of those in attendance and the front-line ministry they are involved in.
3   Nik Ripken, op cit., p. 303.
4   Greater Frontiers Mission:www.globalfrontiermissions.org/gfm-101-missions-course/the-unreached-peoples-and-their-role-in-the-great-commission.

THE 10/40 WINDOW

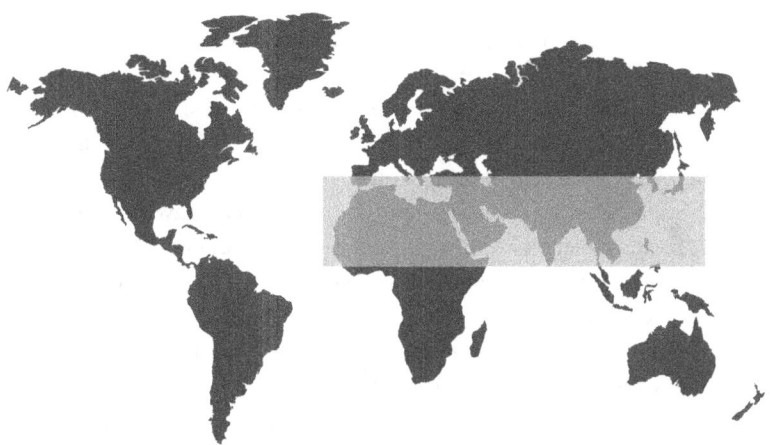

Jesus has changed my life! I cannot imagine what it would be like without knowing Him. I had the privilege of growing up in a family that taught me about Jesus from an early age. I was taken to church and able to attend a strong youth group that discipled me. I then attended a Christian liberal arts college and received a minor in Biblical Studies. I have lived in a county with a population of less than 2,500 people that had more than 200 churches! I have worked full-time in ministry by God's provision through the generous support of ministry partners who also desire to make Jesus known throughout the world. I am humbled, privileged, and thankful.

My heart has been stirred and broken even more by the reality that so many individual people are lost and dying without hope; without Jesus! I also grieve the fact that it is primarily due to the fact that entire people groups have very limited, if any connection with an individual Christian; let alone with a local church. People groups are defined as groups of people who are clustered and united by commonalities such as sharing the same language, culture, and class. A specific subset of people groups is identified by Christian missions and missionaries as Frontier People groups (FPG's). The distinction of these FPG's is they are more specifically identified by the fact that less than 0.1% of the entire population is Christian. More to the point, these least-reached people are concentrated geographically in what is called the "10/40 Window."[5] Even more profound they are found in exceeding numbers in one country: India![6] According to Rick

---

5   The 10/40 Window is a term that represents latitudinal lines on a map between 10 and 40 where two-thirds of the world's population lives and 90% have yet to even hear the Gospel. It was popularized by missiologist Luis Bush in the 1990's to promote prayer and mobilize believers to action to reach them. See: www.jesusfilm.org/blog-and-stories/10-40-window.html.

6   Joshua Project, See: www.joshuaproject.net/frontier/1.

Woods who is the editor of the *Mission Frontiers Magazine,* taking the gospel to India is a daunting task.

> There are unreached people groups in almost every country on Earth. But no other country in the world has a greater concentration of unreached and Frontier Peoples than the country of India. Half the population of all Frontier Peoples, live in India and 90% of all the people in India live in unreached people groups. No other country in the world has such a diverse and complex society with thousands of different communities all separated by caste, language and religion. Each of these communities will likely need a separate movement of disciple-making and church planting—thereby making India the greatest challenge to world evangelization that the global mission force faces today. No matter how you slice the data, the Gospel must become good news in every community of India.[7]

Praise God however because He is still at work! We can receive encouragement from our study of the Scriptures such as what Peter was inspired to write:

> Don't overlook the obvious here, friends. With God, one day is as good as a thousand years, a thousand years as a day. God isn't late with His promise as some measure lateness. He is restraining Himself on account of you, holding back the End because He doesn't want anyone lost. He's giving everyone space and time to change.[8]

Nonetheless, we should maintain our urgency about the spreading of the gospel. I believe all who are concerned about accomplishing the Great Commission[9] and about being a faithful and relevant follower of Jesus in this day and age will realize it is imperative to learn about these FPGs and their countries while doing all we can to reach them. It is God's desire that all people might come to know Him, and if this is His desire, then shouldn't it also be ours?

Of course unreached people groups and unreached people are not just located in the 10/40 window. Many things happening today in our neighborhoods, countries, and world give cause for concern: The Corona virus epidemic; Ebola in Africa; daily shootings in the USA; immigration issues everywhere; threats

---

7   Rick Woods in Mission Frontiers Magazine, May/June 2019; www.missionfrontiers.org/issue/archive/india-the-greatest-challenge-to-world-evangelization.
8   2 Peter 3.9, from Peterson, Eugene. *The Message: The Bible in Contemporary Language.* Colorado Springs, CO: Navpress, 2002.
9   Matthew 28:16-20.

TIMEOUT

Testimony A

Gary, competed with his country's national team in international competitions including the Olympic trials. For the preparation leading up to these competitions, the team's trainer, a believer, was performing weekly injury checks and referring or treating injuries as necessary. During this time, he developed a friendship with Gary. One day Gary asked him to come to his house and look at his father's shoulder injury, which had bothered him for a few years. This led to a relationship between the two families with frequent visits in each others' homes. On these visits not only was he able to give advice on how to deal with the father's nagging injury, but he was able to share stories from the Bible with the entire family and some neighbors. The friendship led to all of them entering into relationship with Jesus (seven people initially). The trainer then began the process of spiritually training this family so they can spread the truth among their people group. While there are many people from their people group in the city where they live, most are located in a different region of the country and are both unreached and unengaged. Unengaged means that they don't have any Christians who are presently trying to share the gospel with them, due geographical, political, language, or other challenges. This family is strategic because they are a family of influence both in the city and their home community, which is a two-day trip from the city. While visiting in their home in the city since they have accepted Jesus, the trainer was able to share with their neighbors and extended family many times and has even assisted Gary and his father in sharing in the heart language of their people group. It is estimated the initial number of people who have heard the truth in their heart language as a result of this family to be at least 30 people! This contact would never have happened without unique access through sports into the local sports community.

of and attacks by terrorists; war in the Ukraine, Syria, Yemen, etc. How should we respond to all that we see, hear, and read? It can be overwhelming. At times, honestly, I just want to ignore anything that does not directly impact my life. Yet I know that God still has a plan. I believe He is still in control, and He still wants to use us to impact our world for Him.

I have found particular relevance to what many of our Christian brethren are experiencing today in the second letter Paul was inspired to write to Timothy. The Apostle Paul who was a missionary to the gentiles, but now found himself in prison and suffering persecution in many forms. As he penned what became the last letter he ever wrote (as far as we know), he was experiencing extreme isolation and loneliness, probably debilitating bitter cold, and an impending, gruesome execution. In this "last will and testament," words written by a persecuted believer for persecuted believers, we read what was foremost in Paul's mind as he addressed Timothy for the final time. He is sharing his heart and giving final instructions, while passing the baton to Timothy and the next generation of leaders.

Paul writes about his priorities: "Sound doctrine; steadfast faith; confident endurance; and enduring love."[10] In specific one key priority stands out among many: And the things you have heard me say in the presence of many witnesses entrust to reliable men who will also be qualified to teach others.[11]

This verse has been discussed in previous chapters already and identified as the basis for *2-T-2-2 Relationships*, but it is worth another look. I believe that Paul understood this mentoring and empowering of the next generation was the only way to leave a legacy that would truly change a community and the world, one relationship at a time. In other words, he is espousing the value and critical importance of *Evangelistic-Disciplemaking*! Shouldn't this also be our response to what we see happening in our world around us, both near and far.[12]

Even as he is instructing Timothy, Paul is reminding him to teach "reliable men" who can then teach others, to pass on all that he has learned. Then Paul shares three different comparisons in the context of his own suffering that applied to Timothy and this work of multiplying disciples that can also be applied to us. These comparisons are:

- A soldier who is called to give up worldly security and commit to endure rigorous discipline[13]
- An athlete who is to train hard and follow the rules[14]

---

10   *Life Application Bible: The Living Bible*, Carol Stream, IL: Tyndale House Publishers, 1988, p. 1872.
11   2 Timothy 2.1-10.
12   For more information I refer you back to chapters 4 and 5 where *Evangelist-Disciplemaking* is discussed at length.
13   2 Timothy 2.4.
14   2 Timothy 2.5.

CHAPTER 10: Sports ministry, the Unreached, and Persecution

- A farmer who is to work hard for the hope of the harvest[15]

Recall the story of Brigadier General Teddy Roosevelt, Jr. from chapter 1 and our examination of the Parable of the Sower in chapter 6.

It is interesting that the other of Paul's main comparisons uses a sports analogy to emphasize his point. In ministry, as in sports, an athlete who is committed in their preparation and plays fairly is a good thing! Why are believers willing to sacrifice in the end? All their suffering, like Paul's, is made worthwhile by the goal of glorifying God, winning and discipling people to Christ, and one day living eternally with Him.

There is one pastor for every 450,000 people in the 10/40 Window compared with one pastor for every 250 people in the US.[16] This illustrates how great a need currently exists, but also how small The Church is. Yes, it is true that many believers around the world face daily persecution and challenges, but thankfully, we know Sports ministry is a bridge that open doors and provides a platform to reach into places of influence and change lives with the gospel.

In the United States, where there are many congregations and a basic Christian heritage, people have access to the gospel even if they are not interested in it. If someone does want to understand it and accept Jesus, it is estimated that they would only have to knock on just six doors in order to find a person who could explain it to them.[17] While this is still a sad reality, it is actually something to rejoice in when compared to the 10/40 Window where an unbeliever would have to knock on at least 30,000 doors before encountering someone who could explain the gospel to them![18] To bring this into clearer focus, compare the numbers: One in six (17%) to one in 30,000 (0.00003%). That is exactly why it is vital that we continue to go to this region of the world.

Paul's priorities as expressed in his letter to Timothy are vital and are what we strive to do through Sports ministry. These are things that all Christians are to participate in, regardless if we live in the 10/40 Window or elsewhere.

The Testimonies found in the Time Outs in this chapter are just three examples of what we have seen happen through Sports ministry and illustrate why I am so convinced that Sports ministry is the answer to the challenge of reaching those who live in the 10/40 Window and beyond.

One of my Sports ministry friends wrote: "Sports is the tool we dig with. The Gospel is the tool we plant with. Let's pray for rain!"[19]

---

15   2 Timothy 2.6.
16   Statistic proved by the Life Giving Network (LGN) (www.lifegivingnetwork.org) during a report presented publicly on September 1, 2019.
17   LGN.
18   LGN.
19   Bubby Bryan, former Communications Director of Uttermost Sports (www.uttermostsports.org); digital newsletter, 2018.

TIMEOUT

Testimony B

Years ago, I was at home in The Netherlands checking my email when I read the following message: "Hi. I am here on a sports training trip and I found your email address through your church website. I am from... (a country in North Africa), and I want someone to tell me what it means to be a Christian. Can you meet with me? Here is my phone number..."

I immediately called the number and spoke to Wallid, the man who had written that email. He was very anxious to meet me so I gave him directions to our village by train and in less than two hours he was sitting on the couch in my living room. After brief introductions I shared the gospel with him. Walid, who came from a Muslim background and a Muslim-majority country, contemplated the risk accepting Jesus as Lord and Savior meant for him. He then said: "This is what I want for my life" and prayed to receive Jesus as his Savior!!! I gave him a Bible that he took back to his hotel room. I have since maintained contact with Walid and tried to encourage him in his faith. I also connected him with other believers in his country. He has continued to do his best to walk with Jesus each day, but it is very difficult. Walid is the only believer in his family. A few weeks ago, I received a message from him. The city where he lives was taken over by an ISIS-affiliated militia. Walid is afraid, but he knows God is with him.

Jesus, the Living Water is the rain we pray for! Might I also add that we need to bring that rain to those that have not heard. Not so long ago our world seemed much larger. Places that used to be so far away have been brought closer through the Internet and social media. We can now communicate easily across the world, and these innovations have sped up the spread of the gospel. I hear many stories from people living in difficult places where we are working who have found a personal relationship with Jesus through something they read or heard online. Add this to the fact that many Muslims are meeting Jesus through dreams and visions, and many Hindus and Buddhists are coming to faith through miraculous healings. Indeed, there is much to be thankful for. We are living in one of the most exciting times in history. God has given us great strategies like sports, recreation, and fitness to use to share His love with others and He is moving!

Audience with World Leaders

Sports ministry has given me opportunity to meet many government leaders and influential people around the world as well. Once in East Asia, our team arrived at the airport so early that none of the check-in lines were open yet. A woman from the airline asked who we were, where we were going, and what we were doing. Then she asked if we could step into a special check-in line at a specific time. I thought she was just giving us extra attention because we were a large group and a sports team. Every fifteen minutes or so she would come over and chat with me. At one point she said that she would like to provide drinks for our team since we were such a nice group.

When our check-in time came she asked me to call the team over and line up our luggage in another lane. We all dutifully complied. Then as a photographer showed up, she informed me that a "vice president" (I assumed he was from the airline company and this was for promotional purposes) would come and ask us some general questions like: "Where are you from?" "How do you like our country?" and "How long have you been visiting?" After some time the vice president still had not shown up, so they stopped checking us in and asked us to wait. After about 30 more minutes, we saw many police cars arrive outside and many security officers standing on the ramp leading from the door into the terminal. Then a crowd walked from the entrance toward us. The man in the middle stopped in front of our team and asked a few questions while cameras rolled and photographers snapped pictures. After three to four minutes, the interview was over and the entourage moved on. As we were left standing there, I turned to an airline clerk and asked who that was. Her response: "That was the Vice Premier of our country." It was quite interesting to me that a team sharing the gospel in this very closed country would be given the privilege of meeting the Vice Premier. We were then given access to the airline's business lounge until it was time to catch our flight back home.

And a Suicide Bomber

While serving with believers in the Middle East, we were able to organize an outreach and play soccer with some youth from a local refugee camp. In broken English, a 19-year old man explained that he was going to be a suicide bomber. He demonstrated how he would attach the explosives to his wrists and waist before telling us he already had been photographed for his "martyr's picture." His friends were treating him like a hero. We gathered him and some of his friends in a circle and boldly prayed that God would intervene and show them the truth

TIMEOUT

Testimony C

"Earlier in the year, I began teaching multiple fitness classes as well as providing personal training to several athletes. Also, I developed a relationship with an owner of another gym and initiated the idea of putting on a fitness seminar for coaches and trainers. I met another rep in the area, and we partnered together for the workshop. The seminar was very successful, and we believe it will lead to additional training opportunities as well as growing the new relationships with those who attended the training. By conducting the class, training, and seminar, God has opened the door to nearly 40 new relationships with locals in my country. I am excited to see how these relationships will deepen as I have time with people inside and outside the gym. I much prefer having an ongoing, legitimate way of connecting with locals. Being welcomed at the gym and becoming part of the coaching staff allows me regular access into people's lives in a way that makes sense to them and gives me credibility and identity as opposed to trying to meet people randomly on the streets or coffee shops."

---

that comes through Jesus! Then I went back to our hostel and cried out to God again and again. I never heard any more about this sincere and yet sadly misguided young man. I often wonder what God did in his heart that day and if he carried out his diabolical plan. Sports ministry gave us the opportunity to share truth and at the very least gave him the chance to change his path.

On the Front Lines

During another major project that I lead in the Middle East, I visited two of our teams serving in villages dominated by a non-Christian religion. One was a group of young women who led two camps for 100 girls between the ages of 14-16. The camps included sports, drama, and crafts. The outreach team built relationships with the girls and many attendees shared openly about their pain, frustrations, struggles, faith, and feelings. Local boys and men were not allowed into the camp, but I was able to attend as a special foreign guest. It was amazing to see how God used this team! Because they were working in a sensitive location, they did not share openly about Jesus unless the girls asked first. The second team led a sports camp for 70 children, boys and girls, in another village. The youth in this country are often called "children of the stone" because their way of dealing with many situations (frustration, anger, and especially seeing soldiers) typically results in them throwing stones. The teams made a noticeable difference in the lives of these children. The local soccer coach said our team "brought life" to his village.

Another door was open through water sports. Utilizing the team member's abilities to train others in swimming, CPR and first aid, multiple opportunities became available to teach lifeguards at various pools, schools, and hotels.

That summer we sent over 300 people from 12 different countries (31 sports teams and 4 prayer teams) to partner with local believers in 32 churches located in 22 cities and villages throughout the country. After the completion of the main project I did my best to compile reports from our team leaders. Based on the information I had at this time I have the following estimates:

- 3,000 people attended sports clinics
- 1,000 pieces of gospel literature where distributed
- 4.000 people heard the gospel
- 250 people made a decision to receive Jesus as their Lord and Savior and were discipled by a local church

Be sure to read Time Out Testimonies A - C on pages 115, 118 and 120 for more personal examples of the doors Sports ministry has opened in the 10/40 Window.

Closer Than We Think

It may seem that all of this is so far away, but if that is what you are thinking you are missing the point. We cannot hide or think that what's happening "out there" overseas will never affect us. A report from the Pew Research Institute projects that within this century, Islam will become the world's largest religion (See Scoreboard 19 & 20 on pages 122-123). We need to learn more about what Muslims believe. We need to understand why there is so much conflict between Muslims, Hindus, and Christians and people of other faiths. We need to reach out and befriend immigrants, those in our neighborhoods and communities who are different than us. In many cases they are coming to us. Some of us need to go into their countries and live out the gospel with the expectation that as we love those we serve we will be able to share the gospel verbally with them. At the very least we need to pray for them and look for ways to show them God's love. Perhaps it will be through sports, recreation, and fitness ministry? We need to ask God for open doors and to be available for how He wants to use us as His light in this rapidly changing world.

SCOREBOARD

#19: Islam Growing Fastest

Muslims are the only major religious group projected to increase faster than the world's population as a whole.

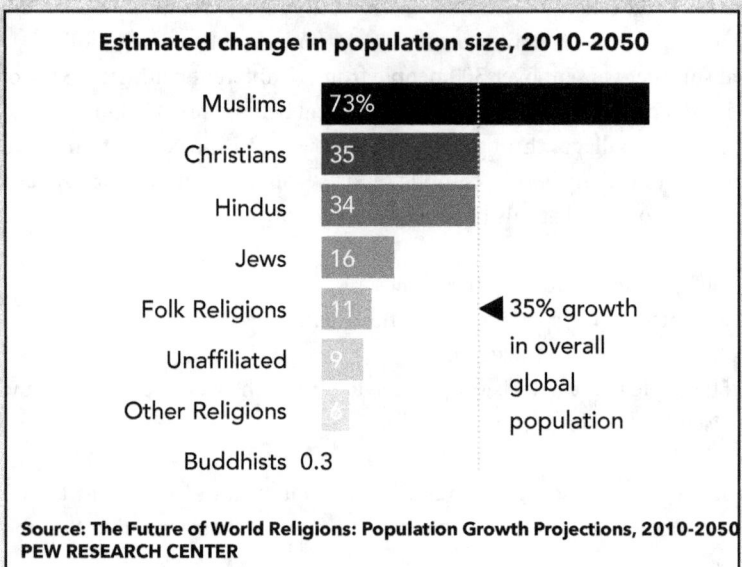

Estimated change in population size, 2010-2050

- Muslims: 73%
- Christians: 35
- Hindus: 34
- Jews: 16
- Folk Religions: 11
- Unaffiliated: 9
- Other Religions: 5
- Buddhists: 0.3

◀ 35% growth in overall global population

Source: The Future of World Religions: Population Growth Projections, 2010-2050 PEW RESEARCH CENTER

A Biblical Insight

Luke writes about the stoning of Stephen and what happened afterwards:

> And there arose on that day a great persecution against the church in Jerusalem, and they were all scattered throughout the regions of Judea and Samaria, except the apostles.[20]

Of course, with them went the gospel to be proclaimed and lived out! Francis Chan relates an account of speaking with a church leader in China who shared five pillars to the growth of the house church movement.

---

20   Acts 8.1.

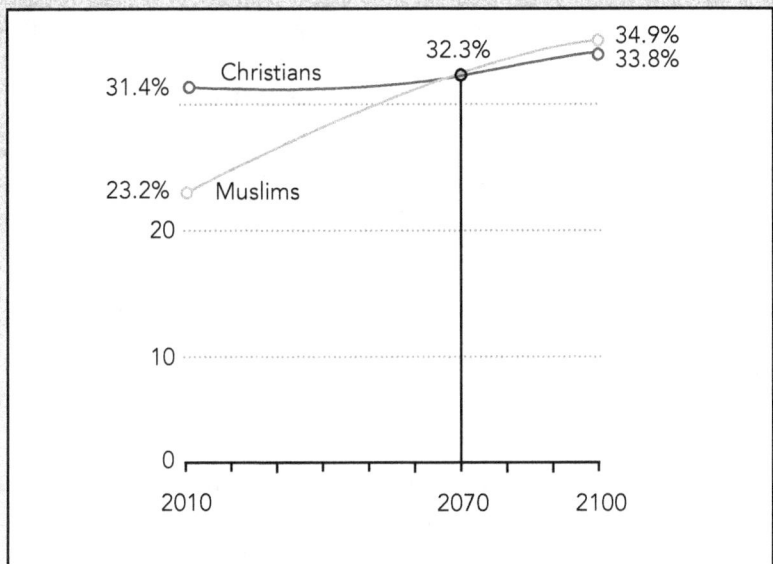

These pillars are:

1) A deep commitment to prayer
2) A commitment to the Word of God
3) A commitment to every member sharing the gospel
4) Regular expectation of miracles
5) Embracing suffering for the glory of Christ[21]

We should all evaluate our own churches and our Sports ministries against these pillars if we want to be most effective. I implore us to do so. How important is prayer and teaching God's Word? Are we discipling our leaders and our

---

21 Francis Chan, *Letters to The Church*, Colorado Springs, CO; David C. Cook, 2018, pp. 134, 135.

converts to share their faith (BUILD / SEND / MULTIPLY)? Are we expecting God to move beyond your own abilities and experiences to even do miracles in your life and in the lives of those you are serving?

Regarding persecution, maybe it has not come to us yet, but that could be because we are not boldly proclaiming Jesus in our communities. I ask myself the question and invite you to ask yourself the same question: "Am I proclaiming Jesus? The more we proclaim Jesus by how we live and the more we verbally affirm Jesus the more likely persecution will come.[22] I am sure that some of Chan's five pillars are more relevant for you and your ministry at this time than others, but in the future all will most certainly find their place.

To my point, we can learn a lot from our persecuted brothers and sisters around the world. If persecution is the seed of The Church then Sports ministries *Evangelistic-Disciplemaking* is The Church's very lifeblood. God has given us no better strategy than Sports ministry that can be/is being used effectively to build His Church; in even the most difficult places and under the most difficult circumstances. No matter where you are ministering in Sports ministry take note! Sport has proven to be a brilliant method of cultural engagement worldwide, but it is particularly helpful in restricted access countries, with people who are different than we are.

Reflection

Commit to pray daily for countries where your brothers and sister are being persecuted for their faith. Ask God to show you how you can get more involved in practically serving them. Learn more about organizations (See Recommended International Sports ministry list in Appendix #13) that are serving in difficult places.

Prayer

Father, be with my brothers and sister around the world who are living under difficult circumstances. Give them more faith, courage, boldness, and hope to stand against the opposition that comes against them. Thank You for their examples of perseverance. Help me to find ways to serve them and to stand strong for Jesus in my own struggles and community.

---

22   For more insight into the Incarnational approach to *Evangelistic-Disciplemaking* described as Proclamation-Affirmation, I refer you the book *Sports Outreach Fundamentals*, pp. 57-60. This is the approach recommended by CSRM and it entails proclaiming the gospel through lifestyle and then affirming the gospel with words.

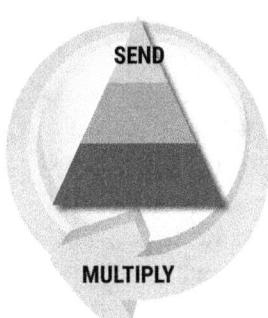

Chapter 11

Missional Sports Communities and A Response to the Present Reality

This shoe will thrive in community.

At the conclusion of a busy summer of ports Ministry in the Netherlands that involved partnerships with more than 50 churches, I was leading a debriefing and evaluation session for 45-50 church leaders. As we discussed the good and bad from the last months, I asked a simple question. "How many new people who participated in your neighborhood sports programs have continued to attend and even join your church as a result of your outreach?" I certainly was expecting a different answer than the one came. Surprisingly, only one leader raised his hand. When called upon he responded humorously-serious: "We have had one and a half persons (the woman who joined was pregnant)." None of the other leaders even flinched to raise their hands. Church members from each congregation had energetically and passionately organized sports camps, sports clinics and community teams, while serving their neighbors. Many significant relationships were established, yet this was the underwhelming result. The mission of our partnerships was to facilitate *Evangelistic-Disciplemaking* in each congregation, but as I reflected on this it was apparent that despite all our best efforts something was missing. As I inquired and probed the leaders more deeply, another leader shared: "We invite all those we meet during our sports outreaches to attend our church. They come once, maybe twice; then then never to enter our doors again. I met some of the them in the neighborhood and asked them why. To summarize, they say that they cannot understand or relate to the 'Christianese' we are speaking and our building is archaic and outdated." My heart broke. We had been successful in moving the congregation outside of their walls, but we had failed to free them from the bondage of their Christian culture and their buildings.

This is exactly way many recent studies have shown that there is a growing *dysconnect*/chasm between those who are Christians/involved in a congregation and those of other religious communities or who are completely secular. Church attendance and participation continues to decline in many countries in the West for this very reason. In addition, there is a growing disillusionment and dissatisfaction with Christianity by many who have become "de-churched"[1] due to their being alienated by The Church. Far too many who claim to know Jesus are not actively living their faith, making disciples or even sharing their faith. They aren't engaged in any *Evangelistic-Disciplemaking* activity because they claim it is too scary or intimidating. How can The Church become relevant again? How can congregations do a better job to engage those who are far from Jesus and His Church? I believe the answer can be found in using Sports ministry to plant *Missional Sports Communities*.

In 2012 I attended a church planting conference where I first heard the term missional community. Since Sports ministry becomes a bridge into the culture and lives of people, it was there that I coined the idea for *Missional Sports Communities*. Religious barriers break down and the common language of sport provides opportunities to share the gospel through the principles and methods that have already been discussed in previous chapters of this book.

Defining Missional and Missional Community[2]

What does it mean to be "missional"? In the article "Defining Missional," Alan Hirsch writes:

> A proper understanding of *missional* begins with recovering **a missionary understanding of God.** By His very nature God is a "sent one" who takes the initiative to redeem His creation. This doctrine, known as ***missio Dei* (the <u>sending</u> of God)** is causing many to redefine their understanding of The Church. Because we are the "sent" people of God, The Church is the instrument of God's mission in the world. As things stand, many people see it the other way around. They believe mission is an instrument of The Church; a means by which The Church is grown. Although we frequently say "**The Church has a mission,**" according to missional theology a more correct statement would be "**the mission has a church.**" A missional community is patterned after what God has done in Jesus Christ. In the incarnation God sent his Son. Similarly, to be missional means **to be sent into the world**; we do not expect people to come to us. This posture differentiates a missional church from an attractional church.[3]

---

[1] Previously discussed in chapter 4. It may be helpful to review that and understand that this is one of four major categories of people when it comes to church, faith and religion.

[2] To better understand this chapter, I recommend the reading of the 3rd book in this series entitled: *Putting The Church Back In The Game: The Ecclesiology of Sports Outreach.* That book discusses ecclesiology as it relates to, and integrates with, the sports world and *The Sports Outreach Community.* You will find in *Putting The Church Back In The Game* how a Missional Community really is a local congregation that is planting another Missional Community and/or growing a local congregation.

[3] Alan Hirsch, "Defining Missional"; http://www.christianitytoday.com/le/2008/fall/17.20.html.

Those of us in The Church (meaning those of us who have accepted Jesus and are part of The Body of Christ...not to be confused with a local church building), must start thinking missionally! Scoreboard 21 details some criteria for how this is to be done.

There are many opinions about how to define what a *Missional Sports Community* is practically. For some, establishing a *Missional Sports Community* is nothing more than a 'small group' extension of the local congregation, but for others it is a precursor to planting a new local church. Global Church Movements (GCM)[4] defined it as a group of 10 or more true followers of Jesus Christ who:

- Gather regularly for worship, prayer, biblical teaching and fellowship
- Passionately seek to love God and obey His Word
- Consistently walk by the power of the Holy Spirit
- Generously invest their time, talent, and treasure in God's Kingdom
- Actively draw people to Christ through life, word, and deed
- Has recognized spiritual leadership
- Seeks to multiply new churches and fellowships
- Is sustained by local resources[5]

SCOREBOARD

#21: Criteria for Thinking Missionally

- The Church going into the world
- A congregation being a tangible example of God's presence in a community
- Local Churches that are outward focused, dynamic and active with people who are far from Jesus
- Christ-followers living out the gospel and connecting with those who have never heard about Jesus

I believe that expecting people to come to our local church and accept Jesus as their Lord and Savior is not pragmatically effective, nor biblically sound. Rather, it is imperative for those of us who are already participating members of a local church to "go into all the world" so we can meet people in their own sports

---

[4] GCM is a ministry of Cru (previously known as Campus Crusade for Christ - CCC).
[5] GCM's list of characteristics as stated in their 2012 prospectus.

environment.⁶ As we have already expressed, the *Dysconnect*⁷ between The Church and the world has become too great. We, The Church, must go to them and stop expecting them to come us!

Striving Together

The Church would greatly benefit and ultimately be much more effective if it would be willing to **strive together** towards accomplishing the Great Commission. To better understand how to so collaborate, a brief study of two Greek New Testament words is offered in the "Good Greek" sidebar (See page 129) to expand this concept of striving together. This presents a better understanding of what it might mean to multiply Missional Communities through Sports Outreach.

The first word is *agon* and the second in *sunathleo*.⁸ They are highlighted in the following two passages.

> Whatever happens, conduct yourselves in a manner worthy of the gospel of Christ. Then, whether I come and see you or only hear about you in my absence, I will know that you stand firm in the one Spirit, striving (sunathleo) together as one for the faith of the gospel.⁹

> Fight (agon) the good fight (kalon agon) of the faith. Take hold of the eternal life to which you were called when you made your good confession in the presence of many witnesses.¹⁰

By standing, fighting and striving together in pursuit of this vision we will be able to change the course of our societies by changing the hearts/souls of those reached through Sports Outreach. When we do, we will be obeying the command to **S-T-R-I-V-E** to build multiplying missional communities through Sports ministry (*Missional Sports Communities*).

Where and How to Begin

Often when someone accepts Jesus on the sports field or in a sports hall, they find it difficult to enter into a local church because the environment is too

---

6   Matthew 28.19f.
7   *Dysconnect* is fully developed in the second chapter of the second book in this series: Greg Linville's *The Fundamentals of Sports Outreach*, Canton, OH: Overwhelming Victory Press, 2018. Dr. Linville maintains congregations are currently dysfunctional in their *Evangelistic-Disciplemaking* efforts and spells the word with a "Y" (*Dysconnect*) so as to highlight and call attention to how dysfunctional The Church's current efforts are.
8   I am thankful for my editor who aided in this brief study and exposition of the athletic words found in the original Greek of the New Testament.
9   Philippians 1.27.
10 1 Timothy 6.12.

Good Greek!

The Greek word for striving together found in Philippians 1.27 is **sunathleo'** (pronounced soon, ath - leo'). It is defined as: "To contend on the side of any one; to co-operate vigorously with a person; to make effort in the cause of or in support of a thing.* This is a compound (two words put together) Greek word. The first word sun means come together and the second athleo is the root for our English word athlete.

In the Greek culture, athletes were striving; one athlete competing with another. Theirs was a pitched battle that took all of their energy, strength, concentration and will to succeed in defeating their opponents. Thus metaphorically, when the Holy Spirit inspired New Testament writers to use this word, His purpose was to communicate to Christian disciples how they were to strive together—as fully trained, conditioned and prepared athletes!

The second Greek word for striving is **agonizou** which is translated: To be a combatant in the public games; to strive; to fight; to strive earnestly. The root of **agonizou** is the word **agon** which is defined as: the place of contest; racecourse; stadium; a contest, violent struggle; agony; anguish.*

So just as in the place where the athletic contests were held (stadiums etc.) and in the same way the athletes competed with one another; Christians are to strive for the gospel and fight our spiritual fights.

*Harold K. Moulton, *The Analytical Greek Lexicon*, Grand Rapids: Zondervan, 1982 ISBN 0-310-20280-9.

— Greg Linville
CSRM Director of Resource Development
Dean of The AGON Institute of Sport Ministry
General Editor - OVP

foreign and uncomfortable to them. Nonetheless, our responsibility remains the same—to grow them into *Dedicated-Disciples*. This includes: a) meeting with them individually to root them in the basics of prayer, Bible reading and personal accountability; b) incorporating them into small groups (*Missional Sports Community*) where their new faith can be nurtured in a setting that is comfortable; c) introducing them to both a traditional weekly worship service and Christian education experience; and d) engaging them in outreach/witnessing endeavors. It should be noted that a sports setting could be a most strategic place where a lot of this can take place.

Sports provides the tool for congregations to become truly missional, and It can be as simple as starting a soccer team of 12-15 people.

For any congregation that is interested to **STRIVE** with others from your congregation, home group, or sports team to reach those far from Jesus and His Church I recommend the following:

- **S**tart with God – pray, fast and plan
- **T**arget a specific neighborhood and/or group
- **R**each out through a *Strategically-Relevant* sports, recreational or fitness activity or event and share the gospel (WIN)
- **I**nvite new players and spectators to join in the fun
- **V**alidate your presence as you build *2-T-2-2 Relationships* by establishing a follow-up community through sports (BUILD). Meet on a regular basis, preferably weekly, at the field, in a gym or sports hall, a private home or yard, or just about anywhere. Seek to embody the characteristics of a missional community listed above and develop *Barnabas, Paul,* and *Timothy Relationships*.
- **E**xpand your ministry by identifying leaders and training them to be followers of Jesus who will also WIN-BUILD-SEND-MULTIPLY[11]

To create an environment for *Evangelistic-Disciplemaking* in your *Missional Sports Communities*, reflect on the points listed in Scoreboard 22 (See page 131, Keys to Planting Multiplying Missional Communities through Sports Outreach).

You might consider using the DMM Discovery Bible study method discussed in chapter 8. God has been using this effectively around the world to make *Dedicated-Disciples*. It can be the perfect complement to a local church Sports ministry. It is an *Evangelistic-Disciplemaking* tool that can bring about the transformation of the community through God's Word and the work of His Holy Spirit. It is based entirely on studying scripture and a key component is finding a *Person of Peace* (which was also discussed in Chapter 8).

---

[11] Review chapter 4 again to refresh your memory on the Sports ministry Pyramid.

CHAPTER 11: Missional Sports Communities and A Response to the Present Reality

SCOREBOARD

#22: Keys to Planting Multiplying Missional Communites through Sports Outreach

1. Pray specifically for doors and for people, that God will bring you to *Persons of Peace*
2. Be available for God to use you
3. Make yourself accessible to others
4. Be bold, go to them, and don't expect them to come to you or your church
5. Learn to speak "secular;" eliminate Christian jargon and language and use sports stories and parables to share biblical truths
6. Accept people as they are, but love them enough to challenge them to grow
7. Use nonreligious methods. People don't want Bible study or worship. Don't assume that they will come to your church. You may need to develop among the believers the mindset that followup activities can be held outside of your church building
8. Don't assume that people believe the Bible to be of any value
9. Don't criticize another religion. Be a peace maker.
10. Affirm rather than condemn. Assume people desire spiritual peace
11. At first, invite people to your house or to the sports field rather than to your church building.
12. Follow the Holy Spirit's leading and remain prayerful in each opportunity
13. Identify people's perceived needs, in this context as it relates to sports and recreation and seek to meet them
14. Help your church to begin programming using the *Sports Ministry Pyramid* model to meet these needs
15. Be committed to the process. To build a good *Missional Sports Community* will take 6-8 months minimum depending on your circumstances

As practical application to begin STRIVING together in Madagascar, leaders who had been trained first prayed and then went out into the community to play sports to share the gospel. Everyone interacted and reached out in different settings. The soccer team was invited by a local coach to share with his five or six teams of more than 120 players who were practicing on the field. When it came time for the sports parable and testimony, many including the coach, made decisions to follow Jesus! Similar sharing took place on basketball courts, with children, and with some local street dancers. Consider what transpired through these encounters:

Martin, a basketball player, identified himself as a "traditionalist." He defined this as meaning he follows the path of his ancestors and not the religion of the colonialists. He could not get past the pain and suffering caused by "the imperialist powers" who came to oppress and enslave his people. A lively and amicable discussion was had before he eventually understood the difference between Jesus and religion.

Josia, a martial artist, was already a believer who is studying law. He was encouraged to use his degree to stand for injustice in the country once he graduates. He agreed to be prayed for.

John, whose friend also listened in but didn't join the conversation, was a soccer player who described himself as religious. He attends church but has never had a personal relationship with Jesus. After explaining the gospel to him he recognized his need to accept Jesus but said he was not ready for that. He agreed to be prayed for and said he would go home and consider what had been discussed.

"Uncle," who was on the sidelines and obviously not an athlete, approached one of our leaders wanting a light for his cigarette. He indicated that he is Catholic and then said: "I know what people like you do. You go into villages and just ask people for money. I have beaten up people like you in the past." He then went into a long rambling diatribe about what kind of people we are and how he didn't want to hear anything from us. He eventually calmed down and even became engaged in a discussion which lead him to feel (as he described it) that God was working in his heart. He eventually agreed that he would explore more about Jesus!

Philip was leading a group of street dancers in an area just next to the main field. A few of our leaders were actually experienced dance choreographers. They engaged with Philip and 5-10 other young men who were there to practice their skills for their group. Testimonies were shared and relationships were built.

It was a great day on many fronts! Many of the leaders shared with me overwhelming thanks for the teaching and said the training has given them new direction, more passion for making disciples, and a heart for reaching their country for Jesus. Plans were made for them to follow-up with those we met and start

CHAPTER 11: Missional Sports Communities and A Response to the Present Reality

Missional Sports Communities with each sports group

As I told the leaders at the beginning of the sports outreach day: **Step out, be bold, and become a missional multiplier through Sports ministry! Just do it for the Kingdom!**

Reflection

How is your view of church affecting your witness in your community? What obstacles do you face in STRIVING to develop *Missional Sports Communities*? How can you overcome these?

Complete the STRIVE Worksheet (See Appendix #9).

Prayer

Father, help me to see the needs of those in my own community. Give me a vision for how to strategically reach them so that as they experience community they can know your love, grace, hope, and peace in their own lives.

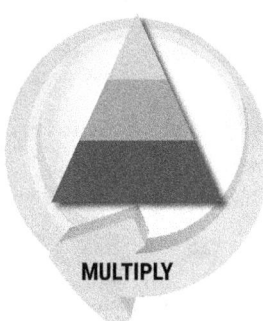

Chapter 12
Building Sports Ministry

This shoe has unlimited potential to accomplish great things!

Starting something new is never easy. It requires dedication, perseverance, and commitment. It also helps if we know that we have a direct calling from God. Building any ministry, including a Sports ministry, is no different, and in scripture we have great examples. To me, the best example comes from the Old Testament book of Nehemiah in which God inspired the recording of how He led Nehemiah to rebuild the wall around Jerusalem.

In that day, a city needed an impenetrable wall to protect its inhabitants from its enemies. In today's world, not having a city wall would be something like living in the most dangerous neighborhood in the most dangerous city in the world and not having locks on your doors or windows. That was the situation for the residents of Jerusalem. Enemies could come and without much resistance steal what they wanted: livestock, personal possessions, and even wives and children. The stress, fear, and pressure of living under such conditions would have been overwhelming. This feeling of helplessness would have been exacerbated for the Jews because Jerusalem had extra significance. It was the "City of God," the location of the temple, their place of worship where Elohim's presence resided. The second temple had already been built at this time, but without walls anything of value that was placed in the temple could be easily stolen. These were the circumstances that broke the heart of Nehemiah and compelled him into action.

What Nehemiah recorded provides us with a good model to follow. As he pursued his mission to restore security to Jerusalem, there is a simple outline to imitate. We must: **Pray** for vision; **Plan** for a mission; and **Persistently Persevere** to strategically implement a Sports ministry and thus, accomplish what God calls us to. These three "P's" are easy to remember and apply.

1) Prayer

The first and most critical key to Nehemiah's success is **PRAYER**. It was through **Prayer** that he started to comprehend God's vision for His people and the city of Jerusalem. It was through **Prayer** that Nehemiah could **Plan** for the mission that was needed to accomplish God's vision and finally through **Prayer**, Nehemiah was empowered to **Persistently-Persevere** through persecution, discouragement and obstacles. Nehemiah models how all of our efforts are to be based and bathed in prayer. We read throughout his writings the why's, when's and how's of his **Prayers**. (See Scoreboard 23 on Nehemiah's Prayers.)

2) Planning

The second key is **Planning**. (See Scoreboard 24 on Nehemiah's Planning.) Nehemiah didn't just haphazardly start working. He was painstakingly intentional and deliberate about the task at hand. We can determine from the dates given that he had spent four months of much prayer and fasting from the time he received the news to when he appeared before King Artaxerxes. Nehemiah must have used his time wisely because when he speaks up, he is prepared to ask for a specific length of time off and for letters requesting safe passage, a supply of lumber, and accommodations. **Planning** entails being *Strategically-Relevant* and *Efficiently-Effective*.[1] As we envision we must prepare and be strategic with our resources in whatever God calls us to build.

3) Persistent Perseverance

The third critical element is **Persistent Perseverance**. (See Scoreboard 25 on Nehemiah's Persistent Perseverance.) It seems it would have been easy to quit, except for the fact that God had called him to this task. We see that Nehemiah pushed on and led his people through difficult circumstances. He stood strong in those situations. Through it all, he remained faithful to his vision and mission. We can see that, as Christopher Eames writes: "Nehemiah was a powerful leader who would not be led along by the masses. His life's work was one of going against the flow—no matter the persecution, be it from surrounding armies or even his own people—and standing up for God, without deviation. His story, as recorded in the Bible, stands as a testament to the work God was able to do through him."[2] His proclamation: "Remember the Lord... Our God will fight for us"[3] carried them through, and amazingly the wall was completed in 52 days[4] after being in ruins for hundreds of years. In the same way we must keep pressing on! Don't give up!

Biblical Success

Be reminded that, while fulfilling your calling may involve actually building a wall or a building, developing a sports field, or other physical structures, your success will be measured by the people whose lives you touch (*2-T-2-2 Relation-*

---

1 See Chapter 4 of the second book in this Institutes of Sports Outreach series which fully explains the *4-Fold Evaluative Rubric*.
2 Christopher Eames, "Nehemiah: A Man and A Momentous Wall," Watch Jerusalem https://watchjerusalem.co.il/115-nehemiah-a-man-and-a-momentous-wall; September 15, 2017.
3 Nehemiah 4.14 & 20.
4 Nehemiah 6.15.

SCOREBOARD
#23: Nehemiah's Prayers

- Praise and worship (1.5)
- Confession of sin (1.6f)
- Seeking mercy and blessing (1:11)
- For wisdom and favor (2:4)
- For God's retribution (4:1-4)
- For protection (4:9)
- For strength (6:9)

SCOREBOARD
#24: Nehemiah's Planning

- He was strategic in what he requested from the king (2:4-8)
- He went on a scouting mission to assess the situation by inspecting the condition of the wall (2:11ff)
- Each tribe was given their own task or portion of the wall to complete (3:1-32)
- He organized the people for protection (4:13, 16-18)
- He took up the broader challenge of the community and stands up to injustice while organizing the city to meet the needs of the poor (5:1-19)
  Likewise, we will be able to comprehend God's Plan for our Sports Ministry as we engage in research, assess our resources and encounter resistance

SCOREBOARD
#25: Nehemiah's Persistent Perseverance

- When he was mocked and ridiculed (2:19, 4:1-3)
- When the evil plans of their enemies came against him (4:8)
- When death threats came against him (4:11, 6:10)
- When lies were Spread (6.5-7)

TIMEOUT

Open Doors in Botswana

We did many different kinds of things in partnership with a sports related para-ministry and local churches including giving sports lessons at schools, sports clinics in villages, prison ministry, and visiting hospitals. We helped them to build many new relationships and contacts. Before we came they had done no sports ministry, so we had great opportunities to share the vision! They plan to do more, so there are great possibilities for the next years.

---

ships) and impact for God's Kingdom. No longer is the building or field just a place for activity. It is a place where orchestrated outreach and spiritual growth can take place, where people can be won to Christ through careful proclamation of the Word and progressive discipleship.

To consider success in sporting terms is to have won. To define "winning" and "losing," the world looks at the scoreboard. Your success of failure is defined by scoring more, or less in the case of golf, than your opponent. The one who finishes second is often forgotten. Take the following example: after a recent Olympics one of the athletes who won a silver medal said that he is not remembered as someone who won silver, but as someone who *did not* win the gold.

But what should our perspective be? Biblical insight to winning and losing that contrasts with the world can be found in the following verses:

Colossians 3:23 – "And whatever you do, do it heartily as unto the Lord and not unto man."

> *Whatever*: any and every aspect of your life (even sports)
> *Heartily*: with your whole heart, with everything you have (mind, body, soul)
> *Unto the Lord*: for God's glory—He is your only spectator and He does not care about the scoreboard.
> *Not unto man*: not for man's glory

Colossians 3:17 – "And whatever you do, in word or deed, do all in the name of

CHAPTER 12: Building Sports Ministry

the Lord Jesus, giving thanks through Him to God the Father."

> Word or deed: actions, thoughts, words, and any situation
> In the name of: as if Jesus Himself were doing it
> Giving thanks: to the one who gave it to you in the first place as a form of worship; Since this form of worship is done as Jesus would have done it, you have reflected the life of Christ in you, which brings glory to God.

1 Corinthians 9:25 – "… They do it to get a crown that will not last, but we do it to get a crown that will last forever." The overarching issue in scripture is that there are temporal things that have little value compared to eternal things.

Luke 9:24-25 – "For whoever wants to save his life will lose it, but whoever loses his life for me will save it. What good is it for a man to gain the whole world, and yet lose or forfeit his very soul?" The Bible admonishes us to seek the things that last, and in doing so, to be willing to lose those things that do not endure. The ultimate loss would be to lose (or not choose) the salvation and eternal life that is promised to those who confess Christ and follow Him.

In other words, while the world uses the scoreboard to determine winning and losing, true winning (authentic victory) can be defined as being a follower of Jesus and being Christlike in motivation, attitude, and effort in the midst of competition in order to bring glory to God. To give everything is what God asks from anyone who identifies as His disciple. Therefore, losing is not following Jesus as a disciple and/or not using your talents and abilities to bring glory and honour to Him to make disciples, to not give all.

Discipleship Revisited

Our ultimate focus then must be on *disciplemaking*! You can review chapter 7 how best to do this, but let's expand it further. The ultimate goal of disciplemaking is to raise up leaders who raise up new generations of leaders. That is, disciples who make disciples who make disciples who make disciples.[5] In my opinion, this is the greatest failure of The Church. In the current Internet age a leader is often identified and marked by how many followers they have on Twitter, YouTube or Facebook. While the greater the number means the greater the potential influence, it does not necessarily make or guarantee a great leader. In *"A Call to Develop Christ-like Leaders"* from Lausanne Paper No. 41, leadership is identified as:

1) A process of influence

---

5 CSRM uses the phrase: *Producing, Reproducing, Reproducers,* to describe the ultimate goal of *Evangelistic-Disciplemaking.*

2) Moving people toward a goal

This process and movement is facilitated by the three functions of a leader that are characterized by the New Testament words for leaders as summed up by The Lausanne Paper.

> In the New Testament, three words are used interchangeably to describe leaders in the local church: elder, overseer, and shepherd or pastor (see Acts 20:20, 28 and I Peter 5:1-3). Each word emphasizes a different aspect of the leadership function. The word "elder" (*presbyteros*), which literally means "older," points to those whose relative maturity qualifies them to serve as an example to others. The word "overseer" (*episkopos*) speaks of one who superintends a task, making sure that the activities of the group align with the vision and the goal. The word "shepherd" (*poimen*, also translated "pastor") speaks of personal care for the health and development of each member of the flock. Each word points to one of the key roles of a leader: to show the way through personal example, to accomplish the task by keeping the group focused on and organized for the goal, and to nurture and develop the people through the process.[6]

Practical Elements

From many years of leading, learning, and making mistakes in ministry, having some success, much joy, much pain, much happiness, much sorrow, and through the enduring patience, unconditional grace, and unending love of my Saviour, I offer you the reader the following points as an encouragement. As you begin to grow in the three-fold role, responsibility and function of being a leader who is committed to *Evangelistic-Disciplemaking* through winning, building, sending, and multiplying, you will be able to...

Show the Way as you:
- Pray and fast for your team and their work regularly
- Be sensitive to God's leading
- Serve your team

---

[6] "A Call to Develop Christ-like Leaders," Lausanne Papers, No 41; Pattaya, Thailand, September 29-October 5, 2004. For a more in depth exegesis of these three distinct words describing Church leadership and their application to SR&F Outreach Ministry see Chapter 8 (and in specific pages 96-102) in the 3rd book of The Institute of Sports Outreach book series: *Putting The Church Back in The Game*.

- Set the example, be a model
- Understand your own strengths and weaknesses
- Don't take yourself too seriously
- Be humble and be a learner
- Don't go back on your word
- Admit mistakes
- Apologize quickly, forgive

Accomplish the Task as you:
- Balance faith and reality
- Stay focused on your vision
- Monitor progress and allow for feedback
- Motivate and inspire your team
- Maintain unity
- Delegate responsibility and authority, release
- Set reasonable goals together
- Work together with other leaders
- Make the tough decisions
- Take the responsibility
- Surround yourself with people who compliment your weaknesses

Develop People as you:
- Keep the lines of your relationships short
- Hold your team accountable
- Protect your team members—from themselves and others
- Respond appropriately
- Be a good listener
- Put your team members in positions where they can succeed
- Know your team member's strengths and weaknesses
- See your team member's potential
- Be a "permission giver"
- Push them beyond what they think they can do so that they can become all that you know they can become
- Share their burdens
- Give private and public praise
- Give correction in private
- Hold your people and tasks with "open hands"

Final Questions

Remember the vision questions from chapter 2? Reflect back on each one as you try to understand and apply them, first to Nehemiah's circumstances and then secondly to your own.

- ✓ What do you think Nehemiah saw as he took up this task?
  - Ask yourself, "What do I see as you begin to take up the task?"
- ✓ Where was Nehemiah's heart?
  - Ask yourself, "Where is my heart?" Are your motives right and pure?
- ✓ How was Nehemiah's faith?
  - Ask yourself, "Where is my faith?" Are you trusting God to use you to do something hard, impossible, or difficult?

If you see and follow Jesus, if your heart is in the right place, and if you have faith to believe God to do the impossible, then you are ready to begin building a Sports ministry!

Reflection

What are 5 principles that you have learned from this book that you want to apply in your life and ministry? Write them down and make a plan. Review the Practical Steps to Build Sports ministry (See Appendix #10) and complete the Planning Worksheet (See Appendix #11).

Prayer

Father, thank You for speaking to me through Your Holy Spirit as I have interacted with all the ideas in this book. Help me to move what I now know from my head, to my heart, to my hands and feet so that I can apply it and become a more effective follower of Jesus… to become the shoe You have created me to be!

May all I do bring glory and honor to You. Amen.

Postscript

The Measure of True Success

The story of the life of this shoe Is still being written.

Now you know my story and the story of The Shoe. Growing up in a small town, in backwoods America, I never could have imagined where my shoes would take me. I am humbled and amazed that God would choose to use me, a simple shoe, in such an amazing way and yet I continue to be more passionate each year about what has become the content of this book. What I have experienced and seen convince me the truths presented here will work and flourish the world over. At the risk of seeming too braggadocios or being misinterpreted, I humbly share this book with you.

My shoes, through the power of the Lord have taken me to many places where I have seen the Lord work miracles. For ten years starting in 2003, I served as the international director for a large European Sports ministry. During that period, I led international projects serving in numerous countries. These projects generally were strategic three-year commitments of investment into congregations within each country designed to empower, equip, and train indigenous leaders in *Evangelistic-Disciplemaking* through sports ministry. During those years we sent 35 staff to serve in Turkey, Albania, Uganda, Greece, Israel, East Asia, South Africa, Brazil, Spain, and the U.K. It was our practice to send 2-6 staff members the first year who would cast a vision and train local churches in the Sports ministry vision. The second year we would send a large number of short-term teams to serve those churches and provide a catalytic opportunity through their presence and ministry. The third year, our staff members would stay in the country and continue to serve the local churches in order to release them and empower them in their ongoing sports ministry of *Evangelistic-Disciplemaking*. Many of the stories you have read throughout this book come from this amazing time of ministry.

Then in 2014 I became international director of a large U.S.-based Sports ministry and currently oversee a growing number of international staff (currently over 20) who serve in nearly 15 countries. These paid and volunteer staff train and serve thousands of churches annually as they seek to develop effective local church sports ministry models.

I am amazed when I consider all that God is doing through this work. Conservatively, in our ministry season that spanned 2018/2019, our staff and partners led trainings for 2,411 pastors, athletes, and church leaders. These trainees represented 1,030 churches and created 808 Sports ministries wherein 994 people accepted Jesus. Additionally, 549 leaders are receiving mentoring in ongoing *Timothy-Relationships*. I praise God for all He has done! To God be all the Glory!

As you consider how God wants to use you to build His Church, I invite you to test the principles found in this book and discover for yourself how to apply them in your own life and ministry context and setting. The next chapter is yours to write and the amazing stories of God's movement are yours to experience.

As God's shoe may you…

> "…run with perseverance the race marked out for (you), fixing (y)our eyes on Jesus, the pioneer and perfecter of faith. For the joy set before Him He endured the cross, scorning its shame, and sat down at the right hand of the throne of God. Consider Him who endured such opposition from sinners, so that you will not grow weary and lose heart."[1]

For His glory!

Dear reader, I would love to receive your feedback and comments.
Please feel free to contact me: pfmyers@runbox.com
Follow me on Instagram @P. F.myers
Friend me on Facebook: Paul F. Myers

---

1 Hebrews 12.1-3.

Appendix #1

EXPLANATORY NOTES FOR THE
INSTITUTES OF THE SPORTS OUTREACH COMMUNITY
BOOK SERIES

DISTINCTIVES OF THIS BOOK SERIES

This is the eighth in the "Institutes of Sports Outreach" series of books which will eventually consist of at least 12 distinct works. While each book could stand alone; the entire series is based on, and united through, the overarching organizational structure of the *3-Tier* Paradigm (see book #2). Each book either builds upon, and/or refers to others in the series. A quick review of the previous books include...

- The first book "*Christmanship*" introduced basic theological and ethical foundations, which serve as the basic apologetic for sports outreach.
- The second book "*Sports Outreach Fundamentals*" outlined the *Level #2 Philosophical-Principles* that serve as the biblically-based, organizational structure for ensuring a *Strategically-Relevant* and *Efficiently-Effective* SR&F outreach.
- Book #3 "*Putting The Church Back In The Game*" was the first entry into *Level #1 Theological-Truths* and established ecclesiology as a fundamental theological foundation for sports outreach ministry.
- Book #4 *The Saving of Sports ministry* is the second of the *Level #1 Theological-Truths* books. It explains how important understanding a theology of salvation is to envisioning and leading a truly *Strategically-Relevant* and *Effectively-Efficient* sports outreach ministry.
- Book #5 *The Mission of Sports ministry* is the third of the *Level #1 Theological-Truths* books. It expresses the true mission of sports outreach is *Evangelistic-Disciplemaking* and the necessity of implementing classic missiological principles into all sports outreach endeavors.
- Book #6 *The Christ of Sports ministry* is the fourth of the *Level #1 Theological-Truths* books. It focuses on how to make Jesus, the Christ, the absolute center and basis of all sports outreach ministry.
- Book #7 *The Ologies of Sports ministry* is the fifth of the *Level #1 Theological-Truths* books. It explores three additional theologies

(Anthropology, Eschatology; Cosmology) and summarizes all *Level #1 Theological-Truths* books.

The series will continue with a number of *Level #2 Philosophical-Principle* and *Level #3 Methodological* books. These books will work together to catalytically enable and empower truly effective Sports outreach ministry.

The oversight for this series of books includes maintaining: a) a consistent editorial board (made up of a strong group of practitioners, academics and editors); b) a general editor; c) individual book editors; d) book section editors; and e) book and chapter authors. What follows in this and subsequent books is the fulfillment of the plan that emerged from an overall vision, and the distinctive perspective, from which the "Institutes of Sports Outreach" book series was conceived. This all contributes to giving this series of books a unique and catalytic place in propelling Sports Outreach into its 2nd century.

Further distinctions and core values of The Institutes of Sports Outreach include: I. Vision; II. Orthodoxy and Orthopraxy; III. History & Theology; IV. Citations; V. Use of Italics; VI. Thoughts on *The Movement;* VII. Thoughts on the Words Church, Local Church and Congregation; and VIII. Capitalization.

I. Vision

This series of books has been envisioned to communicate the *Information* of *The Sports Outreach Community* for the purpose of resourcing, training, connecting and equipping local church Sports, Recreation & Fitness (SR&F) outreach ministers for the end goal of them being able to mobilize, enable and empower their congregations to fulfill the Great Commission. While it is hoped that this series will also prove to be relevant and beneficial for all sports outreach endeavors, it is written by and for local church SR&F practitioners.

II. Orthodoxy and Orthopraxy

One of the key distinctions of this series of books has to do with the intentional target of the material presented. This series is designed to be a complementary blend of Orthodoxy and Orthopraxy.

Orthodoxy is a word that is somewhat familiar to most within *The Sports Outreach Community*, as it is a much used term within Christianity that describes true-to-the-Bible theology and philosophy. However, not everyone would be able to accurately define it, let alone understand its importance and relevance to SR&F outreach ministry. If such confusion exists about the word Orthodoxy, then how much more true would it be about the term Orthopraxy, of which most Christians are unfamiliar. Further explanations are helpful.

Orthodoxy and Orthopraxy derive from a common Greek root: "ortho" –

which means straight, right, or correct. Thus the straightening concept found in both words communicates such straightening will bring about righteousness and correctness. However, the two words each have differing suffixes which sends this correcting righteousness in two different directions.

The suffix "doxy" stems from another Greek word which means doctrine or belief. Its Greek etymological root word is *dexomai*. *Dexomai* connotes a receiving of someone or something, and thus when put together Orthodoxy means to receive and believe a straight, right and correct word from God. "Doxy" pertains to thinking and thus, Orthodoxy has to do with right and correct doctrinal and theological thinking.

The suffix for the second word "praxis" stems from yet a third Greek word which means to practice. "Praxis" has to do with action and activity. Thus, Orthopraxy has to do with the essence of acting in straight, right, correct and/or strategically practical ways. Thus, whereas Orthodoxy deals with correct doctrine and theology, Orthopraxy pertains to right and correct action.

The relevance to sports outreach, and to this book, is that any good Orthopraxy (*Level #3 Methodological Models*) is based upon solid Orthodoxy (*Level #1 Theological-Truths* and *Level #2 Philosophical-Principles*); as explained in many other books in this series. The entire series of books is based upon this *3-Tier Paradigm* which envisions solid theological and theoretical thinking from which *Strategically-Relevant* and *Efficiently-Effective* SR&F outreach ministry can emerge.

III. History and Theology

Theology doesn't develop in a historical vacuum. Moreover, theology shapes history. Thus, an undergirding distinction of this series of books is to highlight historical anecdotes of people, ministries, churches, missions and organizations which will be used to either: a) illustrate theology; or b) provide living examples of why theology (or often the lack of it) is important to comprehending and implementing a *Strategically-Relevant* and *Efficiently-Effective* SR&F Outreach Ministry.

Some of the historical references are ancient, from as early as the 1st Century. However, many will be from the past two centuries; including contributions from current practitioners who share their experiences as they engage in creating contemporary history—both shaping theology as well as being shaped by theology.

It is envisioned and hoped the linking of the theological and theoretical with the pragmatic and practical will enhance not only the comprehension of the reader, but more importantly, this combination will inspire catalytic new visions for *Strategically-Relevant* and *Efficiently-Effective* SR&F Outreach.

These historical vignettes appear throughout the books in the form of special "Time Out" pages.

IV. Citations

Direct quotes are always cited as are more general references that are drawn from specific hardcopy or digital sources; as well as personal conversations. However, some statistical data is assumed without direct referential citing due to the nature of current day search engine capability. With the wonder of the internet, anyone reading this series of books can have the latest data at their fingertips rather than be saddled with out-of-date statistics available at the time of writing. Readers are encouraged to access current trends and research so as to not be unduly, or even wrongly, persuaded by the outdated data that influenced the narratives found in this series of books; some that may well be challenged or disproved by future research. This editorial decision is intentionally offered so as to engage readers in seeking truth, rather than falling into the trap of believing the false truth of outdated statistics. Thus, assuming a book to have an existence far beyond a specific period of time of research, the editors have often opted to not always take the space to provide research data that often becomes out of date within months. However, a quick perusal of the works cited, or any good web-based search would provide any interested reader with the proper references that served to form the basis of an author's assessments and thus be able to make proper assessments of any thesis proposed by authors.

A unique category of citation is the various "side bars/word boxes." All such side bars are original to the authors of the various books, sections or chapters, unless noted otherwise. There are four major categories of side bars: a) Graphs; b) Charts; c) "Scoreboards," and d) "Time Outs." All four have been designed to help the reader contemplate, visualize and implement the content of the narrative. Examples of all four can be found throughout this series of books with the following distinctions.

Graphs show the results of surveys or anything that can be counted and compared. Charts are used to pictorially illustrate the concepts being written about. The third category entitled: "Scoreboards" is used to highlight and/or further emphasize a major phrase or concept found within the narrative, with the thought being the reader is being reminded to "keep score" of the various points being made and/or to score points by applying the data to their own ministry setting. "Time Outs" allow the reader to take a short break from the narrative, to reflect upon an ancient or contemporary historical model or example of what the narrative is describing.

V. Use of Italics

Italics are used wherever words or terms have been repurposed, created or coined by the authors. Italics are also used whenever unique CSRM language is used. This is done for three main reasons. First, italics are used to emphasize the fact that *The Sports Outreach Community* is in need of creating its own language to accurately define, describe and communicate its unique ethos, culture, structure and mission. Therefore, these unique words and phrases are repeatedly italicized. Second, the goal is to not only familiarize the readers with the important transferable concepts put forth in this book series but more to drill the terms and transferable concepts deep into the psyche of the reader; thus the repetitive use of italics. The third reason is to communicate the unique repurposing of words and/or phrases that otherwise might be understood in ways that are different than for which they are utilized in *The Community* and this book. Italics are also used for all foreign language words.

VI. Thoughts on *The Movement*

The phrase that SR&F Outreach Ministries is often referred to is: *The Sports Outreach Movement,* or simply *The Movement.* At the time of writing, this is the term used by most SR&F leaders. OVP however, has taken an editorial stance on calling those involved in Sports Outreach the *Sports Outreach Community.* This is based on the belief that by calling what is done in SR&F Outreach Ministry a movement, subtly communicates all these efforts take place outside the traditional body of Christ (The Church), and becomes an entity unto itself. Thus, this becomes a movement that supersedes, and exists outside of The Church. Rather OVP views this so-called *Movement* as simply one expression of how The Church reaches and incorporates those far from Christ and His Church.

Thus, *The Sports Outreach Movement* terminology used throughout the first books of this series has been changed in all subsequent and future editions to the phrase: *Sports Outreach Community.*

VII. Thoughts on the Words: The Church, Local Church and Congregation

The words "The Church" will be used whenever the universal body of Christ is intended, and both words (The and Church) will be capitalized. Whenever a local assembly of The Church is referenced, it will be done so in lower case (church). Thus, terms such as: local church; congregation; and other words such as assembly will not be capitalized. To help communicate this distinction the word congregation will be used more than local church.

VIII. Capitalization

All words relating to, describing or referencing God will be capitalized. This editorial decision serves to communicate and emphasize the Overwhelming Victory Press (OVP) belief that the triune-God is truly worthy of receiving any and all honor possible. Thus the more commonly capitalized words such as God, Lord, Jesus, Holy Spirit will be joined with any pronouns used to refer to God such as Him, He, His and even at times words that reference God such as Who.

Another special use of capitalization is in reference to the Bible. The words Bible and Word of God, will be capitalized for two reasons. The first is to clearly express the belief and commitment of Overwhelming Victory Press (OVP) to communicate its belief that the Bible is sacred literature; above and beyond all other writings and deserves a place of honor. In a day and age in which the Bible is being attacked, criticized and marginalized, even within much of Christian scholarship, the second reason has to do with communicating OVP's belief and commitment that the Bible is the inerrant, infallible and fully trustworthy Word of God; and that it is fully authoritative for The Church. Capitalization of these words should not however be understood that OVP believes the Bible to be God, but rather His Word.

IX. Thoughts on Gospel Presentations Using Colors

Using colors to verbally proclaim the gospel has been used for decades throughout the world by a dozen or more sports ministries; and used to great effect. This visual demonstration uses colors which are displayed on various items typically worn or used by sportspeople such as wristbands, necklaces, and/or sports equipment. By far, the most commonly used version is on what is commonly called "gospel power" balls.

While there are many variations of how the gospel is verbally communicated via power balls, a basic pattern of how to use the colors displayed on power balls goes something like: God came from a blue sky to a green earth to shed His red blood so we could wear a gold crown. Usually such a verbal presentation of the gospel via a power ball is well received and effective. However, there are times and situations in which the use of colors can be offensive to a particular individual or specific culture. If such a problem arises, it typically has to do with either political or racial overtones of a specific color or two.

For example, there are situations in which the color red carries negative political overtones (red army etc.) or a specific color is considered a bad omen in a specific culture. In these cases it is recommended to change red to scarlet or eliminate the offensive color altogether.

More problematic however, is when an underlying racial or ethnic overtone is communicated by certain colors. It is recommended that extreme caution and sensitivity be applied anytime a gospel power ball presentation is made to a specific race of people who identify with a specific color used in the gospel presentation (yellow, red, black, white).

This is especially relevant when it comes to using black and white in a gospel presentation. In specific, many renditions of the gospel power ball include the color black to represent sin and white to represent being cleansed from sin in the following way...

After the statement about Jesus shedding His red blood, the following is inserted. Jesus' red blood enables our black sins to become white as snow. At this point in the gospel power ball presentation, other variations of the black/white language sometimes include using white to represent purity, forgiveness or being cleansed, while black is used to refer to a sinful or evil nature. To many people in various countries and cultures these references represent a perpetuation of racism that equates black with bad, evil and other negatives, while elevating white as being good, pure or associated with other positives. Such situations can render the gospel ball presentation highly offensive and thus ineffective.

So what's a sports minister to do?
First realize that the colors themselves are neutral and do not intrinsically represent good or bad; evil or purity. Second, understand that black has positive connotations as found in the Bible ("I am black but lovely" - Song of Solomon 1.5) and also in general culture (such as when a business rejoices for being in "the black" financially). Third, sports ministers can be encouraged to use the white and black colors on a power ball to communicate other biblical metaphors or analogies that are frequently used in reference to sin, forgiveness etc. These would include blindness/sight and/or light/darkness. Most importantly keep in mind that the Bible never equates evil with being black (although white is often associated with blessing/cleansing etc.). It's also helpful to note that nowhere does the Bible require using black to describe sin, nor does it state it should not be used in this way.

Beyond these basics, sports ministers are encouraged to consider other biblical principles when it comes to using the gospel power ball or any color-coded gospel presentation. These include: a) using the most strategic and effective methodological models; b) demonstrating loving sensitivity to race, cultures, countries and individuals; c) remaining faithful to a full-orbed, gospel.

So, should a sports minister include the words black and white in verbal proclamations of the gospel?
The basic recommendation is to use the more strategic and effective metaphors (blind/sight) whenever possible…which communicates genuine love and sensitivity. This would still enable the use of the white and black colors on a ball, but embraces a full gospel communication of the real problem…people are blind until Jesus bestows spiritual sight. However, in keeping with the biblical principle of sensitivity to culture, it may be that in certain places and in certain situations not only would it be appropriate to use white and black, but the gospel may be best communicated in black and white terms.

What is CSRM's belief in regards to racism and what is it doing to eliminate racism?

At the time of the publication of this book, the official stance of the CSRM Board of Trustees and Staff rests on a core theological value that condemns racism at any level: personal, systemic, cultural, political and/or economic. This includes a core value of a strong commitment to not be complicit in any activity, endeavor and/or language that perpetuates racism and racist mentalities and expressions. This is evidenced by the very existence of this expanded explanation. While it is true that the use of black and white has been common language for millennia of Christians but with increased social awareness of racism and a growing sensitivity to the potential for language to perpetuate racism, CSRM's International Staff and Board invested significant time and effort in discussing this issue and desires to take every reasonable step necessary to alleviate racism whenever and wherever possible.

The ongoing discussions of CSRM's staff and board of trustees ensure the entire association will continue to foster a gospel-centric, culture that will maintain a strong stance against racism while at the same time not diminish its commitment to communicate the gospel that proclaims the insidious horror of sin, nor neglect to relish the glory of being ushered into God's gracious light and receiving His cleansing.

So, CSRM strongly recommends that the tried and true model of The Gospel Power Ball continue to be used when accompanied by a serious consideration of what is the colors may represent in the local culture and setting in which it is used.

A full copy of CSRM's overall theology can be found via the website and through the various theological books in the Institutes of Sports Outreach series.

A Final Word

To revisit and restate the vision of this series: the laser-focus of this series of books is to enhance and expand the *Evangelistic-Disciplemaking* efforts of individual members and congregations of The Church. This series of books is written by, and for all within, *The Sports Outreach Community* but especially for local church SR&F Outreach Ministers. It is produced by the publishing arm of the Association of Church Sports & Recreation Ministers (CSRM)—Overwhelming Victory Press (OVP)—for all who are called to this most strategic and catalytic outreach of The Church. The prayers of the CSRM staff, Board of Trustees and supporters are that the Lord of the universe will use this series to supernaturally empower all who read this series.

— Dr. Greg Linville
General Editor for The Institutes of Sports Outreach
Director of Resource Development, CSRM 2020

Appendix # 2

Sports Ministry
AND THE MISSION OF THE CHURCH

Mission of the Church

| To reach
UPWARD
in **Worship** | To reach
INWARD
in **Love** | To reach
OUTWARD
in **Evangelism** |

Mission of the Sports ministry

Sports ministry strives to come alongside individual congregations of The Church to mobilize, empower and equip them to accomplish the Great Commission goal of *Evangelistic-Disciplemaking* as seen in the following...

Fellowship & Friendship (*Belong*) [1]
✓ Believer to Believer (Hebrews 10:24; Acts 2:42; Gal. 6:2)
✓ Believer to Unbeliever (1 Corinthians 9:22; Matthew 5:16; 2 Corinthians 5:20)

Evangelism (*Believe*) [2]
✓ Living the Good News (John 14:27; Eph. 4:32; John 13:35)
✓ Sharing The Good News (Mark 16:15; Acts 10:42; 2 Corinthians 5:18)

---

[1] *Belong* is the first of the *5-B's Process of Sports Outreach* of CSRM. Together they fulfill the *1 Defining Purpose of Sports Outreach: Evangelistic-Disciplemaking*. *Belonging* is the first step in a person's journey to become a *Dedicated-Disciple* of Jesus Christ. *Belonging* ushers the unchurched person into a community from which the Gospel is "caught more than taught." Thus, *Belonging* leads to and is often the pre-requisite for *Believing*. The 5-B Process entails going to those who are far from Jesus and His Church for the purpose of initiating and building relationships through sports, recreation and/or fitness SR&F outreaches. See Chapter 5 of *Sports Outreach Fundamentals* for a complete explanation of the *5-B's* and pages 57, 58 for *Belonging*.

[2] *Believe* is the second of the *5-B's Process of Sports Outreach* and describes the conversion of a person who, by faith, enters into a personal relationship with Jesus Christ. *Believing* is most successfully achieved in and through the *Belonging* of an unchurched person to a local church's SR&F outreach community. See pages 58-64 of *Fundamentals of Sports Outreach* for a full explanation of *Believing*.

Discipleship (*Baptize; Behave*) [3]
✓ Grounded in Christ (Eph. 4:12-13; 2 Peter 3:18; Romans 13:14)
✓ Growing in Christ (Romans 8:29; John 3:3; Philippians1:6)

Assimilation (*Become*) [4]
✓ Incorporated into fellowship (Matthew 5:13-16, 22:9; 1 Peter 3:8-9)
✓ Grafted into the Body (Eph. 1:13; 1 Corinthians 12:13-14; Romans 11)

How a Sports ministry Helps the Church
1. Facilitates the Church Mission and the Sports ministry Pyramid (WIN / BUILD / SEND / MULTIPLY)
2. Ministries servant as a tool other ministries in the church can use
3. Great Commission partner – Making true disciples
4. Promotes Body life through opportunities for *Barnabas, Paul, and Timothy Relationships*
5. Culturally relevant bridge / tool
6. Friendship evangelism opportunity
7. Entry level for service for per or new believers
8. Prevents "fallout" and backsliding as people are often more excited to stay involved
9. Discipleship and leadership training opportunities
10. Creates parabolic instruction / *Sports Parables*
11. Promotes applicational faith
12. Potentially cost effective

---

[3] Discipleship starts with a public declaration of faith associated with the 3rd *B of Sports Outreach*. *Baptism* is a very early step in changing the *Behavior* of a new convert. *Behave* is the 4th *B of Sports Outreach* and indicates a radical life change from a secular, self-centered individual to a Christo-centric member of The Church. This change in behavior is where the diligent work of *Becoming* is done. See pages 64-68 in *Fundamentals of Sports Outreach*.

[4] *Becoming* is the 5th *B of Sports Outreach* and is a perfect descriptor because it communicates not only that *Evangelistic-Disciplemaking* is a process but also that *Dedicated-Disciples* of Jesus Christ never arrive, but are constantly progressing in their faith. See page 68 in *Fundamentals of Sports Outreach* for full explanation of *Becoming*.

Appendix # 3

Sports, Recreation, and Fitness Ministry (SR&F) Activity List

This is not an exhaustive list. How to use this sheet:
1. Read through the list and identify what <u>your</u> interest and skills are by circling all those that apply to you. You can expand this exercise further by identifying the interests and skills of those in your church by marking them with a '+'.
2. Read through the list a second time and Identify what interests exist in <u>your community</u> by marking an 'X' above those that apply.
3. Consider the activities that have a circle, 'X' and/or a '+'. This could be a good place to start.
4. Make a plan to use those activities and reach out.

- ➤ **Competitive Team Sports**

Basketball, baseball, football, volleyball, hockey, rugby, cricket, dodge ball, field hockey

- ➤ **Individual Competitive Sports**

Badminton, golf, tennis, table tennis, triathlon/runs, track & field, X-Games, gymnastics

- ➤ **Events**

Sports clinics, 10K or Fun Runs, kids' games, picnics, field days, and all should include a showing of Jesus Film

- ➤ **Recreational Activities**

Arts & crafts, board games, drama, music, puppetry

- ➤ **Wilderness Activities**

Backpacking, camping, fishing, hiking, "four wheeling"

- ➤ **Seniors' Activities**

Walking/jogging, stretching/exercise programs, swimming

➢ **Wellness Activities**
Aerobics/exercise, nutrition & weight control, weight training, Cross Fit, Zumba, Taekwondo

➢ **Outreach Activities**
Leagues, sports clinics, mission teams, prison ministry, including Acts of Service

➢ **Social Recreation**
Ballroom dancing, street dance, square dance, excursions, meals, outings, movie nights, self-defense class

➢ **Special Programs**
Sports Vacation Bible School, programs for the disabled

➢ **Others** – Consider Traditional Games, Recreational Activities, or Sports Popular in Your Country

YOU ARE ONLY LIMITED BY YOUR OWN CREATIVITY!

Appendix #4

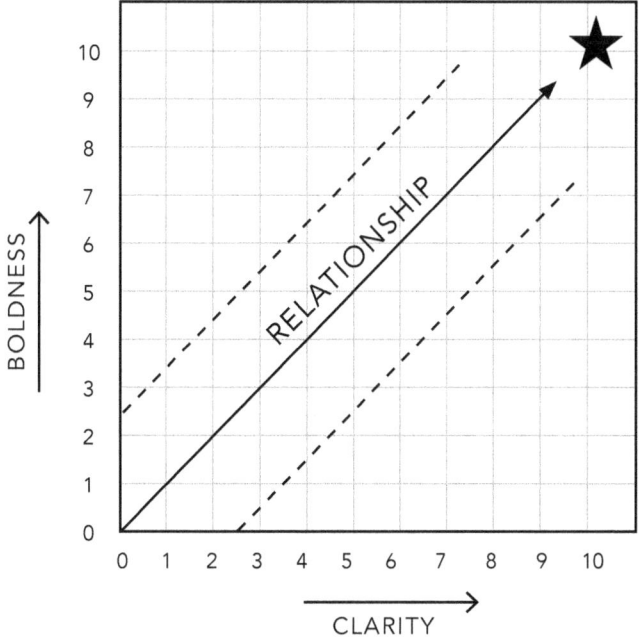

The Mansfield Graph of Evangelism
Ephesians 6:18-20 and Colossians 4:3,4

On the *Mansfield Graph of Evangelism*, take a moment to rate yourself on a scale of 1-10 regarding Clarity and Boldness. The number 1 is low or ineffective and 10 is high or most effective. Ask: how Bold am I in sharing the gospel? How Clear am I when I do share the gospel? Give yourself a rating for each between 1-10. After you have done this, record your ratings on Scoreboard 7 on page 74 and then place an X on the graph where the two numbers intersect to identify where you stand.

Now take a moment and do the same for your church or ministry. This time place a C on the graph where the numbers intersect to identify where your church or ministry stands on the diagram.

The ultimate goal is 'The Star" to be both Bold enough and Clear enough with the gospel so the message is both heard and received. Keep in mind that the boldness and clarity lines often move with culture. In some countries because of security and risk issues you cannot be as bold as in others.

Appendix #5

Evangelistic Event Planning & Programming
Steps for Evangelistic Event Planning

Setting up an evangelistic event (WIN) could be as a start for your ongoing ministry, keeping in mind that you need to have a view of *Evangelistic-Discipleship* from the beginning. Here are some first steps to consider.

1. **Form a Leadership Team**
   - ✓ There is strength in numbers, and this may give you another chance to disciple people who join your team

2. **Strategic Planning**
   - ✓ Identify your target group, the specific group you want to reach
   - ✓ Identify interests & needs and sport/rec/fitness…leisure pursuits using the Sports Recreation, and Fitness Ministry Activity List
   - ✓ Select the event / activity you are going to use

3. **Plan for Evangelistic Activities**
   - ✓ Set your mind on really introducing people to the Gospel. Evangelism does not happen by accident and is also not just informational. Unless evangelism is intentional it is accidental at best
   - ✓ Communicate and advertise the event to your target group
   - ✓ Recruit and train leaders / volunteers for the event

4. **Create your Program**

Steps for Event Programming

1. **Preparation – Who?**
   Establish committees and recruit volunteers (division of labor)
   - ✓ Prayer Team
   - ✓ Registration
   - ✓ Publicity
   - ✓ Program
   - ✓ Follow-up / Discipleship

2. **Content – What?**
   - ✓ Prayer
   - ✓ Devotions (Bible instruction / spiritual truths); testimonies; *Sports Parables*; proclamation of the gospel; drama / skits
   - ✓ Distribution of literature if appropriate (tracts; testimonies; New Testaments; other written material; DVDs)
   - ✓ Post-event invitation (other sports and church events, worship)
   - ✓ Post event activities
   - ✓ Follow-up / Discipleship plan -
     - Identify *Persons of Peace*, engage with them in the discovery process
     - Contact anyone who accepted Jesus and get them into a formal and informal discipleship process and relationships

3. **Evangelistic Opportunities – How?**
   Make the most of every opportunity!!!
   - ✓ T-shirts (include a Bible verse)
   - ✓ Tract w/ ribbon (include a Bible verse)
   - ✓ Certificate w/ gospel
   - ✓ Music
   - ✓ Testimonies & *Sports Parables*
   - ✓ Prayer
   - ✓ Fellowship with tea, coffee, snacks, food
   - ✓ Prizes, post-event ceremony, awards presentation and program
   - ✓ Personal evangelism (prepare your congregation to attend and share one-on-one)

Appendix # 6

Sports Parable Worksheet

Writing Your Own *Sports Parables*

Write a Sports Parable using the following outline.

Title (can be added later, after the parable begins to take shape)

_____

Sports Example (Skill, Position, Attitude, Rule, Game Situation)

_____
_____
_____

Spiritual Principle (to be taught)

_____
_____
_____

Explanation of Illustration / Demonstration

_____
_____
_____
_____

Supporting Verse

_____
_____
_____
_____

Appendix #7

Sample *Sports Parables*

We can use many things from within a particular sport that the audience is familiar with to communicate the gospel message. Usually this can be effectively presented in less than 15 minutes. You are only limited by your own creativity.

Ideas for *Sports Parables*:
- Skills – receiving a pass; dribbling; defense; shooting; rebounding; heading; etc.
- Positions – forward; goalie; striker; coach; center; blocker; pitcher; catcher; etc.
- Attitudes – perseverance; team work; potential; humility; self-control; effort; submission; losing; competition; etc.
- Situations – winning; losing; defense; offense; scoring; missing shots
- Rules – hands; fouls; red card; substitutions; strikes; balls; outs; etc.
- Other

Example # 1 - Boundaries
Every sport has boundaries – sidelines or baselines, for example.

Questions:
1) What happens when you are outside the sideline?
2) What happens when you are inside the sideline?
3) What happens when you are on the sideline?

Answers:
1) You are "out of bounds" and must give up possession of the ball.
2) You are "in bounds" and can keep possession of the ball.
3) You are "out of bounds" and must give up possession of the ball.

Illustration:
Share a personal example or use a story about another person or athlete to continue making your point.

Spiritual Principle:
The Word of God is like that sideline; when you are "inside" (living by those principles) you are within the will of God and living as God wants you to live.

When you violate these principles, represented in this case by the game or rules of the sport, you lose.

Supporting verses:
Joshua 1:8-9; Psalm 119:1-2; 1 John 5:3

Example #2 - Love One Another

Questions:
1) What do you love?
2) You all have friends and so I ask the question, do you love them?
3) You play a sport and I ask you, do you love that sport?

Pick four people who raise their hands and volunteer to come forward, making sure you have even numbers of each gender (i.e., two males and two females or all four of the same). You will see why this is vital under "demonstration".

Illustration:
Focus on one person, asking what he or she loves. Then say, "You say you love [pizza, for example], but what does that mean? I also love pizza, but is that the same as loving people? Or I might love my dog, for example, but I make him sleep outside. Is that love all the same? When I say I love my friends, what does that mean?

Demonstration:
Pair up the volunteers and have them sit down back to back (in most of the world's cultures, it's extremely important that the pairs of people be of the same gender. Absolutely do not pair a male and female together!) Instruct them to interlock their arms and try to stand up. Make it a competition to see which team stands up first. Observe what they do. Which team worked together more? Did they help each other? Once they are finished, make comments accordingly. Have them try it a second time. Ask whether if it was easy for them to stand up. Why did they struggle (or not)?

Spiritual Principle:
One of the best ways to say you love someone is by helping/serving them. Members of these teams had to help each other in order to be successful. The Bible says that love comes from God and that God is love, and when we do

not love one another we do not know God. So when we help one another we are representing God.

Supporting Verses:
1 John 4:7-8

Example # 3 - The Winning Shot

Questions:
1) What does it mean to love someone else?
2) How do you demonstrate love?
3) How do you demonstrate love in playing sports? Does it even matter?

Illustration (basketball example):
Ask for two volunteers. Say: "You are on the same team. Your team is down by one point with only five seconds left on the clock. Who is going to take the last shot? Are you willing to pass up the ball in order to give your teammate the glory?" Let's try it…

Demonstration:
At this point give them a ball and instruct them to pretend that they are in the last seconds of the game. They can either pass the ball or shoot it. Then count down: 5 , 4, 3, 2, 1. Observe what they do: Did one person want to take the shot? Did they pass to each other? Once they are finished, make comments accordingly. If it goes well, have the same team or two other teams do the demonstration again.

Spiritual Principle:
We are called to love one another. We can say it, but unless we act it out, our words mean nothing. God demonstrated it by becoming a man in the person of Jesus who then died for us. His demonstration of love is what defines all other love. Jesus gave His life!

Supporting Verses:
1 John 4:9-10

Example # 4 - Perfection

Question:
1) Who is the best basketball player, football player, or whatever sport you are playing?

2) Is he or she perfect?
3) Are there any perfect athletes?
4) Does everyone make every shot or every goal?
5) Is anyone here perfect?

Illustration:
Ask for two volunteers. Say: "Let's see how close you can get to perfection." Have them shoot ten free-throws or shots, kick ten times at the goal, etc. Play up the competition. Was either of them perfect? One might have been close to perfect, but was he or she actually perfect? Can we achieve perfection? It does not matter how close we get to perfection, we still fall short.

Spiritual Principle:
God's standard is perfection. None of us can achieve it. We try to achieve perfection in sports by practicing, but we never become perfect. Yet, the Bible says that God loves us perfectly, and when I accept Jesus in His eyes I become perfect. Would you like to become perfect in God's eyes?

Supporting Verses:
1 John 4:16-20

Example # 5 – Understanding Your Purpose (The Shoe)

Question:
1) Have you ever thought of what your purpose might be or why you were created?

Illustration:
In almost every sport, participants must wear shoes. Ask for one volunteer. Have him or her remove one shoe as you remove one shoe from your foot. Set the two shoes side-by-side.
Ask: "Which shoe is faster?" Encourage responses from your audience.
Say: "Let's find out. On your mark, get set, go!" Encourage cheering from your audience. Of course they don't move.

To emphasize your point, repeat: "On your mark, get set, go!"
Ask: "What's wrong with these shoes? Why don't they move?"
Solicit answers from the audience until someone says: "You have to put feet in them."
Say: "Now let's see…"

Demonstration:
Have you and your volunteer put the shoes back on and race to a point and back to see which shoe is faster.

Spiritual Principle:
Our lives are just like those shoes. Only after the shoe has a foot in it does it realize its purpose. Only after we allow Jesus to come into our lives do we realize our purpose.

Supporting Verses:
Proverbs 3:5-6; Psalm 139:13; Ephesians 1:4-5; Colossians 1:16; 1 Peter 2:9

Example # 6 – The Gospel Power Ball

The Gospel Power Ball is a sports ball painted in the colours that can be used to share the gospel.[1] Feel free to identify verses that you can use to relate to each concept.

Step 1

Take a partially deflated ball and try to bounce it. Anyone can see that this ball won't bounce. This ball is not capable of doing what its manufacturer made it for. This ball can only then fulfill its purpose when it is filled with air. Without the air inside, nothing can be done with it. And it is the same with our lives. When we do not know God, we are like that partially deflated ball. The only one who can fill us is God Himself, because He is the one who made us.

Step 2

Take a fully inflated ball and explain how to get to know God using the following colors:[2]

Green

Green is for the creation: God created heaven and earth, and He has also created you. He is your Heavenly Father, who wants to have a relationship with you, because He loves you.

Yellow

Yellow, or gold, is for eternal life in heaven where will can wear a heavenly gold crown (*stephanos* in the Greek). God loves you so much that He wants

---

[1] The concept of using colors originated with Preacher Charles Haddon Spurgeon in a message he gave on January 11, 1866 and became what is now known as the Wordless Book. https://en.wikipedia.org/wiki/Wordless_Book.
[2] It is recommended for the reader to read the note in Explanatory Section of this book for a most important explanation concerning sensitivity to the use of certain colors that might be offensive in various cultures and countries.

this relationship to last forever and that we will choose to live with Him in Heaven forever.

Black
Black represents darkness, where there is no light (Jesus), our sins hide: There is one problem that hinders our relationship with God and separates us from Him, and that is our sin.

Red
Red is for the price Jesus paid: Jesus has been punished for our sins and died for us, and so He restored the relationship between us and God the Father.

White
White is for forgiveness: When you recognise you are a sinner and believe that Jesus has died for your sins at the cross on Calvary and accept Him in your heart as your Saviour, then you can know you are forgiven and purged of all your sins and that you will spend eternity with Him. Your sins are washed as white as snow.

Green
Return to green a second time, because green also represents growth: A new life with Jesus has now begun! Now you can live with Him in this life.

Step 3
Many people are familiar with the acronym WWJD – 'What Would Jesus Do?' This acronym can also be printed on the Gospel Power Ball and can be used for communicating the gospel. Assemble the players together and present them with a situation. Then ask them: "WWJD?" On the basis of this question you can present something practical from God's Word relating to the situation.

Step 4
You can use the verse 1 Corinthians 15:57 which can also be printed on the ball. This is a good verse for sports people. We have the ultimate victory only in Jesus!

See Appendix 6 and now use the Worksheet to write your own *Sports Parables*.

Appendix #8

Personal Testimony Example from Paul and Worksheet

Testimony – Telling others about the truth of Christ as he is working in and through your life

Paul's Example - Read Acts 22:3-15
Summarize the three areas he focuses on:

- Acts 22:3-5   His life before Christ

_____

_____

_____

- Acts 22:6-13   His experience receiving Christ

_____

_____

_____

- Acts 22:14-15   His life after receiving Christ

_____

_____

_____

Prayer Preparation:

- Ephesians 6:19-20   • Pray for boldness.
- Colossians 4:2-4   • Pray for clarity and open doors to speak.

My Testimony

My life before Christ

_____
_____
_____
_____
_____

How I accepted Christ

_____
_____
_____
_____
_____

My life after receiving Christ

_____
_____
_____
_____
_____

Life Verse/Challenge

_____
_____
_____
_____

Appendix # 9

Let's STRIVE together in Evangelistic-Discipleship

1. **S**tart with God – pray & fast & plan
   Set aside a specific time _____

2. **T**arget, or in other words to focus on, a specific neighborhood and/or group
   Which neighborhood? _____
   Which target group? _____

3. **R**each out through a specific sports activity and event (WIN)
   Which sports ministry activity will you begin with?
   What are the dates? _____

4. **I**nvite new people (players and spectators) to join you
   Plan a specific time to "walk the streets" and connect with people.
   Play sports, get to know people and explore what is happening in the neighborhood.
   When? _____

5. **V**alidate your presence through being intentional about *Evangelistic Disciplemaking*. Start a Discovery Group (BUILD)
   When and *Where* will your new *Missional Sports Community* meet weekly?
   _____

6. **E**xpand your ministry (SEND / MULTIPLY)
   Raise up new leaders, put them in positions of responsibility, and send them out. As you identify them, write their names here.
   _____
   _____

Appendix #10

Practical Steps to Build Sports Ministry

So now more specifically, as you start to build your sports ministry reflect on the six basic steps to follow as you <u>Pray</u>, <u>Plan</u>, and <u>Persistently-Persevere</u>. Here again I must acknowledge Rodger Oswald for his influence and inspiration for these steps.

The first requirement is a <u>God-given vision</u>. Identify a sports ministry leader. Is this you? You might see the value of using sports, recreation, and fitness for ministry (I really hope you do after reading this far in this book), but who is the best person to implement it? And just because someone is or was a sportsman or woman does not mean that they are the best choice for this position. To find or be the right person you must:

- ✓ Be in communion with God
- ✓ Have a passion that comes from God
- ✓ Have an understanding of the needs, opportunities, and resources available
- ✓ Be available and committed
- ✓ Be able to merge the vision with your church or ministry. It is important to be perceived as – and genuinely to be – a partner, an integral part of the vision that the church is trying to accomplish.

The second requirement is <u>building</u> a ministry team. As you do, be sure to identify and focus on *2-T-2-2 Relationships*. You cannot do it on your own. As you consider people to join you:

- ✓ Personally recruit the individuals for the team that have the vision and bring necessary skills
- ✓ Identify a sports ministry *Timothy* to build into
- ✓ Train the team in the complete vision; sports ministry is about ministry, not activity
- ✓ Develop a prayer team

The third requirement is <u>communicating</u> the vision. Who should catch the sports ministry vision? How do they catch it? Get their attention. Create a desire. Motivate them to action. Do this as you educate them about the vision, the ministry potential, and their participation needed in order to fulfill this vision. You inform them and others as you advertise and promote the ministry. You motivate them as you demonstrate with energy and enthusiasm. You must communicate it to:

- ✓ Leadership – pastor; staff; elders; deacons; ministry leaders; governing body; people of influence
- ✓ Ministry teams – prayer group and program members (evangelism or missions committee)
- ✓ The church body and other ministry staff

The fourth requirement is to <u>develop</u> the program. No longer is the building merely a gymnasium. Key steps are to:

- ✓ Identify resources: Ask: "What do I have?"
- ✓ Places: a park, a field, a parking lot, a sports hall in your community, an alleyway
- ✓ People: coaches; athletes; teachers; prayers; snack-providers; parents; etc.
- ✓ Things: balls; games; goals; etc.
- ✓ Identify your target / focus group (Who is God calling me to reach?) Examples are:
    - elementary-aged children; youth; adults; seniors
    - those who play a specific sport or participate in an activity
    - those who are handicapped, disadvantaged, and institutionalized
- ✓ Identify areas of interest (What is my target group interested in and how can I reach them with the gospel?)
- ✓ Select the event or activity you wish to use
- ✓ Design and organize the program
- ✓ Plan for *Evangelistic-Disciplemaking*.
    - Begin with the mindset that evangelistic activities are planned with a view to making followers of Jesus
    - Remember that evangelism is not an informational issue, and it will not happen by accident
    - Work to make disciples, not converts
- ✓ Communicate the event or activity to your intended audience
- ✓ Recruit and train leadership for the event

The fifth requirement is to <u>maintain</u> the ministry. Starting something can be the easy part. Keeping it going effectively is something else altogether different. In order to do this you must:

- ✓ Educate those who are involved about the vision to keep them sharp
- ✓ Motivate those who are serving through your ministry to keep their passion fresh and alive
- ✓ Inform others about what is happening and praise God for His faithfulness
- ✓ Evaluation – Keep doing what works and improve it

✓ Individual and program follow-up
  • Make sure that you are building into those who are open for learning more about God or growing in their faith.
  • Get them into BUILD LEVEL programs.
✓ Programs – Divide your programs according to the WIN-BUILD-SEND-MULTIPLY model and keep a balance in your activities and mission.

Don't be afraid to try new things, but also don't give up too easily. You will certainly face opposition as you become more successful and visible. Remember that before you can think big you have to think small, one person at a time.

The sixth requirement is focus on <u>discipleship</u>! You can review chapter 7 how best to do this as you do remember that the true measure of success comes down to *Timothy Relationships*, empowering others, raising up leaders, and releasing them into their own calling, vision and mission to follow and serve God.

Gentle Warnings

• Pray and ask God to help you to find a balance between reality and faith as you dream big for God

• Start at the WIN LEVEL on the *Sports Ministry Pyramid*. Identify your target audience then make a plan. Pick one event, activity, or league and do it well. People like to participate in something organized and professional

• Start small. Do not let your grasp exceed your reach

• Don't give up easily. Satan will try to discourage, and challenges will come. Hold on to your vision. Your most fruitful ministry will probably start to come two or three years down the road. Persevere

• Gradually expand. As you develop leadership, participants, and a presence in the community, move forward slowly

• Stay faithful to your goals. Work to develop people. Create fellowship for the believers and friendship with unbelievers; share your faith, disciple, and assimilate those who respond, but also be willing to prune. If an activity or event is not producing fruit, cut it out of the program. The purpose of pruning is to produce greater fruitfulness

Appendix #11

Building Sports Ministry Worksheet

Now it's your turn!

Focus / Target Group (age and characteristics): _____

Estimated Number of Participants: _____

Activity or Event: _____

Projected Date: _____

Overview of Plan (brief summary): _____

_____

_____

Ministry Team Leaders Needed (Name)	Experience Required	Ministry Position (Coach, Prayer Leader, etc.)
1.		
2.		
3.		
4.		
5.		

Action Points	Responsible Person	Completion Date
1. Create a **SCHEDULE** for your activity		
2 Create a plan for doing **EVANGELISM**		
3. Develop some ideas to **RECRUIT** leaders		
4. Develop a plan to **PROMOTE** your activity inside your church and out		
5. Develop a **BUDGET** for your activity		
6. Develop a plan to **FOLLOW-UP** after your program to begin the discovery/discipleship process		
7. Other		

Points of Special Attention:

1. **Prayer Team** _____
2. _____
3. _____

Appendix #12

SPORTS MINISTRY PYRAMID

SEND — **LEADERSHIP**: various leadership programs, disciples empowered to serve

BUILD — **DISCIPLESHIP / SMALL GROUPS / FOLLOW-UP**: Sports Alpha Courses, sports teams, Bible studies/discovery process, clinic/community programs, projects

PERSON OF PEACE

WIN — **EVANGELISM / FRIENDSHIP / FELLOWSHIP**: outreach, league, clinic/community programs, literature distribution, tournaments, match showing

MULTIPLY: new ministries, leaders released to start Winning, Building, and Sending

Appendix #13

Recommended International Ministry List

Check out these ministries to get involved with the practical application of *The Life of the Shoe: Sports Outreach for the World*.

*Note: This listing, compiled by the author, includes organizations that he has had personal experience with and highly recommends. This listing does not necessarily represent an endorsement of this book or its content by these organizations.

Sports ministries

Church Sports & Recreation Ministers (CSRM)
Equipping local churches to change lives through sports, recreation, and fitness outreach.
www.csrm.org

Uttermost Sports
Reaching the unreached in the uttermost parts (Acts 1:8) of the world.
www.uttermostsports.org

Next Move Ministries
Serving churches and the sports world in the Netherlands and beyond by developing *Missional Sports Communities* and more.
www.nxtmove.nl

Athletes in Action – Netherlands
Serving churches and the sports world in the Netherlands and beyond.
https://www.athletesinaction.nl/

MINISTRIES REACHING THE UNREACHED

Global Frontier Missions
Bringing Jesus within reach of every person on earth.
www.globalfrontiermissions.org

continued on page 180

Joshua Project
Bringing definition to the unfinished task of taking the gospel to the world.
www.joshuaproject.net

MINISTRIES SERVING THE PERSEVERING CHURCH

International Christian Response (ICR)
Providing spiritual and material assistance to Christians who live in countries hostile to the gospel, enabling them to proclaim the truth, plant churches - and persevere.
www.christianresponse.org

Open Doors
Committed to aiding persecuted Christians around the globe.
www.opendoorsusa.org

OTHER

Disciple Making Movements (DMM)
Empowering ordinary people to become multiplying disciple makers.
www.disciplemakingmovements.com

Appendix #14

GLOSSARY

New Glossary Terms From This Book

Dumb-Churched (Cultural-Churched)
One of four sub-categories used to describe unchurched-people. The term "dumb" is not used to describe the intelligence or mental capacities of a person, but rather it is used to describe a person who lacks a basic comprehension of, and/or application of foundational biblical truths. Each person within this sub-category has an affiliation and/or familiarity with church but not personally with Jesus. Some may identify themselves a Christians simply because they were born into a Christian family or attended a Christian school. Others may attend a local church on a regular or limited basis but they remain uninformed, or possibly even misinformed, about Christ and Christianity and would not be considered to be a Christian. If they do have a faith, it is very shallow and ineffectual or very new. The *Dumb-Churched (Cultural-Churched)* range from to being what is called a "CEO" (Christmas-Easter Only) Christian, to being more seriously religious (attending services once or more each month). Regardless of their participation in a local congregation, they do not have a growing relationship with God. Those who make up the very religious segment are the "white-washed tombs" that Jesus refers to in Matthew 23:27. They look pretty good on the outside, but inside from their heart they do not know Jesus.

Mansfield Graph of Evangelism
The *Mansfield Graph of Evangelism*, created by Don Mansfield, former staff member of Campus Crusade for Christ (now known as Cru), and named and popularized in the *Sports Outreach Community* by P. F. Myers, is designed to help believers become more effective in sharing the gospel in their own personal life and ministry. It is based on two passages of scripture, Colossians 4:3-4 and Ephesians 6:19, where Paul specifically asks for prayer for clarity and boldness. These two characteristics form the X and Y axis of the *Mansfield Graph*, as described in this book, which then allows the reader to evaluate themselves and apply methods to grow in both areas. The idea is to see the gospel communicated most effectively in every setting as the necessity to be bold and clear is considered.

Ministry Principles In A Sports Jersey

This *Ministry Principles In A Sports Jersey* "connects the dots" between *Level #2 Philosophical-Principles* found in this book and throughout the Institutes of Sports Outreach OVP book series with general ministry principles. These general ministry principles will work when applied in any culture to any ministry tool and medium that does not contradict scripture, thus the sports jersey analogy.

Missional-Sports-Communities

The term Missional Communities is now used by many organizations around the world to describe The Church's response to the current spiritual condition in the world. The basic concept is that believers need to get out of their local church buildings and into their neighborhoods with the gospel to live, serve, witness, and build community. Instead of the old attractional model of expecting people come to a worship service or other activity just because a congregation advertises all are welcome, congregations must encourage and empower their members to embrace the incarnational example of Jesus of "going to make disciples." The phrase *Missional-Sports-Communities* has been in use since at least 2012. Coined by P.F.Myers, *Missional-Sports-Communities* describes thriving sports ministry communities of people who are working together to be The Church as a visible witness for Jesus and establish an ongoing movement of *Evangelistic-Disciplemaking*. Consult with the Nxtmove organization (www.Nxtmove.nl) that has further developed this concept in The Netherlands and around the world.

Person-of-Peace

The concept of *Person-of-Peace* was introduced by Disciple-Making Movements (DMM) as a part of their ministry strategy to plant churches and has become a standard within many ministry circles, including the *Sports Outreach Community*. It is most specifically incorporated by CSRM's International Staff and Global Network Partners in their church planting efforts. It references the person in Luke 10 who welcomed the disciples into their home and received the blessing of peace that was spoken over them. Jesus told the disciples once this person had been identified to stay with them and not move on to another village. The *Person-of-Peace*, in most cases, is not yet a follower of Jesus but the person God had prepared to receive the bearers of Truth or the message of Truth. As the *Person-of-Peace* transferable concept is applied to a sports outreach ministry it may refer to anyone who accommodates and aids the sports minister, even though they have not professed faith in Jesus.

Sports-Parables
The phrase *Sports-Parables* describes a specific methodology to communicate the gospel. It is a way sport can be used (even by and to non-athletes), to reach those far from Jesus and His Church. Based in a methodology modeled by Jesus (Who often taught spiritual messages through parables), simple, sports-related stories are used to create word pictures, concepts and principles to draw in listeners. *Sports-Parables* have many elements and stories that can be used to communicate spiritual truth within every culture. Creative stories and dramas (situational skits acted out) using sports in this way are known as *Sports Parables*. These can be incorporated into almost any sports outreach activity in the process of *Evangelistic Disciplemaking*.

The Sports-Ministry-Pyramid
The Sports-Ministry-Pyramid diagram is used to illustrate effective *Evangelistic-Disciplemaking* within SR&F outreach ministry. Based on the concept of *2-T-2-2 Relationships* of reaching those far from Jesus and then discipling them to reach and disciple future generations of Christians (2 Timothy 2.2). This *Producing-Reproducing-Reproducers* consists of 4 distinct levels of progression: 1) Evangelism (WIN); 2) Discipleship (BUILD); 3) Leadership Development (SEND); and 4) Releasing Disciples (MULTIPLY). *The Sports-Ministry-Pyramid* is both a model for ministry as well as an evaluation tool to ensure a SR&F outreach ministry remains *Strategically-Relevant* and *Efficiently-Effective* in order to move beyond "sports activities," to Bible-based sports ministry.

2-T-2-2 Relationships
This concept is based on 2 Timothy 2.2 and the model of discipleship that was lived out among the early founders of The Church. Howard Hendricks, esteemed professor at Dallas Theological Seminary, introduced a similar concept but with a different order. *The 2-T-2-2 Relationships* transferable concept is based on spiritual relationships that believers have with one another for the purpose of becoming effective followers of Jesus. CSRM's International Director incorporated *2-T-2-2 Relationships* into the *Sports-Ministry-Pyramid* model as a key to *Evangelistic-Disciplemaking*. The essence of this transferable concept is three relationships: 1) a current minister who has intentional and effective relationships with his peers (*Paul-Relationships*), who has 2) been mentored and influenced by an older, more experienced minister (a *Barnabas-Relationship*), and who 3) actively mentors and influences younger, aspiring ministers (*Timothy-Relationships*).

Barnabas-Relationship
The *Barnabas-Relationship* is one of the three *2-T-2-2 Relationships*; is appropriately named after Barnabas who mentored and coached Paul; and is a key element of the *Sports Ministry Pyramid*. A "Barnabas" is an older person in the faith (not necessarily in age) who loves; challenges; encourages; holds accountable and molds the "Paul's" they mentor. A "Barnabas" is a model in both life and ministry that a "Paul" seeks to imitate and emulate. A key distinction of *Barnabas-Relationships* has to do with understanding the need to not only empower the next generation of ministers but also when appropriate, to release the ministry and Gospel work to the future generations of "Pauls" and "Timothys."

Paul-Relationship
The *Paul-Relationship* is one of the three *2-T-2-2 Relationships*; is appropriately named after The Apostle who was mentored by Barnabas, was a peer of other Apostles and a mentor to many "Timothys." *Paul-Relationships* are a key element of the *Sports Ministry Pyramid*. A "Paul" is a co-laborer and true companion (Philippians 4.2f); a peer in life and ministry. "Pauls" love and encourage one another but also keep each other honest and accountable. Paul and the other Apostles were peers and while they shared a common goal for world *Evangelistic-Disciplemaking* each had their unique and specific call. These "Pauls" then became a "Barnabas" to their "Timothys" such as Silas, John-Mark, Luke and others.

Timothy-Relationships
Timothy-Relationships are one of the three *2-T-2-2 Relationships* and is appropriately named after Timothyk who was Paul's protégée and is a key element of the *Sports Ministry Pyramid*. A "Timothy," is a younger person in faith and/or ministry (not necessarily age). Based in the Epistles (1 & 2 Timothy, Titus) and other New Testament sources, the transferable concept of mentoring a "Timothy" entails affirming, encouraging, teaching, correcting, directing and challenging the next generation of Christians and ministers. It also assumes the "Paul" consistently prays for all "Timothys." A key distinction of *Timothy-Relationships* has to do with understanding the need to not only empower the next generation of ministers but also when appropriate, to release the ministry and gospel work to the next generation "Timothy."

Wow Moments
Throughout His ministry Jesus used simple stories that created word pictures to draw in His listeners (parables). Through His parables, listeners could clearly

visualize and understand the gospel and its basic principles and the didactic truths He intended to communicate. His parables often included circumstances or cultural elements that would have surprised or even offended those listening and yet they were accepted. P.F. Myers calls these the *"Wow Moments"* of the parable because Jesus' audience would have gone "Wow!" when they caught His specific point. The *Wow Moments* were connected to the spiritual truth that Jesus was illustrating and were vital to communicating what He was teaching. Within *Sports Parables* are many opportunities to include *Wow Moments* to draw in the audience.

Project-Thinking to Church-Building
The practice of developing on-going ministry. That is winning people to Christ, building them up to become disciples, and sending them out to win others. Sometimes in ministry, as an example, we focus on winning people through one-time *Mega-Events*. This is an example of *Project-Thinking*. We like big events, we like projects, and we put a lot of energy in them. Instead we need to PLAN to "make disciples" who are making disciples who are making disciples. In our language we call them *Reproducing-Reproducers*. We don't just want to do nice projects. We want to engage in activities and ongoing ministries that plant and develop local churches. This is truly accomplishing the Great Commission and putting 2 Timothy 2:2 into practice.

Glossary for this Book Series

1-Foundational Purpose of Sports Outreach
The first transferable concept and the guiding principle of *The Sports Outreach Community*. It describes the end goal of *The Community*: making *Dedicated-Disciples* of Jesus Christ.

2-Dysconnects of Sports Outreach
The second transferable concept describes and defines the two hurdles SR&F outreach ministries encounter in reaching those far from Christ and His Church. The first dysconnect has to do with attracting people from the general community in which they live, to specific local church SR&F activities. The second dysconnect has to do with moving people from the SR&F activities to the broader congregational activities including becoming active participants in traditional worship and Christian Education opportunities.

3-I's

The 3-I's form a *Re-sourcing; Re-training & Re-energizing* continuum for fully equipping SR&F outreach ministers for the purpose of empowering them to envision, plan for, organize, administrate and evaluate a truly *Strategically-Relevant & Efficiently-Effective, Evangelistic-Disciplemaking* sports outreach ministry.

- *Inform* – has to do with the creation, production and distribution of *Re-sources* that are: Christo-centric *Level #1 Theological-Truths*; Biblically-Based *Level #2 Philosophical-Principles*; and *Level #3 Methodological-Models*.
- *Instruct* – has to do with *Re-training* SR&F outreach ministers in how to most effectively utilize and employ the *Re-sources* that have been created, produce and distributed.
- *Inspire* – has to do with *Re-energizing* SR&F outreach ministers with new motivations and inspirations for reaching those far from Jesus and His Church and also has to do with developing ongoing, personal, mentoring, relationships that enables SR&F outreach ministers to become fully equipped for successful Great Commission endeavors.

3-Tier Paradigm Organizational Structure

The third transferable concept outlines the organizational structure of SR&F outreach ministries. Based upon three levels, it builds from a foundation of how to think (theologically); which shapes and informs how to organize (philosophically); out of which what to do (methodology) emerges. Moving from *Why* a SR&F ministry exists to *When, Where* and for *Whom* it is organized to *What* is done; this organizational structure ensures *Strategically-Relevant* and *Efficiently-Effective* SR&F outreach ministry.

4-Fold Evaluation Rubric

The fourth transferable concept describes the four necessary components for ensuring a SR&F outreach ministry will accomplish its goals and objectives which include being Strategic; Relevant; Efficient and Effective.

5-B's Process of Sports Outreach

The fifth transferable concept explains the process of developing a *Repetitive-Redemptive-Relational* ethos and culture within SR&F outreach ministry for the purpose of making *Dedicated-Disciples* of Jesus. It outlines how a SR&F can envision, plan for and implement an effective outreach ministry.

- *Belong*
- *Believe*
- *Baptize*

Glossary   189

- *Behave*
- *Become*

7-Continuums of Tension of the Sports Outreach Movement
The sixth transferable concept outlines the seven most important theological and philosophical issues confronting *The Sports Outreach Community* as it enters its 7th decade.

Accommodation
One of four classical responses and reactions embraced by sport-related individuals who encounter the dilemma of integrating faith and their sport. It describes those who choose sport over faith but try to hold on to both.

Blow-In; Blow-Up; Blow-Out
This *Level #3 Methodological-Model* consists of: a) an American sports team *Blowing-In* to a specific community within a foreign country to play a game against a local or national team; b) having one or more of the athletes verbally share the gospel (*Blow-Up*) and ask for those in attendance to "accept Jesus;" and then c) *Blow-Out* to the next stop on the short term mission trip. This phrase was first used by sports outreach ministry pioneer Rodger Oswald who used it to describe the essence of what all too often occurs when American sports teams engage in short term international mission trips. It is based on a soteriology (theology of salvation) that believes the mission's goal is fulfilled and accomplished when a person "raises their hand" or "prays a prayer" with limited regard to "making disciples" and connecting those being reached with a local congregation.

Building-with-Leaders
Building-with-Leaders is a *Level #2 Philosophical-Principle* that emphasizes the importance of investing in leaders and their development for the ultimate purpose of achieving *Strategically-Relevant* and *Efficiently-Effective* SR& F outreach ministry. This philosophy is the true bed-rock of SR&F outreach ministry but should not be used to dismiss the importance of constructing and maintaining high quality athletic and fitness facilities, which greatly enhance and expand local church outreach efforts. *Building-with-Leaders* is a philosophy that seeks to recruit, *Re-Source*; *Re-Train* and *Re-Energize* local church volunteers to build effective *Redemptive-Repetitive-Relational* opportunities with friends, family members and associates for the purpose of *Evangelistic-Disciplemaking*. This phrase is often partnered with its corollary: *Leading-with-Buildings*.

Capitulation
One of four classical responses and reactions embraced by sport-related individuals who encounter the dilemma of integrating faith and sport. It describes those who not only choose sport over faith but totally abandon their faith in favor of sport.

Christmanship
One of three philosophical approaches to competition and sport; *Christmanship* describes a laser-focused and biblically-based, Christ-honoring ethic of engagement with sport. As compared with gamesmanship that espouses the highest ethic is to win; or sportsmanship which emerges from a philosophy rooted in humanistic relativism and ends with an ethic of fair play etc.; *Christmanship* is an ethic that outlines how to engage in sport for the glory of God and in ways that honors all *Co-Competitors*.

Co-Competitors
A term in the *Christmanship* Ethic used to describe individuals who play on other teams. This descriptive term is used rather than words such as opponent, adversary or enemy.

Competition-Gone-Berserk
Competition-Gone-Berserk is a phrase used to describe how some local church sports ministries have completely abdicated on creating a culture of biblically-based competition (*Christmanship*). Unchecked and unsupervised competition often results in participants experiencing such a negative competitive environment that they choose to not only leave the church league, but more significantly, they decide to have nothing to do with the congregation that sponsors the league. Whether born out of a total lack of any theological structure for competition and sport, or from an underdeveloped *Level #1 Theological-Truth* of competition, the end result of *Competition-Gone-Berserk* is the same…a lost opportunity to reach those far from Jesus and His Church.

Competition-Gone-Soft
Competition-Gone-Soft is a phrase used to describe how some local church sports ministries seek to greatly curtail or totally eliminate competition within all of their leagues and games. This approach is usually born out of an underdeveloped *Level #1 Theological-Truth* that believes competition is intrinsically and inherently evil. This underlying theology leads to a local church sport outreach ministry envisioning and developing a ministry structure that doesn't reward Godly competition and even penalizes anything bordering on

competition. Sadly, the organizational structures that emerge out of such *Level #2 Philosophical-Principles* lead to *Level #3 Methodological-Models* that are not appealing to large segments of those who are far from Jesus and His Church; and thus do not attract them to participate in any of the outreach programs a congregation offers. There are however, specific sports outreaches that are rightfully designed to create less intense competition: a) Low Impact volleyball for beginners; b) Slo-break basketball for seniors; c) basketball clinics for preschoolers; and d) various fellowship leagues of all ages. Nonetheless, for the most part, non-competitive sporting activities do not attract or keep people involved. Any local church that seeks to "go and make disciples" of athletes is encouraged to develop a culture of biblically-based competition (*Christmanship*) that will be managed so as to appeal to, and attract, competitors to participate…all with the end goal of winning them to Jesus.

Core Values
Whereas *Theological-Truths* define and describe the *Why*; *Philosophical-Principles* define and describe the *When, Where & with Whom*; and *Methodological-Models* describe and define the *What* of the *3-Tier Paradigm*; the Core Values define and describe the *How* of the *3-Tier Paradigm*. Core Values have to do with creating an environment of organizational and administrative excellence; an atmosphere of warmth, love and encouragement; and a culture of integrity, punctuality, efficiency and safety. Core Values consider how participants in SR&F activities feel; and are the bedrock of "proclaiming" the gospel through the fleshing out the Great Commandment.

Counting-Conversions
Counting-Conversions is a phrase used to summarize how many congregations, denominations, missions and ministries determine the effectiveness of their *Evangelistic-Disciplemaking* (*Success-Statistics*) endeavors. It describes the fact that many ministries and churches believe evangelistic success is complete and done whenever a person "converts" to Christianity (what is often called getting them "saved"). This end goal of "getting a person saved" is evidenced by one or more of the following: a) raise a hand at the end of a team huddle; b) pray a prayer with a coach or other evangelist; or c) fill out a card in response to a *Platform-Proclamation* of the gospel at a *Mega-Event*. *Counting-Conversions* is linked with the concept of endeavoring to have people make a *Day's-Decision* for Jesus, rather than seeking to "make" life-long *Dedicated-Disciples* of those who far from Jesus and His Church. The key distinction is the ultimate goal of such endeavors. Is the end and final goal to get a person to make a decision or become a disciple?

Day's-Decision
Day's-Decision is one of the "*Double D's*" of soteriology. It is used in discussions concerning topics such as salvation, evangelism and outreach. It is used in tandem with *Dedicated-Disciple* and describes the pragmatic end result of SR&F outreach ministries. Based in a *Level #1 Theological-Truth* of soteriology, it is based in a simplistic theology of evangelism that strives to get a person to "raise a hand;" "pray a prayer;" or "fill out a response card." Any of these end results indicate a person accepted Jesus on a particular day. While proponents of this approach to evangelism would never say they would discourage participation in a local congregation; nor would they state discipleship to be unimportant; nonetheless, this phrase describes those congregations and ministries that tend to not incorporate ongoing disciplemaking methodologies into their overall evangelistic endeavors.

Dedicated-Disciple
Dedicated-Disciple is one of the "*Double D's*" of soteriology. It is used in discussions concerning topics such as salvation, evangelism and outreach. It is used in tandem with *Day's-Decision* and describes the pragmatic end result of SR&F outreach ministries. Based in a *Level #1 Theological-Truth* of soteriology, it is based in the belief that *Evangelistic-Disciplemaking* consists of not only getting a person to "raise a hand;" "pray a prayer" or "fill out a response card." This philosophy believes it is equally important to engage all who have accepted Jesus as Lord and Savior in disciplemaking activities to ensure full spiritual maturity. While proponents of *Evangelistic-Disciplemaking* would never say a *Day's-Decision* is unimportant; nor would they state accepting Jesus as personal Lord and Savior to be irrelevant; they seek to pragmatically incorporate ongoing disciplemaking methodologies into their overall evangelistic endeavors.

Efficiently-Effective
Paired with *Strategically-Relevant*, it is the second half of the *4-Fold Evaluative Rubric*. *Efficiently-Effective* suggests the criteria congregations need to help assess and determine whether or not a local church SR&F outreach ministry is actually accomplishing its goal of making disciples. It defines and describes ultimate effectiveness; and also communicates the importance of basing the organization and administration of SR&F outreach ministry within a strong stewardship ethic.

External Motivational Influences of Competition (EMIC)
EMIC - describes the pressures of competing because of, with, or against external forces such as time, obstacles, challenges of weather or other natural causes, courses (golf, race, etc.) and/or other human beings.

Glossary

Evangelistic-Environments
Evangelistic-Environments describe one of the key aspects of the Core Values of the *3-Tier Paradigm*. The ultimate goal of a SR&F outreach ministry is to create a winsomely attractive and warm environment that facilitates opportunities for congregational members to build relationships with friends, associates and family members for the purpose of having evangelistic conversations.

Evangelistic-Disciplemaking
In essence this describes how to reach and disciple those far from Christ and His Church. This term uniquely defines the *1-Defining Purpose* of *The Sports Outreach Community*. It assumes that "to go and make disciples" entails both going to those far from Christ and His Church (evangelistic outreach) as well as nurturing the faith of newly-born believers and maturing the faith of long-time pilgrims (discipling endeavors). Congregations and ministries can best accomplish their Great Commission goals by envisioning, planning for and implementing, attractive outreaches that no only connect people to Jesus but ultimately end with them as *Dedicated-Disciples*. This *Level #2 Philosophical-Principle* of *Evangelistic-Disciplemaking* is informed and shaped by the *Level #1 Theological-Truths* of soteriology. It is from these theological concepts and philosophical organizational principles then that *Level #3 Methodological-Models* emerge.

Gamesmanship
Gamesmanship is one of three philosophical approaches to competition and sport. It is partnered with sportsmanship and *Christmanship*. It describes a philosophy based on a secularized-pragmatic-ethic of engagement in and with sport. Its highest value is to win; regardless of how. As compared with sportsmanship that is based upon an ethic rooted in the humanistic-relativism of playing fair etc.; and *Christmanship* that espouses engaging in sport for the glory of God and in ways that honors all co-competitors; gamesmanship only prizes winning.

Internal Motivational Influences of Competition (IMIC)
IMIC—describes the pressures of competing because of, or against, internal forces such as one's pride, a personal level of excellence, goal, or a personal unmet ego need.

Leading-with-Buildings
Leading-with-Buildings is a *Level #2 Philosophical-Principle* that emphasizes the "build it and they will come" philosophy for SR&F outreach ministry. This

philosophy has some merit and should not be unduly dismissed. High quality athletic and fitness facilities and equipment do attract those far from Jesus and His Church. However, such facilities by themselves are not enough. They must be missionally-programmed by leaders who envision, plan for and expedite *Redemptive-Repetitive-Relational* opportunities for church members to initiate and deepen relationships with friends, family members and associates for the purpose of *Evangelistic-Disciplemaking*. This phrase is often partnered with its corollary: *Building-with-Leaders*.

Level #1: Theological-Truths
This *Level #1* foundation for the *3-Tier Paradigm*, both informs and gives shape to *Level #2 Philosophical-Principles*; out which emerge *Level #3 Methodological-Models*. These truths form how SR&F outreach ministers think and what they believe. They are the foundation for why such ministries exist (*Evangelistic-Disciplemaking*) and how (Core Values) they conduct and operate their outreaches. Key words: think, believe and envision.

Level #2: Philosophical-Principles
This second level of the *3-Tier Paradigm* provides the organizational structure for SR&F outreach ministries. It is shaped and informed by *Level #1 Theological-Truths*; and is what *Level #3 Methodological-Models* emerge from. This organizational structure defines the *When, Where & with Whom* SR&F outreach ministries envision, plan for and administer their outreaches. Key words: organize and administrate.

Level #3: Methodological-Models
This third level of the *3-Tier Paradigm* emerges out of the *Level #2 Philosophical-Principles* that provide the organizational structure for SR&F outreach ministries. Once a SR&F outreach ministry understands the *When, Where & with Whom* of their SR&F outreach ministries are to reach, they can then organize, administrate and implement their outreaches. Key words: do and act.

Mega-Event
Mega-Event is one of the two *Mega-Models* used at one end of the fourth of the *7- Continuums of Sports Outreach*. The other *Mega-Model* is *Mega-Media*. *Mega-Events* describes one of *The Sports Outreach Community*'s *Methodological-Models*. *Mega-Events* use large and exciting one-time events or activities to both attract those far from Christ and His Church and also to provide a *Platform-Proclamation* for the gospel to be verbally proclaimed to a large group of people. *Mega-Models* is juxta-positioned with *Repetitive-Redemptive-Relational* on the fourth continuum.

Glossary

Missional Programming
As distinguished from programming, the distinctive of missional programming has to do with programming with a clear gospel-centered end-goal. Running a youth basketball league describes a church program. Facilitating a mission to youth through the strategy of a basketball ministry focuses congregational-based coaches on the gospel-centered end-goal of *Evangelistic-Disciplemaking*.

Muscular Christian Era
The forerunner of *The Sports Outreach Community*, muscular Christianity was the term given to describe a particular philosophy that emerged in the early 1800's from Thomas Arnold's Rugby school and George Williams YMCA. It then flourished through the life and ministries of men like Moody, Mott, Naismith, Stagg and the Studd brothers. It culminated in the first few decades of the 1900's when Olympian Eric Liddell inspired the world by both his running to Gold in the 1924 Paris Olympics; but even more so, when he chose not to run on the Lord's Day and thus forfeited at least three other medals. The essence of muscular Christianity had to do with the integration of faith and sport. It devolved over the decades into more of a cultural ethos rather than a Christ-centered missional community.

Ologies
Short hand for the *Level #1 Theological-Truths* of the *3-Tier Paradigm* that inform and shape *Level #2 Philosophical-Principles*. The key and foundational *Ologies* include: ecclesiology; missiology; soteriology; cosmology; anthropology; and Christology.

Orthodoxy
Orthodoxy (not italicized because this is a common theological term) refers to the necessity of establishing theological and doctrinal foundations in general; and in specific it serves to undergird the *Ologies* of sports outreach that provide the basis for all *Level #1 Theological-Truths*.

Orthopraxy
Orthopraxy (not italicized because this is a common theological term) refers to the necessity of establishing biblically-based philosophies from which pragmatic methodologies can emerge. Orthopraxy has to do with the *When, Where & with Whom* of the 2nd level; the what of the 3rd level; and the how of the core values of the *3-Tier Paradigm*. In SR&F outreach ministry, a well envisioned orthopraxy will ensure the successful accomplishing of the *4-Fold Evaluative Rubric* that consists of being *Strategically-Relevant* and *Efficiently-Effective*.

Personality-over-Presence

Personality-over-Presence defines a *Level #3 Methodological-Model* based on a *Level #2 Philosophical-Principle* that organizes SR&F outreaches for the purposes of having a "sports personality" give a verbal *Platform-Proclamation* of their faith, rather than envisioning, planning for and expediting outreaches based on creating on-going *Redemptive-Repetitive-Relational* activities that are focused on empowering local church missionaries to have an ever-growing and deepening presence in the lives of those far from Jesus and His Church.

Platform-Proclamation

The word platform is used in reference to a place from which to proclaim the gospel. Proclamation refers to the verbal proclamation of the Gospel that takes place from various platforms. Such proclamations are almost exclusively delivered to large groups via a *Mega-Model* of *Mega-Media*. *Platform-Proclamation* is a *Level #3 Methodological-Model* that is most usually associated with *Mega-Event*-based outreaches. It utilizes the "platforms" associated with the notoriety afforded to elite athletes and coaches; so they can verbally "proclaim" their faith to the masses.

Proclamation-Affirmation

Proclamation-Affirmation (not italicized because this concept was coined by Jim Peterson) is the *Level #2 Philosophical-Principle* that is shaped and formed by *Level #1 Ologies* such as soteriology (theology of salvation); missiology (theology of missions); and ecclesiology (theology of the Church). These *Ologies* suggest the most *Strategically-Relevant* and *Efficiently-Effective* outreaches are those based in *Repetitive-Redemptive-Relational* SR&F Outreaches. Such outreaches are created to attract those far from Christ and His Church to participate in activities (*Belong* – the first of *The 5-B's Process of Sports Outreach*) in which the gospel is proclaimed through the organization and implementation of quality missional programming; as well as the Christ-like lives of congregational leaders and members. It is hoped these efforts and relationships result in opportunities for congregational members to "affirm" their faith verbally in ways that will encourage non-Christians to *Believe* (the second of *The 5-B's Process of Sports Outreach*) in Jesus and accept Him as their Lord and Savior.

Progressive Intensity Levels of Competition (PIL's)

PIL is used to describe a concept concerning an ascending progression of seven distinct competitive levels within the *Volatility Scale*. Each level brings an increasing amount of intensity to the competition, and this increasing intensity carries with it an inherent potential exasperation for all involved.

Glossary

Producing-Reproducing-Reproducers
This phrase summarizes the hope and end-goal of all SR&F outreach ministries. This hope is based in the *Evangelistic-Disciplemaking* transferable concept, and summarizes the end result of reaching those far from Christ and His Church with the gospel: *Dedicated-Disciples* of Christ who reach others.

Redemption
One of four classical responses and reactions embraced by sport-related individuals who encounter the dilemma of integrating faith and their sport. It describes those who choose faith over sport by attempting to redeem individual sports-people (bring them to faith in Jesus) and also by attempting to redeem (adapt and alter the way sport is organized and participated in) the culture of sport.

Re-energizing
Re-energizing is the third part of the *3-I Continuum* for fully equipping SR&F Outreach ministers for the purpose of empowering them to envision, plan for, organize, administrate and evaluate a truly *Strategically-Relevant* & *Efficiently-Effective, Evangelistic-Disciplemaking* Sports outreach ministry. It defines the efforts to infuse SR&F outreach ministers with new motivations and inspirations for reaching those far from Jesus and His Church. It also has to do with developing ongoing, personal, mentoring, relationships that enables SR&F outreach ministers to become fully equipped for successful Great Commission endeavors.

Repetitive-Redemptive-Relational
Repetitive-Redemptive-Relational is found at one end of the fourth of the *7- Continuums* of sports outreach. It describes one expression of *The Sports Outreach Community's Evangelistic-Disciplemaking, Philosophical-Principles*. This model uses repetitive and ongoing SR&F leagues, classes or activities to attract those far from Christ and His Church; and also to create interpersonal, relational *Evangelistic-Environments* for the gospel to be experienced over a multiple-year, time frame. Based on Peterson's "Proclamation-Affirmation" concept; *Repetitive-Redemptive-Relational* verbal "affirmation" of the Gospel follows long periods of lived out "proclamation." Contrasted to a *Mega-Model* philosophy of gathering a large group of people to large scale event, *Repetitive-Redemptive-Relational* focuses on empowering and enabling, long-term, one-on-one or small group *Evangelistic-Disciplemaking* endeavors.

Rejection
One of four classical responses and reactions embraced by sport-related individuals who encounter the dilemma of integrating faith and their sport. It describes those who choose to leave sport because they cannot reconcile the demands of both. *Rejection* often means totally leaving sport but it can also describe a person who continues to engage in sport but rejects a specific aspect of it such as refusing to cheat; follow the instruction of a coach to purposely injure a fellow competitor or take harmful and illegal performance-enhancing substances.

Re-sourcing
Re-sourcing is the first part of the *3-I Continuum* for fully equipping SR&F outreach ministers for the purpose of empowering them to envision, plan for, organize, administrate and evaluate a truly *Strategically-Relevant & Efficiently-Effective, Evangelistic-Disciplemaking* sports outreach ministry. It has to do with the creation, production and distribution of *Re-sources* that are: Christo-centric *Level #1 Theological-Truths*; Biblically-Based *Level #2 Philosophical-Principles*; and *Level #3 Methodological-Models*.

Re-training
Re-training is the second part of the *3-I Continuum* for fully equipping SR&F outreach ministers for the purpose of empowering them to envision, plan for, organize, administrate and evaluate a truly *Strategically-Relevant & Efficiently-Effective, Evangelistic-Disciplemaking* sports outreach ministry. It has to do with instructing SR&F outreach ministers in how to most effectively utilize and employ the *Re-sources* that have been created, produced and distributed.

Singular-Commitment-Cost
The phrase *Singular-Commitment-Cost* is used in reference to ministries engaging in *Evangelistic-Disciplemaking* outreaches that emphasize there is a cost to becoming a disciple of Jesus. In comparison to Bonhoeffer's "Cheap Grace," churches, ministries and evangelists are encouraged to call people far from Jesus to become life-long, *Dedicated-Disciples*. Rather than simply asking people to "convert" *(Counting-Conversions)* by making a *Day's-Decision*, it is recommended all outreaches clearly communicate becoming a disciple of Jesus costs something! It includes not only receiving Jesus as Savior, but more so, making Him Lord of every area of their life. The *Singular-Commitment-Cost* describes the commitment churches and ministries need to make in "Changing-From" ministry models that strive to be winsome at the expense of proclaiming the whole Gospel; to "Changing-To" outreaches that present the Gospel in its

entirety. It also describes the commitment a person needs to consider in making a decision to become a disciple.

Sportsmanship
Sportsmanship is one of three philosophical approaches to competition and sport. It describes an ethic based on the humanistic-relativism of playing fair; being a good teammate; and obeying the rules of the game. As compared with gamesmanship; a philosophy which highest value is to win, regardless of how; and *Christmanship* that espouses engaging in sport for the glory of God and in ways that honors all co-competitors; sportsmanship values ethics that are based in humanistic-relativism and therefore change according to a shifting societal culture.

Sports Outreach Community
• The phrase that generically describes the unique group within the Church of Jesus Christ that uses SR&F outreach ministry to reach all who are far from Christ and His Church. It has four distinct expressions within local churches: a) congregational-based outreaches; b) sports-related para-ministries; c) fitness/wellness/wholeness based outreaches; and d) recreational/camping experiences and outreaches.
• This community also includes various sports-related, para-ministry models.
• The phrase *Sports Outreach Community* is preferred over Sports Outreach Movement because the former better communicates that this group is part of The Church, whereas Sports Outreach Movement connotes the efforts and activities occur as a separate movement from The Church.

Sports Outreach Movement
The phrase that describes the growing community within the Church of Jesus Christ using SR&F methodologies to reach all who are far from Christ and His Church. It has four distinct expressions: a) Congregational-based outreaches; b) sports-related, para-ministries; c) fitness/wellness/wholeness based outreaches; and d) recreational/camping experiences and outreaches.

Sports-related, para-ministry
Based on the *Level #1 Ology* of ecclesiology (the theology of The Church), the terminology para-ministry is preferred over para-church. It may seem a distinction without a difference and yet this seemingly subtle distinction can have significant and long-lasting negative implications. The word para means beside, and thus outside of. When used in relationship to The Church it communicates being outside of and thus, not part of the universal Church of Jesus. Conversely,

para-ministry indicates a ministry that is outside of and yet beside the Church. There are congregational (often called local church) ministries and there are also ministries not based in congregations.

Sportianity
Sportianity (not italicized because it was not original with CSRM) is used to describe the thoughts, emotions and commitments of people who embrace one end of the *Sportianity-Christianity Continuum*. In essence its context describes people who make sport their highest priority and thus their commitment to, and their involvement in, sport becomes a type of religion.

Strategically-Relevant
Paired with *Efficiently-Effective*, it is the first half of the *4-Fold Evaluative Rubric*. *Strategically-Relevant* suggests the guideline congregations can use to help assess and determine whether or not a local church SR&F outreach ministry is actually accomplishing its goal of engaging those whom are far from Christ and His Church. It is designed to aid local congregations to define and describe the most strategic and relevant sports, recreational activities and fitness initiatives within specific regions, countries and cultures of the world.

Success-Statistics
Success-Statistics is a phrase that describes how individual evangelists, congregations, ministries and missions determine their effectiveness. Some count the number of people who make a *Day's-Decision* as indicated by the raising of their hand, praying a prayer or filling out a card (*Counting-Conversions*) to determine if their outreach was successful. Others see such *Days-Decisions* as but the first step in becoming life-long, *Dedicated-Disciples* and thus their effectiveness is only assessed by the number of people they have labored to "make disciples" of.

The Movement / The Sports Outreach Movement/The Local Church SR&F Movement
To move is to change location and position. A movement then has to do with change, repositioning and going somewhere—hopefully towards a destination. In this series of books there are two terms that are used interchangeably (The Sports Outreach Movement / The Movement) and a third that is very similar (The Local Church SR&F Movement). They can all be used to generally describe the activities of a like-minded group of people who are engaged in Christo-centric ministry that is based in sport, recreation, fitness/wholeness/wellness and camping/outdoor pursuits. This Movement is generally agreed to have started in

the 1940's when a number of activities occurred, beginning with the Venture for Victory initiating its international short-term sports mission trips and ministries such as the Billy Graham Associates began to enable elite athletes and coaches to give a *Platform-Proclamation* of their faith at their crusades and events. It has morphed and expanded both in breadth and depth over the last decades. The phrase The Movement or The Sports Outreach Movement is used to describe and include all four quadrants, whereas The Local Church SR&F Movement is used to distinguish such activities within the confines of congregational outreach.

Volatility Scale
The Volatility Scale is an instrument that has been designed to chart and predict a competitor's experience. By combining the *EMIC, IMIC* and the *PIL's* it produces a measureable evaluative tool that analyzes what athletes, coaches and others will experience in a particular competitive event. *The Volatility Scale* contains four separate quadrants: *Enjoyment*; *Encounter*; *Explosion*; *Exasperation*.

Why; When-Where-With Whom; What
These are all tied to the *3-Tier Paradigm* and are specifically tied to one of the three levels of the paradigm:
• *Why*—is connected with the Christo-Centric *Level #1 Theological-Truths* which provide the basic rationale, ethical foundations for, The Sports Outreach Community
• *When-Where-With Whom*—are connected to the Biblically-based *Level #2 Philosophical-Principles* which provide the organizational structure for *The Sports Outreach Community*
• *What*—is connected with the *Strategically-Relevant* and *Efficiently-Effective Level #3 Methodological-Models* and describes the specific activities of *The Sports Outreach Community*

Without Reach We Have No Revenue and Without Revenue We Have No Reach
This phrase coined by Greg English communicates the local church SR&F outreach minister must balance "counting beans with counting souls." Both the ministry/outreach and the financing of the ministry are important. The financing empowers and enables the ministry and yet the ministry inspires the giving of the finances. The SR&F outreach ministers responsibility is to ensure both occur.

Appendix #15

Works Cited List

Addison, Steve. *Moments That Change the World: Five Keys to Spreading the Gospel.* Downers Grove, IL: IVP Books, 2011.

Anderson, Neil T. and David Park. *The Bondage Breaker.* Eugene, OR: Harvest House Publishers, 2000.

Barna, George. *The Power of Vision.* Grand Rapids, MI: Baker Books, 2018.

Bok, David. "Three Reasons Why." *Discipleship Journal*, issue 4, July 1981.

Bolling, Julian. *Struggle and Triumph* (videorecording). Xenia, OH: Athletes in Action, 2007.

Bryan, Bubby, from *e-Newsletter, 2018.* www.uttermostsports.org/newsletter-archives

"A Call to Develop Christ-like Leaders," Lausannne Papers, no. 41. In: *A New Vision, A New Heart, A Renewed Call: Lausanne Occasional Papers from the 2004 Forum of World Evangelization hosted by the Lausanne Committee for World Evangelization, Pattaya, Thailand, September 29-October 5, 2004*, edited by David Claydon. Pasadena, CA: William Carey Library, c2005. (Lausanne Occasional Papers, no. 30-60). 3 vols.

Chan, Francis. *Letters to The Church.* Colorado Springs, CO: David C. Cook, 2018.

Discovery Bible Study (form) on International Project website. Provides opportunity for people to request Discovery Bible Studies resources. www.internationalproject.org/discovery-bible-study/

Eames, Christopher. "Nehemiah: A Man and a Momentous Wall," *Watch Jerusalem*, 15 Sept. 2017. www.watchjerusalem.co.il/115-nehemiah-a-man-and-a-momentous-wall

Ellicott, Charles. *Ellicott's Bible Commentary: In One Volume, a Verse-by-Verse Explanation.* Grand Rapids, MI: Zondervan Publishing House, 1979.

Elliott, Jim, edited by Elisabeth Elliott. *The Journals of Jim Elliott.* Grand Rapids, MI: Baker Books, 2002.

"Engel Scale," Wikipedia.org. www.en.wikipedia.org/wiki/Engel_scale

Ford, Leighton. "The Arrow Vision" (online article), Leighton Ford Ministries, 6 Feb. 2015. www.leightonfordministries.org/2015/02/06/the-arrow-vision/

"Frontier People Groups" (map and chart), from Joshua Project, a ministry of Frontier Ventures, c2002. www.joshuaproject.net/frontier/1

Green, Michael. *Evangelieverkondiging in de Eerst Eeuwen*. Amsterdam: Buijten & Schipperheijn B.V., 1979.

Hendricks, Howard. *Men of Integrity*. Nashville, TN: Thomas Nelson, 1999.

Hendricks, Howard. Promise 2: A Man and His Friends, A Mandate for Mentoring: Janssen, Al and Larry K. Weeden. *Seven Promises of a Promise Keeper*. Colorado Springs, CO: Focus on the Family Publishing, 1994.

Hirsch, Alan. "Defining Missional." *Leadership Journal*, Fall 2008. www.christianitytoday.com/le/2008/fall/17.20.html

Hudson, Hugh et al. *Chariots of Fire* (motion picture). Burbank, CA: Warner Home Video, 2005. Originally produced 1981.

Hybels, Bill and Mark Mittelberg. *Becoming a Contagious Christian*. Grand Rapids, MI: Zondervan Publishers, 1994.

Jesus Film Project. "What Is the 10/40 Window?" 18 Feb. 2019. www.jesusfilm.org/blog-and-stories/10-40-window.html

Katz, Brandon. "Super Bowl LIV Ratings Show Signs of Life Amid Multi-Year Dip" (online article). Observer, 3 Feb.2020. www.observer.com/2020/02/super-bowl-tv-ratings-nfl-chiefs-49ers-viewership/

Keller, Helen Adams. *"Three Days to See"* published in Atlantic Monthly (January 1933)

Kelly, Matthew. *An Introduction to Postmodernism (and Why It's Not a Bad Word)*. Youth Specialties, 2004.

"Know God's Word" (online article), Precept Ministries International website. www.precept.org/know-gods-word/

Life Application Bible: The Living Bible. Carol Stream, IL: Tyndale House Publishers, 1988.

Life Giving Network (LGN). A report presented publicly, 1 Sept. 2019. www.lifegivingnetwork.org

Linville, Greg. *Christmanship: A Theology of Competition and Sport*. Canton, OH: Oliver House Publishing, 2014.

Linville, Greg. *The Mission of Sports ministry*. Canton, OH: Overwhelming Victory Press, (forthcoming)

Linville, Greg. *Putting the Church Back in the Game: the Ecclesiology of Sports Outreach*. Canton, OH: Overwhelming Victory Press, 2019.

Linville, Greg. The *Saving of Sports ministry: The Soteriology of Sports Outreach*. Canton, OH: Overwhelming Victory Press, 2020.

Linville, Greg. *Sports Outreach Fundamentals: Biblically-Based Philosophical-Principles for Strategically-Relevant & Efficiently-Effective Disciplemaking*. Canton, OH: Overwhelming Victory Press, 2018.

Maxwell, John C. *Developing the Leader Within You*. Nashville, TN: Thomas Nelson Publishing, 2012.

McCown, Lowrie and Valerie J. Gin. *Focus on Sport in Ministry*. Marietta, GA: 360 Sports, 2003.

McNeal, Reggie. *The Present Future: Understanding Current Realities in the Church*. San Francisco: Jossey-Bass, 2009, c2003.

Outlook Web Bureau. "ICC Reveals Astonishing 2019 Cricket World Cup Viewership Numbers; India Vs Pakistan Broke Records" (online article). 16 Sept 2019. www.outlookindia.com/website/story/sports-news-icc-reveals-astonishing-2019-cricket-world-cup-viewership-numbers-including-figures-from-record-breaking-india-vs-paki/338795

Oswald, Rodger, author of many sports ministry manuals and videos. Campbell, CA: Church Sports International, published in the 1990s and 2000s. For individual titles, search in www.worldcat.org

Packard, Joshua. "Meet the 'Dones'" (online article). *Christianity Today/Pastors*, Summer 2015. www.christianitytoday.com/pastors/2015/summer-2015/meet-dones.html

Perkins, John. *With Justice for All: A Strategy for Community Development*. Ventura, CA: Regal Books, 1982.

Peterson, Eugene. *The Message: The Bible in Contemporary Language*. Colorado Springs, CO: Navpress, 2002.

Pew Research Center. "The Future of World Religions: Population Growth Projections, 2010-2050" (online article). 2 April 2015. www.pewforum.org/2015/04/02/religious-projections-2010-2050/

Qu-ran. *The Glorious Quran: Arabic Text and English Rendering* [by] Muhammad Pickthall. 10th revised edition. Des Plaines, IL: Library of Islam, 1994. Distributed by Kazi Publications, Chicago.

Reilly, Rick. "Life of Reilly," 23 Dec 2008. ESPN Website www.sports.espn.go.com/espnmag/story?section=magazine&id=3789373 Story relating to high school football game between Grapeville Faith and Gainesville State School.

Ripken, Nik. *The Insanity of God: A True Story of a Faith Resurrected*. Nashville, TN: B&H Books, 2013.

Spurgeon, Charles H. *Morning and Evening*. New Kensingon, PA: Whitaker House, 2001.

Stetzer, Ed. *Christians in the Age of Outrage: How to Bring Our Best When the World Is at Its Worst*. Carol Stream, IL: Tyndale House Publishers, 2018.

Tamasy, Robert. "Out of the Nursery." *Discipleship Journal*, issue 23, Sept./Oct. 1989.

"Unreached People Groups" (online webpage). www.globalfrontiermissions.org/gfm-101-missions-course/the-unreached-peoples-and-their-role-in-the-great-commission/

"What is a DMM?" (online article) on website: Pursuing Disciple Making Movements in the Frontiers www.dmmsfrontiermissions.com/disciple-making-movement-what-defined/

Whitney, Donald S. *Spiritual Disciplines for the Christian Life*. Colorado Springs, CO: NavPress, 1997.

Woods, Rick. "India, the Greatest Challenge to World Evangelization" (online article). *Mission Frontiers Magazine*, May/June 2019. www.missionfrontiers.org/issue/archive/india-the-greatest-challenge-to-world-evangelization

www.ingramcontent.com/pod-product-compliance
Lightning Source LLC
Chambersburg PA
CBHW072004110526
44592CB00012B/1199